Planning and Design Strategies for Sustainability and Profit: Pragmatic sustainable design on building and urban scales

2004

Adrian Pitts

ELSEVIER

AMSTERDAM • BOSTON • HEIDELBERG • LONDON • NEW YORK • OXFORD
PARIS • SAN DIEGO • SAN FRANCISCO • SINGAPORE • SYDNEY • TOKYO
Architectural Press is an imprint of Elsevier

Architectural
Press

Architectural Press
An imprint of Elsevier
Linacre House, Jordan Hill, Oxford OX2 8DP
200 Wheeler Road, Burlington MA 01803

First published 2004

British Library Cataloguing in Publication Data
Pitts, Adrian C.
  Planning and design strategies for sustainability and profit: pragmatic
  sustainable design on building and urban scales
  1. Sustainable architecture – Economic aspects   2. City planning –
  Economic aspects   3. City planning – Environmental aspects
  4. Sustainable development
  I. Title   720.47

Library of Congress Cataloguing in Publication Data
A catalogue record for this book is available from the Library of Congress.

ISBN   0 7506 54643

For information on all Architectural Press publications
visit our website at: www.architecturalpress.com

Typeset by Keyword Typesetting Services Ltd
Printed and bound in Great Britain

Contents

Acknowledgements and credits

All undertakings of this nature require the aid and support of many people, and thanks are due to all those who have helped in some way. I would particularly like to thank Edward Ng and Hanwen Liao for their written contributions that have been incorporated into the texts of the case studies for Hong Kong and Sydney. Edward Ng and Chan Tak Yan are thanked for their help in obtaining images to support the Hong Kong case study. Also grateful thanks are due for helping to obtain images to: Clive Knights for Portland; Eva Dalman and Göran Rosberg for Bo01; Lisa Nutt for Austin; and Susan Thomas for Chattanooga. Alan Gledhill (Leicester City Council) is thanked for his comments and discussions and for the provision of illustrations to accompany the Leicester case study.

I would also like to thank the following: Brian Edwards for useful comments at the inception of this work; Jane Homewood for some of the initial inspiration to confront the topic, and for information that aided the Melbourne study; Mike Street for background discussions about local government operation in the UK; Peter Smith for ideas and information that have arisen from our previous collaborations; Faidon Nikiforiadis for help in preparing some illustrations; and last but by no means least, Janet, Alison and Daniel for their support and understanding over many months of preparation and writing.

Illustration credits

Plate 7: Leicester City Council
Plates 16 and 17 and Figures 7.6 and 7.7: Austin Energy Green Building Program
Plates 18 and 19 and Figure 7.10: Clive Knights
Plate 28: Göran Rosberg/Ronny Bergström, Malmö City Planning Offices
Plates 29 and 31 and Figure 7.14: Jan-Erik Andersson/Eva Dalman
Plates 33, 34 and 35 and Figures 7.17, 7.18 and 7.19: Edward Ng and Chan Tak Lan
Figure 7.1: Leicester City Council/EDAW
Figures 7.8 and 7.9: Electric Transit Vehicle Institute/Advanced Transport Technology Institute

Note: In this text the now more generally accepted definition of one billion is used, that is 1000 million.

Part A

The background: sustainability in context

Chapter 1

Introduction

The environmental imperative

There is now great concern for the environmental degradation that is being caused by the depletion of natural resources, pollution of air, ground and aquatic environments, global warming, and a general lack of concern for the earth's natural ecosystems. The importance of the contribution made to unsustainable practices by development of buildings and the built environment is also often underestimated. This is a worrying situation since the time-lags prevalent in environmental systems dictate that changes in outlook and action are needed now, not at some point in the distant future. To combat this situation, integrated approaches are required both to address public awareness, but also public concerns, and to encourage the professionals who have a responsibility in this area, in order to make possible the necessary improvements in environmental and sustainable design and development.

The scope of this book is not just concerned with planning, or design, or sustainability, or profit, or indeed any one topic; indeed, it is the focus on single issues and single viewpoints of many interest groups and sources of information currently available that can create difficulties. This text attempts to offer a more integrated approach, to address the issues and to suggest some solutions based on research into current good practice. It aims to provide support for new integrated and dynamic thinking that can lead to development of a sustainable built environment in ways that can be subscribed to by a broad section of society. It describes how strategic and urban planning with strong leadership can be interlaced with the design of regions, cities, towns, neighbourhoods, building clusters and individual buildings. The development of accounting methods for sustainability to enable demonstration of it as a profitable alternative to normal operation is also a key element. Overall, there is a focus on how to produce a more sustainable future using good environmental and energy-efficient planning and design techniques in pragmatic ways, and on solutions that are also economically, socially and culturally strong.

In modern societies there seems to be a greater focus on *rights* than on *responsibilities* and an attitude which pays more attention to *price* rather than *value*. There also seems to be a fragmentation of the processes that could deliver holistic solutions to some of the problems being faced within the built environment. Unfortunately it is only in the adoption of holistic and reasoned approaches that sustainable design can be fully assessed, optimized and promoted.

It is also disappointing that obvious opportunities to make real strides forward in terms of environmentally focused sustainable design are not being taken. The proposals of the long-awaited UK government initiative *Sustainable Communities: Building for the Future* (issued in February 2003) still seem to place the main emphasis on location and zoning style planning that is primarily linked to economic regeneration. Environmental matters are addressed, but it is not clear that they will receive the priority they deserve; although economic and social components are important, neither can be resolved if the environmental issues are not tackled.

This text attempts to encompass a variety of approaches and scales, providing guidance as to the infrastructure necessary to achieve successful sustainable development. In this it supports a revival in a revised form of a strategic planning approach that is long term, wide ranging and community based, together with the adoption of assessment and accounting procedures that enable environmental costs and benefits to be better examined and incorporated into strategic decision making.

Focus and content

Sustainability and the built environment

Sustainable development is now commonly classified as having three main components: economic sustainability, environmental sustainability and social sustainability (this final element sometimes being referred to as *equity*, thus giving the so called *three Es*: economics; environment and equity).

This text has a particular focus on the environment, and more particularly the built environment, for it is buildings, their design, construction, management and use, which are responsible for so many negative influences that limit the potential for sustainable development and growth. It is also the built environment of the city and urban areas that comes most under the spotlight. The reasoning is attributable to the fact that the world's population is undergoing a continuing urbanization process and it is cities and urban areas that create many of the problems whilst also requiring the greatest resources to sustain them. And yet, perhaps in a contradictory sense, dense cities also have features which encourage certain environmental benefits. That is not to say that rural areas are not important, since some examples of good or alternative practice are to be found in rural developments; it is rather that urban areas present the greatest challenges and they are also places where greatest potential to change things for the better exists.

Buildings as a whole have also been identified as representing the sector with most potential for improvement to meet the targets for reducing the threat of climate change. Climate change is not the only environmental and sustainability issue facing the planet, but it is one that both underlies and links so many others. Buildings are resource intensive in construction and operation; they also produce enormous quantities of waste during the construction process, during their period of use and occupation, and also at the point of their eventual demolition. Their location also affects significantly other resource- and pollution-associated activities such as transport and local ecology.

Although the text is research based, it also includes many facets of what is already accepted good practice; concepts and examples from around the world are investigated and evaluated and features are drawn together for consideration. A conscious decision has been taken to emphasize positive development and opportunities rather than to dwell on the negatives; this is undertaken on the basis of the translation of Voltaire's maxim expressing the concern that 'the best is the enemy of the good'. The author is a strong advocate for the position of enacting what can be done now, and building upon it; if modest improvements in sustainable building become the norm, then it becomes easier to proceed with the larger changes, as long as the trap can be avoided of believing that enacting only a few small changes will be enough.

Structure

Part A of the text, *The background: sustainability in context*, examines the current position in general terms and explains the problems being faced in relation to urban and suburban development. It is within the city and town context that the problems and issues of sustainability are most acutely exhibited and it is right that the focus should be here. Many issues are, of course, relevant to more rural areas too. This part includes a brief review of the development of cities and urban areas within an historical context. The review is furthered by consideration of the drivers for change, in which those factors that make it inevitable that mankind will have to confront issues of environmental sustainability, and at an appropriate level and scale, are detailed.

Part B, *Planning and designing for sustainability*, helps to identify the roles, developments in thinking, attitudes, technologies, techniques and processes which are needed and which can be used to achieve more sustainable urban design, development, construction and operation. The chapters therefore act as a guide to good environmental planning and design practice. They indicate how buildings and their surroundings can be designed to minimize environmental impact and also to offer opportunities for optimizing sustainable development. Part B includes a section on the techniques that are required to assess performance, for without them it is difficult to measure progress or compare options.

Part C, *Exploiting the potential*, focuses on the ways in which a sustainability-focused approach can lead to benefits for all. It illustrates how governments, designers, developers, building occupants and operators, and others can work together within a framework that includes an urban and strategic planning point of view. The discussion involves how to encourage opportunities that are both environmentally and commercially sound.

A large component, not just of this section but also of the whole text, is the description and evaluation of a series of case studies that embody some degree of good practice or understanding. As already stated, the intention is to emphasize the positive rather than the negative; not every idea, scheme, policy, programme or action results in immediate and overwhelming success; however, by building together the potential of the good ideas, a more sustainable outcome is possible.

There is also a bibliography that lists useful sources of further information, both printed texts and internet websites.

The development of the urban built environment

The archaeological evidence of human urban settlements extends back about 5000 years; such settlements arose from the improvements available in terms of living conditions that the habitation of more permanent communities offered to their occupants. It is interesting to note that one of the underlying causes of this change in lifestyle was the climatic changes that followed the last glacial period which ended about 8000 years ago and which enabled different forms of agriculture to develop. The question might be posed as to what effect the climate change expected in the near future might have on modern lifestyles and expectations, and whether it will have equal impact in lifestyle and well-being.

There is evidence of primitive planning even in the earliest settlements found in various parts of the world including China, India, Egypt, Asia Minor, ancient Mesopotamia and the Mediterranean. The size of settlements at this prehistoric time were relatively small and these were not true cities by modern-day standards, and it was not until the rise of the Greek and Roman civilizations that cities of 100 000 or more in population began to develop (though cities of such a size only became common in the last 300 years). In more recent times, the United Nations has identified urban areas as those with more than 20 000 inhabitants living in close proximity, though in some countries places with as few as 2500 occupants are considered urban.

The development of substantial towns and early cities was also accompanied by the initiation of new social and political structures which eventually led to collective activities, which included control over planning and development processes; these had such significant effects that they are still visible in the present day. It would seem that regulated planning was only possible when the settlement had reached a particular size for it to be seen to have benefits by the inhabitants, and re-emphasis of this role for modern urban sustainability is now required.

The original towns came into being because of two changes: firstly in agriculture, whereby a surplus of food production was possible in the countryside, which could then provide for the needs of the town; and secondly in transportation, allowing the movement of food and other goods (the wheel having being invented about 3500 BC). Such towns were rarely out of walking distance of their supporting mechanisms, however, and the distance to a stable water supply and its capacity were important limitations. Collective settlements had a number of positive features which, on balance, made these initial urban places more effective in enhancing the quality of life for their occupants.

In the past, urban living was more effective in the production of wealth and culture than its rural hinterland, but it was not without cost and then, as now, the by-products in terms of wastes and disturbances to the natural ecological cycles caused problems. Current generations should not be surprised that environmental degradation continues to be generated; however, the scale and effect of such problems in the present day has consequences for the future of the planet in ways incomprehensible when towns and urban areas first began evolving. Yet it is significant that even in those early urban areas settlement planning encompassed traits of environmentally sensitive design which took account of the effects of solar radiation on buildings, traits that seem sadly lacking in many modern counterparts.

Population density in the earliest towns was also surprisingly high and is estimated to have been equivalent to about 50 000 inhabitants per square kilometre, as high as the densest neighbourhoods found in modern high-rise cities such as Hong Kong. A severe drawback in these circumstances, then as now, is the quantity of waste that must be disposed of and the supply of everyday necessities. Density of inhabitation has many consequential effects and will be returned to several times in the course of this work.

Historically, the nature and form of urban areas have undergone a long but inconsistent evolutionary process with the most rapid changes coming in the most recent 250 years with rapid urbanization accompanying industrialization. The industrial revolution started in the second half of the eighteenth century, beginning in western Europe and centred in the UK. The explosion of technological advancement led to rapid development of new machines and systems and more efficient ways (at least in terms of the workforce) of producing goods. This in turn led to increasing demands for manpower and raw materials and drew more and more people to live and work in towns and cities.

The planning of the expanding towns and cities and of the new dwellings required to house the workers was often based on a rigid grid pattern with little regard for anything but to fit the largest numbers into the smallest space. There were a few exceptions such as the urban villages developed by the more benevolent factory owners such as Titus Salt, as demonstrated at Saltaire (see figure 1.1). Here a variety of more pleasant dwellings was constructed, but these developments were relatively rare. The industrialization of urban areas did not simply increase the population, it also distributed them in a very different way to that found in pre-industrial urban life. Industrialization led to the urbanization of the mass of the population with the industrial city requiring high levels of centralization to support production, distribution, exchange and banking. Before

Figure 1.1 Saltaire: Example of well designed, environmentally pleasant workers' houses

industrialization as much as 90 per cent of the population was rurally based; after it, it was as low as 10 per cent.

The speed of urbanization has been greatest during the last 50 years and now almost 50 per cent of the world's population lives in cities. Continued urbanization puts great pressure on resources which have to be moved into the urban area to support the lives of its inhabitants. The desire for sophisticated comfortable places to live and work, and for the typical features of modern lifestyles, also multiplies the resource usage, waste production and pollution generated by urban areas.

There have been major variations in the patterns of expansion, however. In the UK and USA the typical model involved those households with newly acquired wealth tending to move away from the urban centre, not to the periphery or immediate suburbs, but to the outlying edges of the city and semi-rural space. This was in stark contrast to the desires of pre-industrial times to live in the centre. This movement is also associated with the greater availability of transport systems to support the separation of residence from workplace and commercial centre. This pattern has not been universal, however, and in some of the more regulated and planned major European cities the core area has continued to be occupied by wealthy citizens, with poorer people confined to surrounding satellite areas. In some cities the reasons for this were not just cultural but also financial as incentives were offered to stay in the centre. This alternative has not avoided all current urban problems but has certainly placed them in a different context.

In the UK and USA the migration led to greatly increased need to travel for work, retail and social activities and to consequent transport problems, leading to increased energy use and pollution. Ironically, then, the desires of certain people for a more pleasant environment in which to live have actually led them to contribute to its problems and potential destruction.

Perhaps the biggest change has been the complete separation, both physically and conceptually, of the inhabitants of a city from the means to support their activities. Whilst cities can be very efficient in some respects as a result of their density, there are also many inefficiencies in the support systems. Collectively, the citizens of the major cities seem to show a lack of knowledge and understanding of the consequences of their lifestyles for the wider environment and the ability of the earth's natural systems to sustain such lifestyles. Such a situation naturally leads to a requirement for sophisticated strategies and planning activities simply to enable large cities to function; however, many cities are now reaching the limit of practicality, and of sustainability.

One of the most significant changes brought about by the industrialization process has been the almost complete reliance on non-renewable fossil-fuel-based energy sources to provide the power, not just to drive the industrial processes but also to support the infrastructure including construction, buildings and especially transport. Peter Droege, the noted academic and urban designer, has investigated this reliance and coined the term *fossilism*, which he explains as representing the 'unique and brief development period in society, economic systems, cultural meaning, urban form and architectural expression...expected to last no longer than roughly three centuries (1750–2050), as a brief era driven and marked by an all encompassing, global dependence on fossil fuels'.

This reliance on fossil fuels is at the heart of the current debate over sustainability and in fact acts as a clear indication of the unsustainability of many facets of modern life. The developed world can be expected to enter a period of post-industrialization and indeed *post-fossilism* in the next 50 to 100 years, perhaps earlier, yet it seems the lifestyles being led cannot yet move forward and transcend the reliance on old technologies and ways of thinking. Development over the last 250 years has thus probably created the most worrying environmental situation in the history of mankind.

In the following chapter consideration is focused on the various factors that demand attention and act as drivers for change in both practice and perception if the sustainability of the planet is to be maintained. Many are related to the current unsustainable reliance, within urban contexts, on fossil fuels.

Chapter 2

Drivers for change

Introduction

This chapter aims to support change and development in planning and design practice by showing that the earth's systems are already in a perilous state of unsustainability. The following sections present some of the overwhelming evidence as to why changes in thinking and practice are required. The information is subdivided into broad sections dealing with environmental, economic and cultural/societal issues, but in reality all are so interdependent that they cannot be considered or dealt with in isolation.

The underlying theme of all of the problems is the inefficient and wasteful use of the earth's natural resources, the damage that the consequential pollution causes, and the inequitable and detached nature of the distribution of resource use and of pollution effects that currently exists. By far the greatest threats are those associated with global climate change, which is both symbolic of, and often related to, the whole range of other sustainability issues. An excellent set of starting points for a review of issues is provided in the reports of the United Nations Intergovernmental Panel on Climate Change (the IPCC), the most recent of which was published in 2001. The messages of these reports have been widely disseminated but, because of the caution of the scientists involved, the most prominent conclusions reported often give the impression that there is an undue level of uncertainty. This weakness is then exploited by lobbyists wishing to protect a particular commercial position, and they suggest through the media that the two sides of the argument are of equal weight and that major changes should wait until it is resolved. The result is that necessary action is not being carried out or is delayed. In fact, any modest study of the details of the IPCC reports will readily create alarm as the true potential impacts are understood.

Environmental drivers

Climate change

The evidence shows that the average global temperatures rose by modest but significant amounts during the twentieth century; such changes are small by comparison with some of the very worrying future scenarios. The 1990s was the warmest decade on record (since the 1860s, when full records began) but, more than that, the 1990s was probably the warmest decade in the 1000 years for which good quality proxy evidence of temperature levels exists. In the last 30 years there has also been a reduction in snow and ice cover in the Northern Hemisphere of about 10 per cent and a retreat of mountain glaciers in non-polar regions over the last 100 years.

There have been other worrying changes in climate. Average sea levels rose by between 0.1 and 0.2 metres and rainfall increased over continental northern latitudes during the twentieth century, with a decrease in rainfall for sub-tropical zones. Over mid- to high latitudes of the Northern Hemisphere in the second half of the last century there was a significant increase in cloud cover and of heavy rainfall events. The El Niño phenomenon, which causes more extreme climatic events in the Pacific region, has increased in intensity and persistency since about 1970.

These changes in climate are in part, of course, due to natural variability and natural events, but the IPCC has concluded that emissions of particular gases arising from human activities have altered and will continue to alter the atmosphere and the climate of the planet for many years to come. The process by which this occurs is generally termed the *greenhouse effect*; figure 2.1 indicates the generalized processes of this greenhouse effect. The greenhouse phenomenon means that the earth's surface and atmosphere are about 33°C warmer than would otherwise be the case, and indeed without this process it would be too cold to sustain current human life. The problem lies in the fact that the concentrations of the greenhouse gases in the atmosphere have been rising at an alarming rate over the last 250 years, a period coincident with industrialization and mankind's use and exploitation of fossil fuels.

Carbon dioxide concentration in the atmosphere has risen by more than 30 per cent since 1750 and, despite considerable climatic and geological variations in the earth's history, evidence indicates that the current levels have not been exceeded for at least 420 000 years (and probably not even during the last 200 million years). Since carbon dioxide is the most prominent greenhouse gas and is also the by-product of fossil fuel use, it would seem, even though human activities represent only a relatively small fraction of the overall cycle, that significant disturbances to the natural cycles have been created by mankind. Figure 2.2 shows a representation of the evidence linking carbon dioxide concentrations with climate change and is derived from data presented in the journal *Nature* in 1990 which itself was determined from evidence in ice core samples. Of the most recent 20 years' worth of increases in anthropogenic emissions, about 75 per cent

Figure 2.1 The greenhouse effect

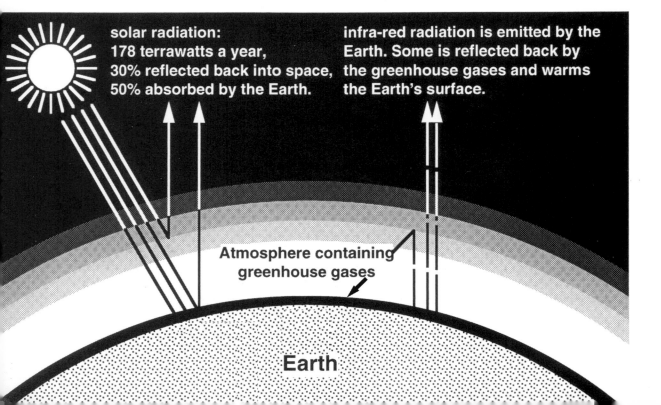

solar radiation:
178 terrawatts a year,
30% reflected back into space,
50% absorbed by the Earth.

infra-red radiation is emitted by the Earth. Some is reflected back by the greenhouse gases and warms the Earth's surface.

Atmosphere containing greenhouse gases

Earth

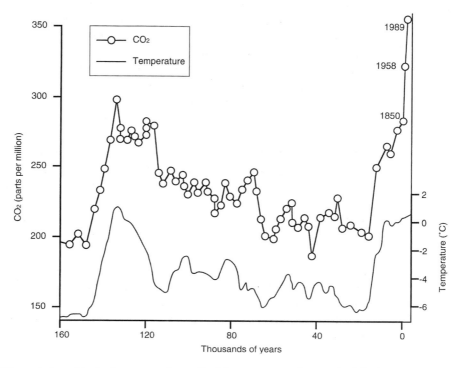

Figure 2.2 The relationship between carbon dioxide concentration and global temperature

of the change arises from fossil fuel burning and the other 25 per cent is mainly due to deforestation and land use change.

A gas with even more greenhouse effect is methane, the concentration of which has increased by 151 per cent since 1750 with about half of the increased emissions being anthropogenic in nature. As global temperatures rise, the natural processes that produce methane are enhanced, further exacerbating the problem. As the concentrations of these greenhouse gases rise, it is natural to assume additional warming will occur.

The IPCC's reports are based on the use of detailed geological and climatic information in conjunction with sophisticated scientific models for the prediction of the future climate. The IPCC admits that the models cannot simulate all aspects of climate but that their performance has been improved, and their accuracy has been demonstrated by being used to reconstruct climate history, which is then compared with actual experience. There is now confidence that the rise in sea levels during the twentieth century occurred as a result of global warming; the levels are projected to rise by between a further 0.1 to 0.9 metres by 2100. Though these rises may seem modest, they are very significant and alarming for small islands and for low-lying coastal areas, especially considering the concentration of major cities along coastlines. It has already been suggested that existing tidal barrages (see figure 2.3) and flood defences will need modifying to cope with anticipated changes, especially when one considers the combined effect of higher sea levels together with more extreme storms to create surges in the level. In 1953 major floods along the whole east coast of England resulted in much devastation and more than 300 deaths; further problems are almost inevitable.

Most of the sea level rise is due to thermal expansion of the oceans, which will continue for many decades as the lower depths also become warmer as a result of surface warming; absorption of heat by the sea is one reason why air temperature rises have so far been moderated. Other researchers have suggested even greater sea level rises could eventually

Figure 2.3 An example of a river tidal barrage: sea level rises and storm surges may threaten their effectiveness

be caused by the gradual melting of ground-based ice sheets such as in Greenland and the Antarctic. It is also clear that fossil fuel burning will continue to have a large impact on atmospheric concentrations of carbon dioxide in the twenty-first century and beyond. At present about six billion tonnes of carbon equivalent material is emitted worldwide each year (equivalent to about one tonne per person on the planet); however, this average masks wide variations from half a tonne or less in much of the developing world, through two to three tonnes in Europe and many industrialized countries, up to about six tonnes per person in the USA. The problem of increasing concentrations is exacerbated by the fact that natural absorbers of carbon dioxide, such as the oceans, will take up a smaller proportion of emissions in the future. The predictions are for carbon dioxide concentrations to reach between 540 and 970 ppm (parts per million) by 2100, compared to 250 ppm in 1750. Even to stabilize the carbon dioxide concentration at a much raised level will require anthropogenic emissions to be reduced to 1990 levels, and this does not take account of the pressures created by the natural tendency for increase in emissions from developing countries.

In its 2001 report, the IPCC produced a series of 35 scenarios to project future climate. In every one, global surface temperature is predicted to rise significantly, with a range of increase between 1.4 and 5.8°C by 2100. These predictions are higher than had been expected in its previous report and the rate of warming will be much greater than that already experienced in the twentieth century; it is also projected that land areas will warm more rapidly than the average giving even more cause for concern.

A further problem is that the long-lasting nature of the emissions that are linked to climate change, and the inherent time lags in the system, mean that not only will the effects persist for several centuries, even if emissions are stabilized, but temperatures will continue to rise to unprecedented levels. Greater variability in weather patterns will also occur, implying more storms, more periods of flood and drought, and more desertification. More extreme weather patterns also lead to soil erosion and thus even less potential for plant material to grow and to be able to absorb carbon dioxide through the process of photosynthesis.

The effects of climate change will thus cause the need to rethink building design to cope with such changes, especially in coastal cities where a potential rise of almost a metre in sea level combined with more frequent storm surges would be catastrophic. The disturbances to water cycles will also cause problems for those areas already affected by scarcity of water, and the international tensions over availability of oil could become dwarfed by those that might occur over availability of water for agriculture and other uses.

The evidence from geological and other records does show that, in the distant past, the earth did undergo a number of climate variations with enormous consequential effect. This cannot be used as an excuse to ignore the issues now, however; for the first time in the history of the planet human activities are having a significant impact on global climate and no-one fully understands the implications of where this will lead. It is suggested that climate change following meteor impact caused the disappearance of the dinosaurs, creatures which ruled the earth for much longer than humankind has so far achieved. The geological records do not identify what was the trigger for great changes in the past. It would seem prudent, essential in fact, to err on the side of caution and not to gamble on that trigger point now.

Mitigation options

In the IPCC report on mitigation scenarios, which examine the methods that might be used to reduce emissions to the atmosphere and thus reduce the risk of global climate change, buildings figure very prominently. They are responsible for some of the greatest emissions (about 25 per cent globally but up to 50 per cent in individual countries) but also have the potential to effect the greatest improvement. The IPCC has indicated not only that building-related emissions could be reduced by about 40 per cent by 2010, and by about 60 per cent by 2020, but that most of these reductions could be reduced at negative net direct costs; that is, by using market encouragement and taking a longer term view, the savings from reduced fossil fuel use will outweigh the costs of implementing measures. Buildings provide the largest single contribution to the suggested emissions reduction targets; further, a reduction in transport associated with building use could also make a substantial contribution to the reduction targets.

Ecological factors

Potential climate change will obviously have an impact on ecology as the environmental conditions vary in ways unseen for many thousands of years. Ecology and the natural flora and fauna of an area are already under threat, however, from the destruction of habitats that occurs with the procurement and processing of resources being consumed for construction products. The building process, when insufficiently regulated and guided by strategies and planning, causes significant destruction and disturbance of natural ecology. Further, the winning and processing of the materials required for building and the disposal of wastes from the construction industry also damage the natural environment. The reasons for this are often that the environment is seen as a cheap means of supporting construction needs without construction bearing the full costs of the damage caused.

On a broader level, the changes in the natural world which continue in line with inappropriate strategic planning mean that the world will continue to struggle to feed its population, and the changes in weather patterns already mentioned will severely affect crop production. Some commentators have taken pleasure in the expectation of the ability to develop a UK wine industry to rival that of southern Europe; the reality is that increased crop production for some could be outweighed by the loss of growing potential elsewhere. Warming is likely to be at such a rate that current natural flora will be unable to adapt and move fast enough and will thus be lost, and this will have serious consequences for the food chain. The potential for spread of diseases may also be enhanced as the conditions ripe to support malarial mosquitoes move north to cover a significant fraction of countries thus far unaffected, including perhaps even the UK. The natural wealth of the earth's forests, freshwater and oceanic ecosystems has already been affected severely by global climate change, and has decreased by more than one-third since 1970.

Resources and wastes

The phrase *ecological footprint* has been used to describe the impact of resource use by a city or country. It explains the area of land required to support a particular area in terms of water, food and materials. The support areas needed are usually tens if not hundreds of times the size of the urban area they provide for and reflect the developed world's financial ability to buy up the resources it needs from the poorer nations of the world to support its lifestyle. In the longer term this is clearly unsustainable since developing countries will gradually increasingly compete for the finite resources. All nations will have to become much more efficient in utilizing resources, and it is disappointing that the techniques already developed for greater efficacy are often restricted and not available (at reasonable cost) to the very developing nations in which potential for wasteful practices must be modified.

Economic drivers

The damage to the natural environment caused by inappropriate and ill-considered short-term development can also have longer-term economic and financial consequences. Already, in many cities of the world, traffic congestion causes major problems, not just in terms of air pollution but also in terms of time wasted in traffic jams. In the UK the estimated annual cost of traffic congestion is over £20 billion with a further £10 billion or more in environmental and social costs associated with traffic.

The almost total reliance on the use of the private motor vehicle is being tackled in some places and with some techniques, but is a very difficult and emotive problem to solve since the wider use of the motor car has been one of the most significant liberating social changes of recent decades. In order to provide some workable solutions and strategies, the planning of their execution is needed at a broad scale. It is not just about control of car use but also about where people live and work. Businesses regularly report on the costs of traffic congestion but seem only to have one solution to propose: the building of more and wider roads. A more complete and integrated approach is needed.

A further economic driver for change lies in the consequences of climate change. The severity of storms, the increased flooding, and the risks of subsidence caused by drought have all led to increased damage to property and rising insurance claims. In the 1960s there were about 20 major disasters, leading to claims of about $30 billion; in the 1990s there were about 70 disaster events, with claims adding up to $250 billion. The world's insurance and re-insurance companies view the prospect of climate change, with the attendant consequences for more severe weather and storms, with great alarm. It is no accident that many companies already fund research into climate change, its effects and possible remediation measures. One of the world's largest insurance companies has already predicted that, if the current trends continue, the international insurance industry will be bankrupt by the year 2065. It has also recently been suggested by some radical proposals in the UK that the occupants of houses currently situated in flood risk areas will have to relocate; their properties worthless and redundant, having become uninsurable and unsaleable. This could affect many tens of thousands of properties.

A joint project by the United Nations Environment Programme and major insurance companies has estimated that the losses due to extreme weather, damage to ecological and agricultural systems, loss of land and water problems are costing about $300 billion per year on a worldwide basis. There are also many hidden costs as the frequency and extremes of rain and drought cause gradual erosion of foundations for properties and other structures, resulting in ongoing expensive maintenance and remediation.

In many countries the costs of disposal of wastes are already rising steeply, and as both the places where wastes can be safely disposed of disappear and the regulations concerning waste treatment increase, then there is further financial pressure to be more efficient.

One of the mitigation processes suggested at the international Kyoto summit meeting was that of emissions trading, whereby the countries exceeding their targets for emissions would be able, in effect, to buy the spare capacity from developing nations. This would provide those developing countries with the financial means to avoid the highest carbon-intensive industrialization process followed in the already developed countries. Overall there would be a tendency to reduce emissions and their associated costs. The targets agreed in Kyoto still fell far short of those necessary to combat climate change, however, and problems continue to build up since there has been a general retreat from the measures agreed at Kyoto, with the USA and others refusing to endorse and implement the agreement in its current form. Despite this, there is still the prospect of some emission trading and perhaps in some parts of the world a *carbon tax* approach. It is therefore prudent in economic terms for planners, companies and individuals to explore and plan for less carbon-intensive and wasteful activities.

The impact of environmental risks is also being recognized in the distribution of funds from national and local government agencies. With a modest degree of planning and assessment these agencies are able to direct public funding towards groups that embody or encourage better environmental and sustainable practices, and these actions provide a further economic focus. Economics also drives change through the understanding that the development of new, less wasteful and less polluting technologies will be favoured in the future and that the introduction of system efficiency improvements will also help to reduce capital investment costs.

Buildings and the built environment are important in these economic areas because of the significance of the construction sector within the economy as a whole and because of the longer-term costs that will be incurred by not implementing more sustainable practices. As the significance of longer-term costs of unsustainable buildings becomes more obvious, this should lead to encouragement for appropriate design; otherwise, the buildings risk becoming unusable.

Political, cultural and societal drivers

In addition to the environmental and economic factors, there are ranges of other drivers that further promote change. In recent years there has been a substantial upgrading in building regulations in the UK that has meant a more important focus on energy use. Though such change was long overdue and still leaves some areas of concern, it has placed a stronger emphasis on elements of sustainable design. There have also been major changes in planning guidance (in Planning Policy Guidance notes and associated documents) offered by the UK government. Some of the causes of the revised guidance have been the now-acknowledged need for a substantial housebuilding programme to meet future needs. It has also been acknowledged that the simple expansion of housing into the countryside is not the best answer to these needs as it both increases the development costs and increases urban sprawl, with consequent commuting and traffic problems. A greater emphasis has therefore been placed on the use of previously developed land, closer to town centres and with existing social, cultural and transport infrastructure.

In the UK, in recent years, there has also been a significant increase in general public spending in urban areas, particularly to support regeneration programmes and for the alleviation of poverty in the worst zones. This spending, however, has not been fully coordinated, with various government departments attempting to improve specific quality of life indicators. As a result there are aspects that have been ignored, particularly in the development of an urban policy which controls or channels all relevant funding and to support good sustainable design. As citizens improve their lot there is still a tendency to move out to the leafy suburbs; what is required is strategic planning and policy which makes the most sustainable areas, often at the heart of a city, attractive and pleasant to live in. Rehabilitation of an area needs to be beneficial and attractive to all for better social cohesion and practical sustainability.

Arising from the first Earth Summit in Rio de Janeiro was the concept of local action within the so-called Local Agenda 21 (LA21) programme. This spawned a number of support organizations and networks that have led to more active focus and planning at the local level to address sustainability issues. LA21 has also enabled activists within local areas to help develop *bottom up* approaches, and this is further reflected in increasing public concern and public pressure to adopt more sustainable practices. Unfortunately, the potential ideas behind LA21 have not been fully exploited. In the UK, although the national government describes the initiative in glowing terms, it is not an obligation for local authorities to be involved, nor is it supported by specific financial or other incentives. In the future this must be rectified in order to build on the excellent work that has already been done and to realize its potential. At the most recent Earth Summit in Johannesburg, the proposal was adopted to move from Local *Agenda* 21 to Local *Action* 21. The time is now ripe for this change to be made possible, and local strategies and planning are key components.

In another sphere, and particularly in association with the private rather than the public sector, the involvement of clients in the building design and procurement process is now becoming more common, even in the UK. The result has been more emphasis on longer-term issues such as sustainability and running costs.

A final driver for change is the now more obvious level of inequality in the world between the developed nations of North America and Western Europe, and the developing world. This inequity of use of resources and imposition of the effects of pollution is, at the very least, making some people question the morality of the business-as-usual scenario.

The next steps

In this book many examples of good practice will be quoted, but the perception is that in many cases the changes are happening not because of a planned concept of urban sustainability but often in its absence. There is thus a strong argument to reinvent the professional role of the strategic urban planner or urban development manager; a person armed with the knowledge and expertise in the field of sustainable planning, design, construction, and even subsequent operation. But this professional must also work with the local community, organizations and businesses to develop more locally focused plans. There is the need for strategic planning to permeate each level of the process and scale of development. In subsequent chapters guidance is presented for planning, design and construction with the aim of promoting more successful, and indeed profitable, sustainable development.

The crucial thing is that action needs to be taken now; the self-reinforcing nature of many of the environmental drivers for change, combined with the long time lag between cause and effect, means that the planet could be faced with runaway global warming in the near future—a daunting prospect for future generations.

Part B

Planning and designing for sustainability

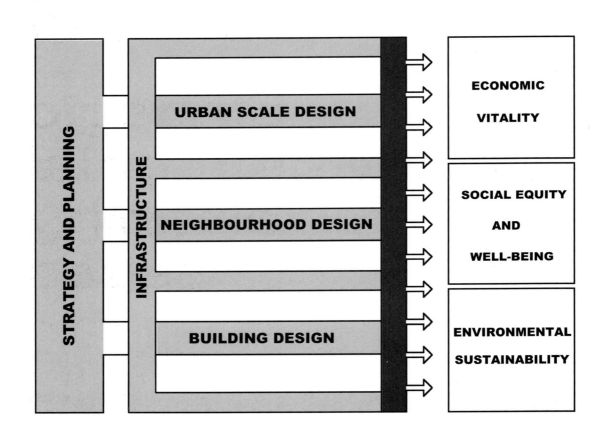

Chapter 3

Strategic environmental planning issues

Introduction

This chapter considers the environmental issues that must be addressed in a broad strategic way in order to achieve successful sustainable design of the urban and built environments. An effective approach to these issues requires planning at a level that can support integrated development within an urban context. The image at the front of this part of the text shows in a diagrammatic form the interaction between issues at various scales, including the crucial role for strategic planning.

There are many facets of development that might be considered important for sustainability and in this section they have been subdivided into the areas of *built environment, energy, transport, water* and *wastes and pollution*. Key features need to be addressed strategically and in a coordinated way because new policies and regulations may need to be developed or revised, and they must be consistently and fairly applied in a way which shows understanding of the overall picture, not just single narrow issues.

It is also clearly important to recognize that buildings and the construction process not only have effects on the local and further distant environments through both direct and indirect routes, but also that features of the environment affect buildings, their construction, their design and their performance; that is, it is a two-way process. For instance, changes in climate affecting weather patterns may require adjustment to regulation and policy for buildings so that they are safe and appropriate for that new climate.

The role and need for strategic planning

The whole building design and procurement process is very complex and encompasses development and construction from the urban and regional scale down to that of the individual dwelling. This range of scale may lead to a level of disconnection and separation between the tasks and professions involved in the overall process, and also between them and the local communities for which the development is planned. This disconnection means that professional groups such as urban planners, architects, builders, structural and services engineers, landscape designers and transport/highway engineers can frequently work in some degree of isolation and with the potential to execute, at best, less than optimal solutions and, at worst, contradictory ones. In attempting to achieve sustainable development the consequences of failure at this level are much greater because of the paramount need for systems solutions that take a holistic approach. One of the best means to promote better integration is through the definition of plans and policies at the urban or city level that recognize regional and national priorities and issues, but that also enable more local, neighbourhood concerns to be taken into account. Such plans and policies need then to be extrapolated to explain operation down to the building scale.

The involvement of local communities in formulating the criteria against which development is judged, and in the approval process, can be very fragmented at the present time and this means that single emotive issues can sometimes dominate to the exclusion of an overall understanding. This is unfortunate because the bedrock of long-term sustainable development is the production of an environment that matches the needs and aspirations of the whole local community in a balanced and objective way over a long timescale of 25 years or more. The planning and strategy development needs to enable involvement from the local community to occur more freely and, by providing information and resources that get the local community involved, there is a much greater chance of a more generally acceptable, broader, and long-lived strategy being adopted.

In the future the so-called *knowledge economy* may deliver new forms of involvement and control; however, the processes and timescale associated with this concept mean that action is still required in the interim to maintain sustainability. As a component of this there also needs to be strategic and ongoing development of information transfer networks such as broadband internet access. This can have the additional benefit of encouraging home working, thus reducing pressure on transport systems. It is also appropriate to consider controlling the type of buildings and building qualities (including creating places and spaces of real value) that are encouraged or permitted in new development. This may necessitate the use of expanded and more appropriate planning development controls than currently exist.

A criticism of much of the architectural movement for sustainable design is that it has delivered good examples in individual buildings or small groups of buildings, but that this has yet to be transferred to the mainstream or at a larger scale. Success at larger scale is a very necessary component for demonstration purposes and also because true sustainable development is most effective at larger scale. This again requires action at strategic planning level. The stance on scale is further supported by the Charter of European Cities and Towns towards Sustainability (the Aalborg Charter), signed in 1994 by a host of city representatives, which stated: 'We are convinced that the city or town is both the largest unit capable of initially addressing the many urban, architectural, social, economic, political, natural resource and environmental imbalances damaging our modern world and the smallest scale at which problems can be meaningfully resolved in an integrated, holistic and sustainable fashion'.

In this context a number of enabling concepts and actions are required. This can be promoted by the formulation of strategic plans and policies that set the framework for effective operation. *Agenda 21*, which was the Rio Earth Summit programme to guide global activity to support sustainable development, also has, as a key theme, local participation. There is scope to develop this area further.

Another reason for the need to promote a revised strategic planning function lies in the range and separation of bodies now providing guidance and, more importantly, funds for the enabling of urban development and regeneration. In many countries there exists a plethora of government ministries, non-governmental and quasi-governmental organizations which feed-in both finance and influence to various levels of development within the built environment. As these are often directed at specific regeneration issues, it can mean that the potential to influence overall urban sustainable design is lost. One might say that the challenge of coordinated strategic planning is to ensure that the value of the whole is at least equal to the sum of the parts, hopefully more, but certainly to ensure that the lack of coordination does not make it less.

As an underlying aim, one could take the following quotation from the UK Urban Task Force report, *Towards an Urban Renaissance*: '. . . the well-governed city must establish a clear vision, where all policies and programmes contribute to high quality urban development. In partnership with its citizens and its business leaders, the city authorities [should] have a flexible city-wide strategy which brings together core economic, social and environmental objectives'. It goes on to report: 'In this context, local government should be based upon principles of subsidiarity, mediation and partnership. It must combine strong strategic local government, which can provide long term vision and which can consider in a holistic way all the major needs and opportunities of a town or a city, with the engagement of its people'.

One of the greatest pressures for development in the UK comes from the need to build for the growing numbers of households. The number of new dwellings required in the next 20 years has been estimated at about 3.8 million and this will mean a substantial increase in development activities to meet needs. It arises from a number of causes including changing demographic patterns, household size, and the need to replace older stock. The placement and location of such large numbers of new properties has been of great concern because of the consequential environmental impact this will have. The general presumption dictated in the most recent government guidelines is that such new dwellings will, to a significant extent, reuse land already within urban areas. This includes the redevelopment of existing buildings, including changes of use, and an increase in average dwelling density in development to make more efficient use of land.

In addition to reuse there will also be some new extensions to existing urban developments, and some entirely new urban areas are also planned, mainly in the south-east of the UK; but even so, these new towns will represent only a fraction of the total and the expectation is that such new communities will have a strong sustainability focus. The purpose behind this thinking is that size is important; small, entirely new communities encourage unsustainability since they are rarely large enough to support local-area social and cultural services necessary for everyday life, and are often some distance from established employment locations. This means that not only does new infrastructure need to be provided but that also the occupants of such areas have significantly longer journey distances, normally by private motor vehicle, to access the facilities and services associated with larger urban areas and to travel to work. At the same time the new development encourages relocation, by those who can afford it, out from existing older urban areas, making them less viable and sustainable. The need for appropriate strategies and plans is clear if a more sustainable rather than a less sustainable outcome is to be achieved, and though the above description applies principally to the UK, facets of it are mirrored elsewhere.

Strategic planning can be defined in several ways, however. In addition to the development of the strategies themselves, it should encompass use of benchmarking and target setting, analysis of trends and performance, and the setting of goals for achievement. These features are interlinked and might be expressed in the diagrammatic way shown in figure 3.1.

Arising from the above discussion and examining options for best practice, one could recommend a series of actions that should be included in strategic planning activities:

- Coordination of environmental, economic and social requirements.
- Embodiment of approaches to issues which can operate over time-scales set at short, medium and long term (up to 30 years); and the

Figure 3.1 Strategic planning as part of a complete interlocking process

formulation of a range of overall objectives linking different scales of development and influences.

- Involvement of a wide group of stakeholders, particularly including local communities.
- Inclusion of positive elements from Local Agenda 21 initiatives.
- Inclusion of assessment of performance, targets and goal setting, and feeding back of results.
- Ensuring that the overarching issues of: built environment, energy, transport, water, and wastes and pollution are addressed in a coherent manner to avoid conflicts.

In what follows, the main environmental areas identified above are examined in more detail. The aim is to help demonstrate the means both to satisfy the demand for development and to address issues of sustainability.

The built environment

Clearly, in new urban development, or in redevelopment of existing areas, the buildings themselves will have an important environmental impact. Strategic planning considerations should encompass issues of size, location, nature and type, density, quality and the disturbance to local ecology and landscape. The site and local climate are also important factors which are dealt with in more detail later. In the following sections a range of topics is examined at a broad level and issues are highlighted, along with appropriate recommendations. The bibliography at the end of this book includes a number of useful sources to permit more detailed follow-up on the issues identified.

Size and placement of development

The planned development and expansion of urban areas and the creation of new urban areas are very important for long-term sustainability and must be addressed through sophisticated and detailed planning approaches. Planning control in many countries, and particularly in the UK, has until recently been seen as a relatively static zoning procedure, with applications for development considered against general regulations and policies which could be far removed from the local situation and which failed to take a truly holistic view. There may be conflicts between national and local requirements, which suggest the need for strategic planning that links the two. Obviously a key determinant is whether the development occupies new land separate from existing urban areas, whether it is adjacent to existing urban areas, or whether it is within existing urban areas. As part of the process it is necessary to have a good knowledge of the ecological, topographical and geological issues that impact on a development, and the acquisition and employment of such data may be best accomplished as part of strategic planning activities.

The optimum size of development is also important. A completely new urban area may need to be planned on a basis of having a population of at least 20 000 in order to provide for sustainability of its local infrastructure. Smaller additional development within existing urban areas may be easier to integrate but will still require enhancement of local facilities.

Some of the most awkward planning issues arise with the placement of substantial development adjacent to existing areas and the consequent objections from the local area's residents. The new development 'may require new facilities and amenities to support it and it is more likely that both existing local residents and potential new residents will favour development if substantial, good quality and attractive additional community facilities are also specified and included.

Figure 3.2 Care over scale and location is required for new urban development

In the recent past, new development was often carried out on clear *greenfield* sites. There are many advantages to starting with a clean sheet; for instance, the layout and planning can be performed so as to maximize environmental benefits such as daylight and solar heat gain, or control of air flows. There is also the opportunity to plan the location of amenities and facilities in order to maximize benefit for the local inhabitants. Unfortunately, many of the opportunities for optimum layout and design were not carried through in the past because of the natural desire by developers to maximize profit (and minimize cost). This, combined with a lack of understanding of the consequences, resulted in low environmental benefits. Local facilities and amenities provided in the development may not have been appropriate for the needs of the community, thus limiting the development of community spirit and often encouraging travel by private vehicle to access distant alternatives.

The re-use of existing land or occupation of so-called *brownfield* sites has much to recommend it. Urban sprawl and the degradation of green areas are reduced; it is also likely that existing infrastructure can be modified or enhanced to cope with the new redevelopment. There are also other benefits in the revitalization of an area and the encouragement of new investment.

When development occurs within existing areas and is linked to renovation and refurbishment of existing structures, there may be requirements for the preservation of character or historical record in particular neighbourhoods and buildings; each of these creates additional complications. The preservation of important examples of building style and type can be justified, as can general styles within an area; however, the insistence on exact replication of unsustainable features in every case may need reconsideration. An example might be retention of single glazing in replacement windows when superior double-glazing with matched appearance might be a more sustainable alternative. Planning strategies thus have to be more flexible in this regard.

Another area that requires consideration relates to possible risks of building on previously used land. Depending upon former use, there may be contamination or other technical considerations that limit redevelopment. Clear strategies concerning redevelopment policy and responsibilities must be set out so as to avoid future conflict.

There are of course already some very good examples of reuse, but it is clear that the enormous potential for improving the sustainability of existing property must also be addressed and actions taken. Older, perhaps derelict properties, such as the former woollen mill converted to retail and commercial uses shown in figure 3.3, can be brought back into new use rather than being allowed to decay. Other buildings have been converted

Figure 3.3 Old industrial buildings can be used for new commercial opportunities such as this bookshop in a converted mill

for domestic use; the example shown in figure 3.4 is that of a derelict mill planned to be converted to apartments with high insulation standards, heat and electricity generated by a sustainably managed woodchip fuel source, and additional power generated by 400 square metres of photo-voltaic panels to be mounted on car ports.

Building types

The types of buildings planned for in new or redevelopment schemes, in terms of their function (residential, commercial, retail, industrial or lei-sure), is another key factor in achieving successful urban environmental design. In recent times there has been great emphasis on *mixed-use*

Figure 3.4 A derelict mill which is to undergo complete refurbishment including many environmental design features

development in which a variety of building types are located in close proximity. The reasoning behind promotion of mixed development is that, by creating such areas, the need for travel to work by private vehicle can be much reduced, local facilities become more viable due to increased local demand (from the local workforce as well as local residents) and community spirit is encouraged. There also needs to be consideration of *urban grain* and positioning of strategic building types on a local level so as to optimize opportunities for linkage.

The quality of buildings, both in general aesthetics and in environmental terms, is also important. In the UK, the Commission for Architecture and the Built Environment (CABE) has argued for the importance of good design and, as will be seen later, good environmental design can be a profitable development component. Strategic planning can encompass traits which focus on the benefits of good design in ways that allow longer-term sustainability to be included too if *best value* principles are invoked on this scale. One concern at present is that the value or benefits of development are viewed in a disjointed manner and individual buildings can be difficult to assess in isolation because important factors at the urban scale are rarely included in the analysis. If the boundaries of a development are set at the broader scale, a number of alternatives can be considered; that is, not only should the building on its own be efficient and effective, but it should also be efficient and effective (and of good quality) within the context of its neighbourhood or urban area.

In new development there is also a need to encompass flexibility for potential future uses. As is now evident, the lifetime of many buildings exceeds the timescale over which they might be used in their initial capacity. Robust planning and design that allows for reuse rather than demolition is a preferable and more sustainable option that also maximizes the future value of the building. This must be linked to specification of materials and choice of construction techniques that provide long operational life and opportunity for modification without wholesale refitting or refurbishment. Wherever possible, construction materials available locally should be preferred so as to reduce transport costs and pollution, and also to aid the local economy.

There are also benefits to be gained from the development and distribution of information packs for homes and businesses to explain purposes and modes of operation of any sustainability-oriented features.

Density

Over recent decades the density of residential development, measured in terms of numbers of dwellings or habitable rooms, has been in a process of decline, particularly in suburban developments, with the consequent creation of urban sprawl. In the UK, densities of 90 dwellings per hectare were quite common at the start of the twentieth century whereas this had dropped to as low as 20–30 dwellings per hectare at its end. Many people consider that reversing the trend and encouraging greater densities is the main method to deliver sustainable urban development. The situation is somewhat complex, however. High densities may deliver the intensities required to support transport and local amenities and facilities, but the resulting buildings may not be visually appealing and may not encourage a variety of occupancy or integrated communities. There are also issues related to density that affect environmental performance and effects on the surrounding area.

The vitality of urban areas depends to some extent on a good mix of household and occupant types. It may therefore be more effective to combine a variety of building types to suit a variety of needs and at a variety of densities. Some of the recently planned new neighbourhoods (see Ashton Green within the Leicester case study later) have a higher density close to the main commercial and shopping areas and transport routes, combined with lower densities elsewhere. The use of such an approach can still deliver the average densities required for sustainability but with potential for a better, more integrated community, particularly when the local amenities are well planned and matched with the overall scheme.

Landscape and ecology

The natural resource of the site is its land and ecological systems. Protection and enhancement of these features helps to promote a feeling of well-being and also creates a more pleasant place to live. Ecological systems in themselves can also contribute to the absorption and recycling of certain wastes. Figure 3.5 shows green landscape close to the centre of Sheffield.

Ecological and biodiversity surveys should be carried out and an inventory of local attributes catalogued, particularly to discover whether the development impacts on sites of special scientific interest or special ecological habitats. It is also important that access routes to development sites should minimize habitat disruption and that development should ensure preservation of local natural habitats. The creation of new habitats such as wildlife corridors and the building of wildlife capacity is an opportunity that should be encouraged.

Figure 3.5 The integration of green landscape

Good initial ecological planning should be carried out with a view to establishing the longer-term viability of the area. Preparation for subsequent management can be developed through building partnerships with local groups so as to preserve and enhance the local ecological features. Planting programmes for urban trees and community orchards might be considered, and space for allotments and even city farms might be considered where appropriate.

Recommendations—Built environment

1. There is a need to carry out a community-based local environmental, economic and social appraisal to inform the development process and develop strategic planning and suitable supporting guidance. If there are any planning constraints that apply, such as for historical conservation, it will be necessary to set in place strategies or approaches to resolve conflicts that may arise.

2. If a new community is being built, involvement of participants at the earliest point after the initial construction phase is suggested, with the aim to create a new identity with prominence given to environmental issues. If development is associated with an existing local community, that community should be involved in the planning process and encouraged to have continued involvement during and after process completion; planning for integration with the existing community and facilities/amenities is crucial.

3. New developments must ensure provision or expansion of suitable additional community facilities to match needs. Needs for a housing mix appropriate to the area must also be met. Major commercial and industrial development providing employment should be planned to have easy access to community hubs and local centres, with transport links and facilities.

4. If the site has been used previously, examination of issues related to its strategic position, classification and needs is required, particularly if the site is affected by previous landfill activity. Site requirements for decontamination or treatment and the methods to be used must be addressed to ensure its long-term stability.

5. Provision for green open space and parkland should be made within the proposals, appropriate to the size and scale of the development, and suitable means of access in relation to residential areas should be ensured. These should be set within a broad long-term strategy for ecological maintenance and development.

6. Materials and methods of construction should be encouraged that reduce environmental impact and optimize potential for future re-use.

Figure 3.6 A park in Barcelona, a city with high standards in design of outdoor space

Overall, the aim should be to create a pleasant public realm that relates to the local context, provides key facilities and develops amenities, all with sustainability as an ongoing and integrated element.

Energy

The reduction of fossil-fuel-based energy use is a key issue for environmental sustainability and can be greatly assisted by the more informed and strategic development of energy planning at an early stage. There are opportunities to optimize supply opportunities as well as to reduce demand. The use of energy in buildings, mainly to create acceptable and comfortable indoor environments, consumes between 40 and 50 per cent of primary energy in many developed nations, which means that planning

40

and design is an extremely important influence on overall use. Buildings have conventionally been seen as energy and resource consumers, but perhaps a new view is now emerging in which the building itself begins to be designed in order to make net contributions to the resource system by both reducing its energy demand and acting as an energy source.

The means for energy production and supply have normally been seen as quite separate from the built environment and urban planning. ✳The world's developed economies are characterized by centralized or large-scale power generation, fuel processing and energy supply systems. These can be located some distance from the end user. This has a number of consequences, not least from the disjunction and separation of awareness of the user from the effects of the use, particularly in terms of pollution, damage to the local ecology, and intrusion into the landscape.

The current relatively small use of renewable and alternative energy sources is likely to increase, with improved economies in their operation, recognition of their beneficial environmental effects, and encouragement from national governments. Renewable energy plants and systems often operate at more local and indeed even individual building scales; policies and strategies for successful integration are needed, however, taking an urban viewpoint. Such sources can also offer some exciting alternatives for incorporation into the urban landscape, and perhaps a greater degree of understanding in planning approval is required from an aesthetic point of view for the use of a variety of alternatives within the built and local environment. There will also need to be changes from a technological standpoint, since current distribution and cost systems are predisposed towards centralized systems.

Figure 3.7 shows a small-scale rural wind farm that can produce renewable energy for the electricity grid from 500 MW, 35 metre high turbines. These turbines are located in a rural area but there is often objection to new turbines in a variety of locations, urban, suburban and rural, because of the visual and noise impacts. Such objections need to be understood and resolved through better planning that also addresses public understanding and perceptions of alternative sources of supply. Often there is gut reaction against change, but, given that change is inevitable, choices as to the best alternative must be made.

Development of policies and methods of controlling and enhancing the use of alternative energy sources are therefore needed. This is particularly important if buildings are developed to be energy providers rather than consumers and if alternative fuel sources are to be used. Combined heat and power (CHP) systems, which provide heat as well as electricity, offer some useful options but the balance between the two forms of energy supply and the schedule of demand is important for the viability of the

Figure 3.7 Wind farm

system. The matching of supply and demand within local areas and the connection of loads to the system need consideration at urban planning scale because of the importance of the mix of building types and activities. Alternative building forms, orientations and design features may be necessary to provide for, or enhance, the energy supply potential of the alternative technologies.

One alternative energy source is the burning of municipal waste; however, in addition to the concerns over air pollution, the building itself impacts on the local visual environment (figure 3.8). Less intrusive is the photovoltaic array on the façade of the Northumberland building in Newcastle (figure 3.9).

Figure 3.8 Alternative energy sources such as municipal waste incinerators also have some environmental impacts

In addition to new means of supply there are also other issues that can be dealt with at an urban planning level, such as the choice of energy source and illumination devices used for community facilities and street lighting. Light pollution and energy consumption can both be better controlled and reduced.

Recommendations—Energy systems

1. Strategic neighbourhood energy plans should be developed that incorporate issues such as layout and form of the built environment and energy conservation techniques. Information and advice

Figure 3.9 Northumberland Building: re-clad façade incorporating photovoltaic array

to improve energy conservation as an ongoing target should be made available to householders and businesses to optimize performance; free or subsidized energy surveys should be available. Policies to deal with fuel poverty issues are also required.

2. Strategic planning of supply and connections is required to permit ease of modification for installation of new energy sources and for monitoring and control systems to improve energy performance. The routing of supply networks should be coordinated with other service systems.

3. The potential for development of renewable energy harnessed on-site or at neighbourhood scale should be supported. Inde-

pendent energy supply companies can be used to optimize opportunities and fuel choices, including green energy sources.
4. Visual, noise and safety concerns that arise from use of renewable energy sources should be addressed positively.
5. Measures to optimize street lighting and traffic light performance should be taken, using the latest energy-efficient technologies.

Transport

The major consumers of energy and creators of pollution in the developed world are buildings themselves, but a further and growing problem is created by the transport systems that enable the population to travel between buildings. The development of many cities has meant the dispersal of population to outlying areas some distance from places of work and commercial and retail centres, making transport more difficult to plan and operate. Congestion and wasted time in use of transport is becoming an increasingly important concern. There has also been a marked increase in the reliance on private vehicles for movement and an increase in distance travelled. Movement and transport systems are thus some of the key elements of successful sustainable urban design, not just because of the potential to reduce congestion, pollution and energy use, but also because of the sense of community and connectedness that good movement systems provide.

Several factors require attention; the matching of local transport policies to development requires an understanding of the range of citizens' needs, particularly in the provision of safe and secure systems designed to meet required periods of use, service frequency and length of journey. The proximity of transport systems to local facilities, amenities and workplaces is important, as is the availability within principal housing zones.

Safe pedestrian routes and appropriate provision for cyclists is also required. Several commentators have used the so-termed 'Five Cs' as a way of expressing the needs of the local community, particularly for pedestrian movement. These are:

- *Connectivity*: networks for pedestrians need to connect the places they require to travel between, serving all major needs and providing a choice of routes. Easy access to public transport is required and opportunities for movement through safe green routes should also be provided.
- *Convenience*: primary routes should be direct and avoid awkward landscape features. Crossing roads should be easy and not require extended waiting periods.

- *Comfort*: paths and roadways should be of suitable width (two metres for most uses, three metres for paths shared with cycles) and constructed from suitable materials, avoiding steep slopes on primary routes. A sense of safety from positioning and surveillance should be created.
- *Convivial*: routes should be well lit at night, be suitable for meeting and chatting (away from noise and fumes) and designed to be aesthetically appealing.
- *Conspicuous*: routes should be easy to find and follow with clear signage, landmarks and surface treatments.

Integration of transport systems linking buses, trains and other public transport, and also with private vehicle use, is needed and may involve planning new road layouts and transport networks to provide optimum solutions that take account of traffic surveys and traffic impact assessments. Controls on private vehicle use and of congestion, including measures and regulation to enforce full costs, including pollution effects, are now becoming a reality. Limits on car parking both at home and in the workplace can be used to encourage use of public transport, but only if the right types of public transport are available.

Environmentally friendly public transport provision should also be encouraged with low pollutant emission vehicles and alternative fuels, such as electrically powered tram systems. In the following list the requirements are summarized and incorporate additional elements normally recognized as good practice.

Recommendations—Movement and transport systems

1. Regional transport planning is required to meet the challenges of allowing people, goods and services to move between domestic, commercial, retail, community and industrial locations.
2. Any newly planned building development must be assessed against existing transport plans and strategies, and proposals for how such new development will interact with existing provisions must be made; travel surveys and traffic impact assessments will be required.
3. Proximity and connections between new residential development and main employment, retail and commercial centres should be assessed. The location of planned community centres and the mix of building uses must also be considered. Catchment areas for bus routes and public facilities and amenities should be analysed in connection with proposed transport plans. Development should seek to maximize opportunities for access to primary

Figure 3.10 New transport networks may include electric tram systems

public transport corridors through and around the residential areas that then link to employment, retail, commercial and amenity centres.

4. In planning public transport, provision for adequate shelter against the weather must be made together with real-time information provision for services operating at sufficient frequency to encourage use.

5. Local transport nodes should allow access to more major urban areas and links to other forms of transport such as trains.

6. It is important to lay out development with the concept of enabling *walkable* neighbourhoods; the separation of vehicles, cyclists and pedestrians is desirable; height variations and kerbs should be used to separate use where needed. Access for disabled and other citizens of restricted mobility must be considered.

7. Cycling should be encouraged as an alternative to car use for suitable distances, and cyclists should be provided with segregated lanes and optimal contiguous and direct routes where possible. Secure cycle storage places must be included in development proposals to facilitate use, and workplace facilities for cyclists (such as showers and changing facilities) should be encouraged.

8. The number of private parking places should be limited—perhaps to about one place per dwelling. Parking should be secure and visible for surveillance. The visual impact of parking areas must also be considered.

9. Additional charges for parking and parking spaces away from the home might be considered, and charges or restrictions on road use may have to be considered to reduce congestion problems in urban areas, but these should be combined with improved public transport provision.

10. Charging or restriction policies should show favour towards communal cars and those using alternative fuels or with low emissions.

11. Reduced use of private vehicles may necessitate strategies to ensure access for delivery, loading and unloading.

Water

The sourcing, supply and disposal of water are each proving to be increasingly problematic issues from a range of perspectives. Periods of more extreme weather have led to both drought and flood conditions being experienced, each posing risks for the built environment. Improved design and construction of urban areas can reduce a number of the difficulties encountered; a strategic approach is needed, not least because of the infrastructure issues that are raised. Water poses issues on two fronts: firstly, its supply and use; secondly, the disposal of water, either as a component of sewage or, and perhaps more importantly given changes in precipitation levels, as rain or stormwater runoff. There is a need for alternative systems to differentiate supply as well as to deal with runoff, particularly at times of storm; storm water should in fact be seen as a resource to be collected and used, or harvested, where appropriate.

Water is a scarce resource in many parts of the world, and yet, in many developed countries, potable water is used for all processes including watering the garden, cleaning the car, flushing the lavatory as well as drinking and for food preparation. At the same time as water shortages are being reported there has been a marked increase in variability of weather patterns, exacerbated by the operation of water drainage and runoff systems close to, or beyond, capacity levels. Excess water in the form of rain can lead to substantial problems for drainage systems, which are made worse by the building of new development on flood plains, and by the covering of large areas of water-absorbing ground with solid urban surfaces such as roads, paths and concrete, and hard surfaces over garden areas. The natural water flow patterns can be altered quite substantially

Figure 3.11 Alternative water collection for use at the Hockerton housing project

and this causes major problems for existing systems and potential for increased flooding. The flooding associated with river flows may be further enhanced by coastal flood risk—many of the defences erected in the past may not be able to cope with exaggerated water levels as storm surge risk increases, combined with rising sea levels.

Strategic planning actions and design initiatives can be used to help with the setting and application of performance targets for developments. There are also opportunities to differentiate the collection, processing and use of water according to source and use. Water consumption can be affected by the choice of appliances within buildings. In new or re-development the use of hard surfaces and water-absorbing capacity must be considered and there is now much greater specification and deployment of sustainable urban drainage systems. Of course, general groundwater issues, hydrology, watersheds and water quality must be encompassed in strategic approaches.

Recommendations—Water systems

1. A local assessment in relation to strategic water management should be included in development proposals. Urban landscape should be designed with care and a suitable mix of permeable and non-permeable surfaces linked to replenishment of ground water.
2. There is a need to develop and encourage easy-to-understand water classification systems to allow for different uses. Greater use of recycled greywater and rainwater collection should be made for non-potable needs.
3. Policies to encourage water meters to be installed in prominent locations are suggested to allow ease of monitoring. Low water-use appliances, such as toilets, washers, showers and spray taps, should be installed to help reduce consumption.
4. Greater use of on-site waste water treatment in the form of reed beds, passive systems and so-called *living machines* should be made, and incentives offered for their use.
5. Rain and stormwater collection systems are required to divert runoff from conventional systems. Sustainable urban drainage systems (SUDS) should be considered as a matter of course in new development (figure 3.12). Swales, basins and filter drains help to reduce problems of surges and flooding. Advantage should be taken of the use of ponds and other water features to help control water flows and provide local amenity.
6. Development on river or tidal flood plains should not normally be planned.

Figure 3.12 Sherwood Energy Village site: sustainable urban drainage was pre-installed as part of its infrastructure

Wastes and pollution

In the UK, about 470 million tonnes of waste is produced each year; of this 28 million tonnes is household waste and 75 million tonnes is produced by business premises. Construction waste is also a very significant fraction of the total, at 72 million tonnes, and this occurs as demolition and refurbishment wastes or as the by-products of new build. There are also significant amounts of waste material now produced in urban areas as synthesized, rather than natural, materials, which can pose specific disposal problems either because of an active pollutant threat or through the long life of the material before it is naturally broken down. The conventional means to deal with many of these wastes has been to bury them in landfill sites, a solution particularly favoured in the UK, with a number of environmental consequences. As the current sites begin to fill and pressure against new sites is exerted by local inhabitants, alternative means of disposal need to be developed, including recycling.

Production of wastes and pollution within the urban environment can be reduced and controlled by a number of processes. Though household waste is only a small proportion of the total waste that a developed society produces, it is symbolic of wider concerns and the most visible component for the general public. Methods for dealing with domestic waste should therefore be a prominent part of an overarching strategy for commercial and industrial wastes and, of course, construction-generated waste.

Policies and procedures for dealing with wastes are therefore required at urban level and also need to be based on a national approach in order to avoid simple transference of problems to neighbouring areas. Local authorities in the UK are beginning to introduce more encouragement for recycling; these policies are long overdue since in the UK at present less than 10 per cent of household waste is normally recycled (in some areas less than 5 per cent), compared to 40 per cent and above in many areas of Europe. Wider provision of special recycling collections should be encouraged (see figure 3.13).

Figure 3.13 Opportunities should be created to recycle more waste, as in this green bin scheme in the Kirklees area (UK)

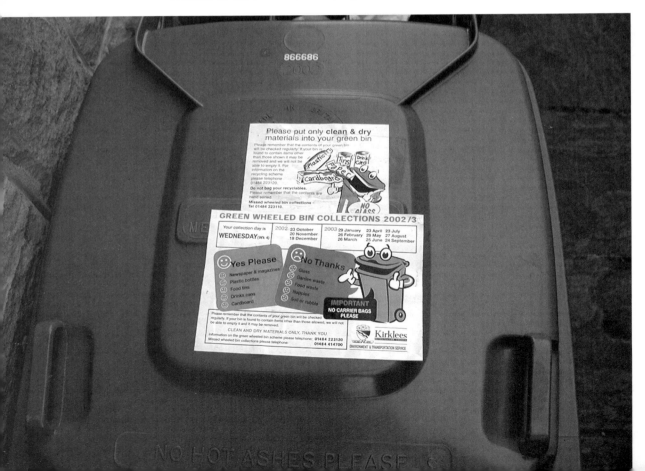

In the case of building design and construction, the initial choice of materials and construction techniques can affect eventual waste generation. Planning policies and site design for subsequent reuse/recycling/reclamation need to be better defined. Active use of recycled, reused and reclaimed materials should be encouraged through policies and planning.

In urban areas, a waste disposal strategy that includes composting facilities and recycling facilities can promote much more efficient systems for dealing with such wastes. Collection of wastes should be designed as part of new development, as at the Bo01 City of Tomorrow site (see figure 3.15) which is also discussed in the case study chapter. Other pollution and wastes policies should aim to encourage a change of business culture concerning wastes, seeing such material as a potential future resource.

Air quality, noise pollution issues, the effects of wastes and sewage/foul water treatment on local aquatic environments, are each deserving of inclusion in an overall policy. The burning of waste may have an energy benefit, but this must be weighed against environmental issues such as the release of contaminants to the air.

Recommendations—Wastes and pollution

1. Strategies should be used to reduce construction waste at the time of new development or refurbishment. Encouragement to reuse materials from the site or from nearby sites should be provided, and life cycle assessments undertaken to provide the decision makers with the information on alternatives.

2. Strategic decisions about waste should be taken with the involvement of the local community since alternatives to current practices can be made workable only if the community subscribes to the modification of behaviour.

3. Provision to separate waste streams should be made at the household level but with ease of collection and disposal at the community level. Use of different systems at different scales and appropriate storage options for wastes are required. Recycling facilities should enable ease of sorting into necessary categories. Suitable materials might be sold to realize their value, thus creating an income stream to encourage the community to recycle. Novel and easier-to-use disposal systems should be planned as part of the development infrastructure. Distances to be travelled by householders for recycling should be minimized.

Figure 3.14 Conventional construction activities produce significant quantities of waste materials

Figure 3.15 Waste disposal chutes designed as part of the integrated site infrastructure at the Bo01 development in Malmö

4. Provision for composting suitable waste should be made—perhaps on a community or neighbourhood basis.
5. Air, water and soil quality should be monitored on a regular basis to assess the impact of wastes and pollution on the local environment.
6. Alternative disposal processes such as pyrolysis, gasification and the clean burning of waste for energy recovery should be considered within wider policy options.

Implementation of strategies and planning

As already stated, strategic planning has great value at the urban city or regional level in that it should both connect upwards with broader regional and national policies and plans and should also have dialogue with the more local township or neighbourhood level. The body most suitably placed therefore to undertake and coordinate such a task is the local authority, council or similar level of government. This level also offers the chance for interaction with elected representatives of the communities that are being served, and provides sufficient size that the employment of specialist advisors and other professionals becomes viable within the process.

In order to coordinate and facilitate the process it is recommended that a small team of planners and managers with appropriate skills be established within the local council. There should also be investigation of potential development in terms of community and cultural issues; the built and natural environments; and resources and finances. The local community should be involved in developing and testing ideas for development which enable the proposal and evaluation of policies that lead to the creation of a wide-ranging strategy. The local community and stakeholders can then be included in the development of an agreed neighbourhood plan. The powers and facilities of the local council or authority should be used to promote the chosen strategy and support activities that contribute to its execution, including the monitoring and review of performance, with information fed back on the success or otherwise of the various stages of operation.

Application of laws, regulations and controls

The local council or authority is normally charged with ensuring that legislation, regulations and controls are applied within its area of jurisdiction. These may have been set at international, national or local level and it has a duty to apply these fairly but comprehensively when dealing with issues of sustainability. The functioning of revised strategic planning should ensure that policies and regulations are well integrated, and this may also require some degree of flexibility in application.

Although environmental sustainability must be coordinated with economic and social issues, there should be a predisposition towards placing the environment as the prime consideration, for without it the other two cannot function in the longer term. There are a number of assessment techniques that can be employed (these are described later) and they should be more frequently used in determining appropriate actions.

Indeed, procedures that involve monitoring, measuring, targeting and goal setting should be integrated into strategic planning so that feedback produces improved results. The public discussion of such elements can be beneficial too since the community is enabled to be more connected with the decision-making process and it also permits better understanding of issues of sustainability and their evaluation.

Control of development through the planning process needs to have a more local, neighbourhood dimension than at present. The operation of strategic planning can facilitate this by providing the framework and the information for the more localized plan. The enthusiasm generated by Local Agenda 21 operation and actions can be built upon here to provide a more formalized series of processes through the formulation and operation of so-called Neighbourhood Action Plans (NAPs). Local resource management should be incorporated, as well as an understanding of dealing with wastes and pollution at the local level.

A problem in the UK context is that individuals and relatively small groups can have a disproportionate effect on development by focusing on single issues, particularly if the agitators are well educated and able to use procedures to their own particular advantage. Many of those either proposing or opposing change are very parochial in their interest; they are often said to reflect the NIMBY ('not in my back yard') approach. Plans developed by a neighbourhood would require a more comprehensive approach, in effect providing strategic planning at the small scale, and all members of the community must face up to issues rather than passing them on; they would have to balance competing influences. Strategy planning, by being proactive rather than reactive, can be a means to wrest the initiative from narrow-focus and narrow-minded groups. The devolution of a certain level of power has risks but should also encourage those currently unlikely to become involved in urban scale decision making to take a role.

Strategies for the local council or authority

There is much that can be achieved by way of using the activities of the local council to indicate new, more sustainable ways of working. The council will often have duties to deal with a number of environmental issues and it will also be a major energy consumer. Simply by altering its own activities, it can provide better support to environmental sustainability. Its employees can be influenced to act in a more sustainable way whilst at work and this may also have a knock-on effect at home. Rewards for members of the workforce who suggest more sustainable ways of operating can be offered as an incentive.

In encouraging changes in methods and practices and by creating points of focus, the profile of various technologies and techniques can be raised in the local community and this may mean they surpass the initial take-off level and reduce the burden of marketing costs for new initiatives. This is also a useful strategy for encouraging new businesses to grow.

In summary, there are several specific areas in which the local council or authority should develop policies:

- Monitoring and conservation of energy use in council buildings.
- Policies affecting fuel type and fuel use in council vehicles.
- Monitoring and conservation of water use in council buildings.
- Use of alternative energy sources for council premises, including purchase of alternative green energy from suppliers.
- Reduction of wastes and encouragement for reuse, recycling and alternative disposal methods.
- Development and adoption of assessment methodologies that might also be applied outside the council.

Improving the sustainability of local businesses and organizations

Important though raising the sustainability performance of the council itself may be, the environmental impact of the businesses and industries working within its boundaries is likely to be more important by several orders of magnitude. Most businesses are, of course, focused on financial sustainability in the first instance; strategies to make the operation of businesses more sustainable with better financial results are therefore valuable tools.

Issues of the built environment's impacts, good principles of urban planning, neighbourhood design and building construction need to be embodied in general guidance provided by the strategy-planning body to inform the needs of local organizations. Some means of achieving these aims are as follows:

- Promotion of best practice procedures through the production of guidebooks, factsheets, and provision of data on exemplars of good practice.
- Adoption of local versions of assessment and rating schemes for new developments and redevelopments, with permission for development linked to performance standards.
- Publicizing schemes which make the public aware of the environmental performance of organizations and which can therefore lead to modified purchasing behaviour.

- Adoption of purchasing policies that favour more environmentally sustainable products or services.
- Provision of direct and indirect financial encouragement to use more sustainable practices by such actions as: the offering of rebates on taxes or costs of development; the provision of grants for the carrying out of particular sustainability-related measures; and the offering of low-interest-rate loans for environmental improvement measures.
- Imposition of taxes in such areas as transport (congestion charging or road tolls), taxes on parking in certain areas, and charges made for collection and disposal of wastes, to encourage changes in practice.

Encouraging sustainability in the wider community

The local authority may offer encouragement for change to more sustainable processes and practices by the levying of charges on less sustainable alternatives, the granting of permissions and the offering of loans, tax rebates or grants for more environmentally sensitive solutions. The key to this is information provision, however, and strategic planning must provide the framework for elucidating information about new development in a form digestible by non-specialists.

One means to encourage more public understanding and participation is to focus on issues of quality of life and human well-being, terms that most people understand. Of course, underlying these broad terms are complex listings of factors that have been identified as influencing them and can be used to measure the benefit or otherwise of changes to the urban environment, albeit in sometimes rather indirect ways.

Summary

The range of topics covered in this chapter has been wide; the purpose has been to introduce the generic issues within suitable categorizations and to stimulate thinking about themes that must be part of the subsequent design processes. These issues are not only relevant to local authority planners but should also be of concern and interest to designers, local communities and the general public. Ideally, a process planning methodology is required which not only indicates the information flows that are needed between the various players and components of the whole system but which also develops the feedback loops and links between the scales of development.

Overall, perhaps, some of the most coherent support for more and better strategic planning is provided by extracts from the key proposals of the UK's Urban Task Force report: 'Give local authorities a strategic role in managing the whole urban environment, with powers to ensure that other property owners maintain their land and premises to an acceptable standard' and 'make statutory development plans more strategic and flexible in scope, and devolve detailed planning policies for neighbourhood regeneration into targeted area plans'.

In summary, good strategic planning initially helps the city or region and its citizens to create a vision of future development that is both realistic and forward looking through a process of participation and partnership. It should then develop practical policies and strategies and lead activities and processes to support that vision so that the desired outcomes can be achieved.

Chapter 4

Designing the built environment

Introduction

Whereas the previous chapter focused on planning of the built environment from a strategic perspective, this chapter deals with the detail of the more practical implementation, ranging through urban, neighbourhood and building scales. The prime focus is on good quality, environmentally sensitive and energy-efficient design opportunities that may be exploited.

The importance of an urban approach

In recent years, in the UK, there has been some increased focus on cohesive sustainable urban design. This has been prompted by the work of the Urban Task Force led by Lord Rogers of Riverside, also now associated with activities of the Office of the Deputy Prime Minister. This shows the importance of a *synthesis* approach and the need to address issues at the appropriate scale. Unfortunately, at the same time it has seemed that large tracts of central government funding, made available to support regeneration, were provided with a narrow focus and have produced at times a less integrated and potentially less successful outcome, at least from a sustainability perspective.

The Commission for Architecture and the Built Environment (CABE) has taken a lead in attempting to reconcile the issues and to integrate good design and sustainability in the development and regeneration process. Nevertheless, potential still exists to give a stronger role to strategic planning and urban policy in order that the buildings and environments created serve the longer-term sustainability needs rather than simply the immediate need to solve a particular problem or deliver a single building project. The necessary synthesis could be incorporated into a redefined *masterplanning* activity.

Masterplanning

In order to satisfy sustainability needs in modern urban design, the masterplanning activity should not be solely concerned with zoning for activities and spatial planning at the broad scale, as it may have been in the past. It must be more sophisticated and include three-dimensional physical planning for both buildings and public areas; it should, further, also be further multi-dimensional in taking into account temporal variations, the social and cultural concerns of the local community, and the overarching environmental issues. It should involve the evolution of a design strategy, the production of design codes and a plan for implementation and management. The masterplan must clearly express the policies derived from the strategic planning process and should take into account health, equity, environmental quality and resource efficiency. It should set the scene to develop the character of an area by incorporating transport access; the ways in which key features can knit together to form urban communities or villages; the planned density and mix of uses; and the positioning of key features such as local centres, landmarks, parks and facilities.

Masterplanning in the twenty-first century should also be more aware of environmental sustainability issues, though this can only happen with the support and understanding of the local community. The masterplan must make explicit reference to the results of environmental assessments that should be carried out, and these assessments need to enable the impacts on quality of life and well-being for communities to be understood. Comparative information on alternative scenarios should also be provided.

Emphasis on the quality of the built environment should also be incorporated and expressed through the planning and subsequent design and construction functions. Such quality helps create the places that people wish to live and work in, and sustains them over a longer period.

The importance of local climate

It is also essential that in future development a clearer relationship is established between buildings and their local climate at macro/regional level as well as at the local microclimatic level. Such relationships existed in the past when buildings were designed on the basis of collective experience and understanding of the climate, materials, skills and technologies available, and local conditions. Sometimes the understanding was less precise than would be required to design for the sophisticated needs of present-day building occupants, and this also indicates a need to understand modern assessment techniques and tools to improve the design process. A lead in this area must be taken at urban level in order to set the correct climatic framework for design; a framework that shows understanding, integration and expertise that are not always available at single project scale (even though this is where the impact may be felt). It is necessary to develop strategies at urban scale to ensure consistency and viability. Issues concerned are:

- Site layout, exposure and orientation.
- Form, size and layout of new building.
- Relationship to and effect of surrounding buildings.
- Relationship to and effect of surrounding topography and landscape.
- The effects of development on the functioning of already existing buildings and systems.
- Interaction with local microclimate.
- Use of passive and active design features matched to the climate.
- Choice and use of materials and construction.
- Choice and use of building services systems.

Policy and planning issues

A number of aspects of urban scale design, and to a lesser extent neighbourhood and building design, have policy and planning components and should be considered in a strategic and managed manner.

Specification of development

The general specification and expectation of the urban plan should be modified to take greater account of sustainability. The process should commence with locally based appraisal and information exchange and permit the production of development briefs, neighbourhood design guides and masterplans. In each facet of the process, the existing situation must be examined as well as the future potential for enhancement or improvement. Some elements should be performance based rather than specification based and be flexible to allow for gradual development and evolution.

The location and planning of urban and neighbourhood centres may require a more interventionist or managed approach than at present in order to enable urban forms to evolve. Control of building activities will also need to take into account climatic factors and interaction with surrounding buildings. Situations cannot be allowed to occur in which a well designed sustainable building is in the future made unsustainable by poorly executed changes to its surroundings. Current theories about grain and scale within development may need to be modified to take greater account of the environmental and climate issues.

New and revitalized local urban centres ought to be seen as key elements of sustainable development. The centres need to have some retail focus but also provide access to other commercial activities and employment as well as the normal community facilities and amenities. By bringing together these elements, the critical mass needed to support the economic viability of the area is created, but, further, there are great environmental benefits from the potential for reduced travel distances and improved public transport. The linking to transport hubs, and the provision of services to meet local needs in pleasant surroundings, are self-reinforcing issues and should also develop in relation to neighbourhood urban centres.

The density of development is crucial to a number of other issues such as transport and the functioning of local and urban commercial and retail centres. Uniform density can be both visually boring and lacking in vitality; it is also unnecessary since gradations of density can be developed to allow flexibility. Highest densities are required close to the centres of activity and transport, but care must be taken that high density does not create demands on the surroundings that are unsustainable.

Urban layout and density will also have an important impact on the potential to exploit alternative or renewable energy sources, either because of the possible locations that are available for construction of generating plant or with respect to its feasibility for use because of inappropriate demand schedules or mix of demand from a development. In planning, care should be taken to avoid decisions that overly restrict future options, and the need for current and future distribution systems must be taken into account. Policies may also have to be developed that address changing circumstances; for instance, well-designed buildings may not need the heating and cooling systems currently typically specified and provided as a matter of course. As a result, planning guidelines and their interpretation may need modification.

Similarly, policies and regulations applied at urban level relating to water systems may need modification to allow for collection, storage, and use of a greater variety of sources. Already water/rain collection systems are being used in practice, as are sustainable urban draining systems. Similar and alternative systems are also likely to become more common in the future. Waste water disposal to other than conventional foul water sewers, such as reed beds, is also likely to develop, and urban planning will have to account for the different needs in both local land planning and approval of systems.

Building materials and construction techniques are already being changed to meet the demands of sustainability. This can result in the design of buildings with alternative appearance or use of different building practices. Traditional planning regulations at the urban level can conflict with such changes in practice, and understanding will need to be shown, together with adoption of more flexible policies (or at least a more flexible interpretation). A relaxation of approaches is likely to be required particularly within building conservation areas, and the application of building codes will also have to be adjusted.

Access to transport systems

General transport issues have been considered in the previous chapter; here the concern is to examine elements of the layout of an urban area and the locations of facilities required for that area to function, and the distances between dwellings and those facilities. Figure 4.1 illustrates optimum and recommended maximum distances that should be aimed for in order to promote a successful community. The list is not comprehensive, but indicative of requirements. The distances to bus stops and local centres are particularly important in determining use of private car travel; however, in order to encourage workers to use public transport it is just as vital that the location of employment is well served, as well as the housing areas in which the workforce lives. It is also important that the planning must incorporate some degree of anticipation of developments likely over a long time period. Though the details are most relevant to the UK, the general features have wider applicability.

Feature	Neighbourhood										Urban Area		City		
	100m	200m	300m	400m	500m	600m	700m	800m	900m	1000m	2000m		3000m		5000m
Play area	■	░													
Local shop	■	■	░	░											
Bus stop	■	■	■	░	░										
Post office	■	■	■	■	░	░									
Playground/small park	■	■	■	■	░	░									
Primary school	■	■	■	■	■	░	░	░							
Natural green space	■	■	■	■	■	░	░	░							
Public house	■	■	■	■	■	░	░	░							
Local shopping centre	■	■	■	■	■	░	░	░							
Local transport hub/rail	■	■	■	■	■	■	■	■	░	░					
Local community facilities	■	■	■	■	■	■	■	■	░	░	░				
Health centre	■	■	■	■	■	■	■	■	■	░	░		░		
Church/meeting hall	■	■	■	■	■	■	■	■	■	■	░		░		
Secondary school	■	■	■	■	■	■	■	■	■	■	░		░		░
Playing fields/sports facilities	■	■	■	■	■	■	■	■	■	■	░		░		░
District centre	■	■	■	■	■	■	■	■	■	■	■		░		░
Major shopping facilities	■	■	■	■	■	■	■	■	■	■	■		░		░
Large natural green space	■	■	■	■	■	■	■	■	■	■	■		■		░
Cultural/arts facilities	■	■	■	■	■	■	■	■	■	■	■		■		░
Leisure/entertainment facilities	■	■	■	■	■	■	■	■	■	■	■		■		░
Hospital	■	■	■	■	■	■	■	■	■	■	■		■		■
Major cultural facilities	■	■	■	■	■	■	■	■	■	■	■		■		■

Key: ■ = best practice   ░ = recommended

Figure 4.1 Optimum distances between dwellings and the key features of the urban environment that support them

Open space

Much attention is focused on the layout and design of buildings, but attention should also be paid to designing the spaces between them. This is often the missing link in making a community work. Good landscape and other features can aid this process, but it is necessary to make the correct strategic decisions at the earlier urban design stage. The positioning of landmark buildings and structures, and the use of squares, streets, courts and other features, helps to encourage public use. Open space and provision for green areas are crucial in terms of modifying the local solar and wind climate, and the activities that are expected to occur within such open areas should be designed with climate in mind.

Open green space and parkland therefore need to be planned in conjunction with building. The concepts of *green lungs* or green networks of interconnected spaces have been advanced to enhance access, climate, biodiversity, water absorption, general amenity and recreational opportunities. Green areas can also be integrated with urban forestry and tree planting as well as offering opportunities for composting of suitable wastes.

The planning of these spaces needs to consider their linkage and networking and suitability to the facility and function they provide. Interconnection and routing are important so as to engage with all suitable public areas and encompass a logical hierarchy. The places must create a sense of safety through surveillance and frequency of use, and also by engaging the interest of the local community. The spaces should be suitable for a variety of groups of different ages to use, and features such as public gardens can be incorporated as focal points in urban centres. With regard to many of these issues, good environmental design can aid and improve the operation and benefits and it is also important to design for linkages to smaller or private spaces around dwellings.

Not all open space has to be open to the weather; the use of *wintergardens* (large scale free-running but enclosed conservatories or glasshouses) as vehicles for creating environmentally pleasant spaces is now being developed in urban areas (see plate 1). Such spaces can also encourage greater community-focused activity.

Materials of construction

The choice of building materials and the sourcing of any particular item can have a significant environmental and energy impact. Influence over choices can be made through the adoption of appropriate strategies and controls for development. Such policies can also influence the methods of manufacture and may encourage prefabricated construction off-site as a means of improving efficiency, reducing waste and increasing recycling through design for future disassembly. A balance is needed, however, since such construction can sometimes lead to increased transport use.

In developing policies in this area there should be assessment of the environmental impact of techniques for extraction or production and minimization of transportation of materials and other resources. Estimation of the impact on the *in-use* energy consumption of choice of materials should be made, and materials with intrinsic pollutant or toxic effects should obviously be avoided. Use can be made of environmental rating systems to assess the impact of materials, to inform policy decisions and to encourage appropriate choices in design.

Planning for new building technologies

Some issues arising from incorporation of new technologies require consideration at urban policy or planning level; also, new, more sustainable building practices often have effects on the appearance and construction techniques used in development. In some countries, the UK perhaps being a good example, planning policies are often very conservative; this can discourage use of some very worthwhile alternatives.

Earth-integrated or underground structures in which one side or perhaps even the majority of a building is covered with earth can be a very useful technique both to reduce the visual impact of development and to provide more insulation and thermal capacity. The modification to heat flows through the structure is normally very advantageous and has been recognized by some cultures for many years; unfortunately, in places where such types of development are unknown, planning policy may inhibit development. In one of the case studies later, the Hockerton housing project is described, and this provides a good example of the use of this technique.

The use of thick layers of insulation in construction as a means to improve energy performance can also cause problems because it may mean

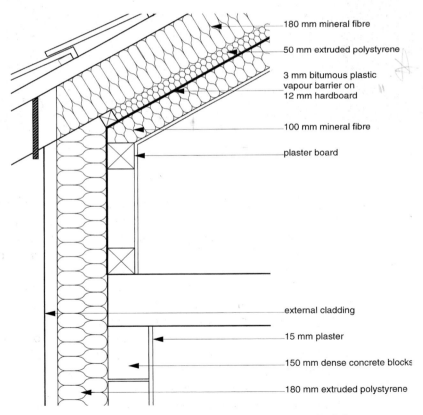

180 mm mineral fibre

50 mm extruded polystyrene

3 mm bitumous plastic vapour barrier on 12 mm hardboard

100 mm mineral fibre

plaster board

external cladding

15 mm plaster

150 mm dense concrete blocks

180 mm extruded polystyrene

Figure 4.2 Example of construction section for a highly insulated building

Figure 4.3 Experimental house at Freiburg using transparent insulation materials

that the wall cavity size is increased beyond that which normal regulations permit. There are also cases where the transfer of moisture across cavities that contain insulation materials is poorly understood. In both situations there is a case for a more enlightened application of policy and regulation.

In some cases good attention to passive heating measures and high insulation standards has meant that properties do not need conventional heating systems, even on the coldest of winter days. The lack of such heating systems sometimes means that these properties are categorized as *unimproved* and it may be more difficult to borrow money to buy them or to gain permission to build them. This is clearly illogical and there needs to be better understanding in planning and design systems and by mortgage companies and property developers.

Novel building technologies may result in different shapes or colours of buildings, which can mean that better environmental design or use of building-integrated renewable energy alternatives may be rejected due to poor policy or planning guidelines. Insulation techniques such as the use of the transparent insulation materials or aerogels can result in a difference in external appearance, as can novel glazing, shading and daylighting systems, the implications of which need to be taken into account in planning at the urban level since it is at such a level that modifications can be considered and implemented.

Some of these issues are beginning to be dealt with, but as well as the conservatism of the planning system there can be an in-built conservatism within the local population that must also be addressed. There is no simple solution, except to continue to expose modern design and technologies to greater public scrutiny and, hopefully, subsequent understanding.

Neighbourhood and site planning

This section concentrates on design at the neighbourhood scale and the various site features that impact on energy-efficient and environmentally sound design. Neighbourhood and site planning should also follow on from, and be intimately linked to, urban scale planning.

The phrase *climate-sensitive design* has attained a level of credibility and acceptability in recent years. Such design is sometimes referred to as *bioclimatic architecture* and it is certainly something that requires inclusion at neighbourhood scale. In essence, this approach acknowledges that the interaction of solar and other climatic factors with the building and its surroundings will determine the local external environmental conditions which subsequently have an impact on internal environments and the comfort level of the occupants.

There are a number of issues that should be encompassed at this scale:

- Assessment of the effect of, and relationship to, buildings and other features at the site boundary of the proposed development.
- Evaluation of the optimum positioning and width of access roads, thoroughfares and pedestrian pathways, and their relationship to building heights.
- Maximizing the environmental benefit to the site as a whole of landscaping, water features, planting trees and other vegetation and consideration of the effect of the positioning of walls, fences and other obstructions.
- Planning the basic orientation of building and façades with respect to solar influences and determination of the environmental impact

of sunlight and shade, and understanding the effect of site slope and topography.

■ Choice of appropriate form and massing of buildings and building grouping.

■ Designing to take advantage of the benefits of the local wind environment and reduce wind problems.

■ Assessment and reduction of environmental noise and other local pollution issues.

These climate-oriented features have the potential to reduce both winter heating demand and summer overheating or cooling requirements if integrated into site development. A further benefit is the increase in general level of occupant comfort and the creation of a more pleasant environment in the outdoor areas of the site. Also, the durability of building materials may be increased and maintenance costs reduced by the mitigation of adverse weather impacts. Site design decisions thus have an important influence at the microclimatic scale and must be well understood and applied in practice; the difficulty is that they can sometimes be contrary to other planning issues, so a good rounded appreciation and judgement are vital.

Once a site has been defined and an assessment of the impacts that cross over the boundaries has been made, it is possible to move on to detailed planning of the site itself in terms of form, layout and orientation.

Form, layout and orientation of development

Community facilities and amenities should be at the heart of neighbourhood development and should relate to local commercial, retail and workplace areas, as well as to the local housing. The design of mixed-use development in which housing, retail, commercial and leisure activities can be planned in close proximity is a popular solution. The combination of different activities at different levels of a block can give a good integrated mix and still offer access to green outdoor space, as illustrated in figure 4.4. Design for good mix is important so as to support good environmental practices with regard to transport but also to allow opportunity for community-based heat and power systems, which require a balanced variety of energy demands. The density of development, as related in the previous section, is also an important factor in determining the viability of local facilities. Planning must therefore involve a multi-dimensional appreciation of the factors.

The shape and size of the buildings, either as blocks, as groups or as individual elements, has an effect on key environmental concerns. The design in this respect should take account of the surrounding to the site, in particular existing buildings, and assessment of the impact on sunlight,

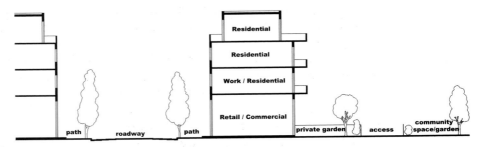

Figure 4.4 Integrated mixed-use development within the same block

daylight, shade, air flow and other factors should be determined at the outset. There can, however, be points of contradiction in the design of neighbourhoods between optimizing solar benefits and dealing with needs to maintain a particular appearance or control security. Orientation, spacing and distance are key features, but in suggesting design options one should not be overly prescriptive; each neighbourhood must reflect a degree of integration of factors and its own character. Figure 4.5 shows a solution to street design that provides privacy through appropriate spacing and planting.

Urban block arrangement also impacts on environmental design and sustainability. Blocks should generally have a defined perimeter to separate public and private areas, though in dense urban settings the perimeter should not be monotonous, for both aesthetic and environmental reasons. Also, the orientation and style of blocks should not be too rigid, though it would be best to optimize design to allow southerly aspect (that is, with the longer dimension of rectangular blocks east–west), but the short dimension should not be so narrow that it creates self-shading. Central areas within blocks and courtyards should be oriented for best effect; courtyards in particular offer climatic benefits during both summer and winter periods.

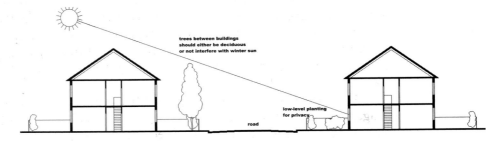

Figure 4.5 Planting and spacing is important to maintain solar access and privacy across streets

Normal design recommendations in the UK are that blocks should aim for open cluster appearance with approximately 60 per cent building, 40 per cent open space.

Spacing between blocks and buildings should consider daylight (used to offset the need for artificial lighting) as well as sunlight. Where blocks face either across roads or across central areas, the space opposite a major building element should be left more open. Such blocks allow daylight and sunlight in, and do not require such wide streets for maintenance of privacy; however, block corners need particular consideration to avoid problems. Within blocks, the use of different heights for different functions (dwellings and workspaces) can help make best use of solar gain whilst avoiding overheating; size of individual units or buildings should favour depth over width, or aim for a square plan. The shape and type of roof can also be modified to reduce overshading and the angle of units within a block can be modified to give better solar access. Block design should consider the positioning of buffer areas and the possible use of colonnades to provide shelter.

Landscape and external features

The choice and use of appropriate landscaping techniques around buildings for climatic purposes, and as an element of aesthetic design in its own right, is clearly important. What is often more difficult is the measurement and quantification of the exact benefits that accrue in energy or environmental terms. The most measurable effects are associated with site layout to optimize solar influences. Some quantifiable measure of improvement can also be derived by considering the effects of shelter and windbreaks on air movement.

Shelter, shading and windbreaks can be created by topography, by the planting of shrubs and trees and by the construction of walls, fences and other devices. In order to optimize the effect due regard must be given to the orientation with respect to the sun and to prevailing wind directions. Data are available to assess the degree of shading which particular trees provide and the time period for which they function (see table 4.1). Topography and fences are normally static throughout the year, but their effect is not, and design should be related to the effects during key seasons.

The spaces between buildings, and between buildings and the fences, hedges and walls that surround them, are particularly important. Wind-tunnelling effects need to be avoided, as do shapes that create downdraughts; and sufficient space should be allowed to prevent unwanted overshading. If space is limited, some screening can be provided by trees

Table 4.1 Approximate solar shading coefficients of single tree crowns (derived from data in *BRE Digest 350: Climate and Site Development*)

Tree type (common name	Jan	Feb	Mar	Apr	May	Jun	Jul	Aug	Sep	Oct	Nov	Dec
Ash	0.45	0.45	0.58	0.62	0.85	0.85	0.85	0.85	0.85	0.65	0.45	0.45
Beech	0.55	0.37	0.2	0.2	0.55	0.9	0.9	0.9	0.9	0.55	0.55	0.55
Birch	0.4	0.4	0.4	0.6	0.8	0.8	0.8	0.8	0.6	0.4	0.4	0.4
Chestnut	0.4	0.4	0.57	0.74	0.9	0.9	0.9	0.9	0.65	0.4	0.4	0.4
Elm	0.35	0.35	0.35	0.52	0.69	0.85	0.85	0.85	0.69	0.52	0.35	0.35
Lime	0.4	0.4	0.4	0.57	0.74	0.9	0.9	0.9	0.9	0.65	0.4	0.4
Maple	0.35	0.35	0.35	0.52	0.67	0.85	0.85	0.85	0.69	0.52	0.35	0.35
Oak	0.3	0.3	0.3	0.47	0.64	0.8	0.8	0.8	0.8	0.64	0.47	0.3
Sycamore	0.35	0.35	0.35	0.55	0.75	0.75	0.75	0.75	0.55	0.35	0.35	0.35

or shrubs trained over a framed wire mesh or some other device. Solid walls are less beneficial than porous screens, but they can still be useful and may act to retain solar heat from the day into the evening to provide outdoor comfort conditioning. Where planting extends over a range of heights, the denser vegetation should be closer to the ground.

The planting of trees, shrubs and other flora has further benefits: some plants may be used on slopes up to about 70 degrees as an alternative to erecting a retaining wall; they also act to remove carbon dioxide from the air and generate oxygen. The aesthetic effect and feeling of well-being that can be created by appropriate landscapes can do much to enhance environmental satisfaction with the built environment, which goes hand in hand with good energy and environmental policies.

Attention should be paid to the location and positioning of landscape features, green interventions and landmarks; they can affect the way in which routes and access points in the development are used. Ideally, major shelter belts should be positioned at the perimeter edges of the development and strategically placed throughout the development to break up wind flow; also, ground roughness should be maintained to break up wind flows. The ratio between a shelterbelt height and the distance to the building should be 1:3 or 1:4, though smaller-scale planting should be used around buildings and outdoor play areas.

The type of planting used should be suitable for the purpose and position; heights of major shelterbelts may be as much as six to eight metres, but their obstruction to view and solar benefits must be considered;

issues of screening for privacy need also to be taken into account. For more localized wind shelter, perforated screens, fences and hedges usually perform better than solid walls because they do not cause such dramatic variations in air flow, which can otherwise lead to increased levels of turbulence; 40–50 per cent porosity is best, with a greater degree of openness at the top and more solidity at the base.

Where possible, planting should provide shade and cooling opportunities for summer as well as reducing excessive wind speeds; areas under trees are generally cooler in the day and warmer at night than their more open surroundings. Ponds, fountains and other water features can also be used to modify local climate through evaporative cooling. Water features should also be incorporated to maximize potential for sustainable drainage systems and use of passive water treatment systems such as reed beds. The type of surface finish and the thermal capacity of the materials used in landscaping at ground surface level affect the absorption and reflection of solar radiation, and these factors can also be used to modify local climate.

Sunlight and shade

Whether one is attempting to encourage or exclude solar radiation from impinging on the building, it is necessary to appreciate the degree to which *solar access* is available, so that likelihood of solar heat gain can be determined. Sunlight and shade patterns cast by the proposed building itself should also be considered as these will affect nearby buildings and landscape. Graphical and computer prediction techniques may be employed to determine solar effects, as well as techniques such as the testing of physical models with a heliodon or similar device.

The spacing between buildings is very significant if overshading is to be avoided during winter months when solar heat gain is most advantageous in cool or temperate climates. For parallel rows of dwellings, the spacing between the rows has an important impact on shading and solar access, and this is sometimes greater than the impact of the orientation of the rows, taken over the whole year. Particular attention must be paid to the slope of the site, which may result in greatly increased building spacing in order to maintain access; in northern latitudes south-facing slopes are obviously to be preferred (and vice versa for southern latitudes). Figure 4.6 indicates how the distance between buildings must be increased to accommodate building height and roof shape. Figure 4.7 shows the difference in spacing required between similar buildings but on opposite slopes.

Solar access benefits may be obtained by placing individual, or low density, buildings to the south side of a site and tall buildings, rows or

Figure 4.6 The effect of building height and roof shape on required spacing to permit solar penetration during winter

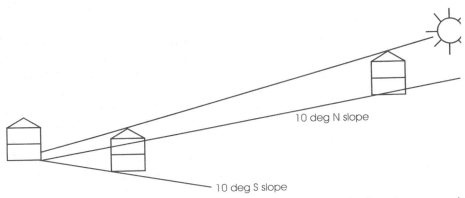

10 deg N slope

10 deg S slope

Figure 4.7 The effect of site slope on spacing between buildings to maintain solar access in winter

terraces towards the north (reversed for southern hemisphere sites). For housing schemes, rows of terraced dwellings are better placed on roads with an east–west axis whilst detached housing is better for a north–south axis.

Trees can also provide obstructions to solar access. However, if they are deciduous, they perform the dual function of permitting solar insolation to reach the building during the winter whilst providing a degree of shading in the summer; spacing between trees and building is critical.

Air flow

The effects of ventilation and air flow are important both around the exterior and through the interior of buildings and they can have both beneficial and negative impacts. The influence of the wind environment is at a larger scale than the individual building, and the local neighbourhood and site planning are both important considerations. At the present time there is encouragement in the UK and countries with similar climates to avoid use of air conditioning by enhancing natural ventilation in summer months. At the same time, excessive heat loss caused by infiltration of cold air in winter periods should be minimized. These two types of requirements are contradictory and solutions must be differentiated at the design stage and matched by design of the local neighbourhood surroundings.

In order to reduce the potential for air flow in winter periods, the overall building dimensions should be kept to a minimum to reduce the effect of wind pressures. In addition the larger building dimension should avoid facing into the predominating wind direction (that is, the long axis should be more parallel to the prevailing wind flow) and, overall, long parallel rows of relatively smooth-faced buildings should be avoided. Sheer vertical faces to tall buildings are also a problem as they can generate substantial down-draughts, which can obstruct pedestrian access and even be dangerous. Tall buildings should ideally have a façade that is staggered and steps back with increasing height away from the wind; and on small buildings, flat and low-pitched roofs should be avoided as these tend to increase air pressure differentials. Buildings can be grouped in irregular arrays, but within each group the heights should be similar (no more than a variation of 2:1) and spacing between them kept to a minimum. If the aim is to maximize ventilation opportunity, then obviously the recommendations above can tend to be reversed and this may enhance cooling effects.

The use of features to encourage air movement can also create problems around buildings in the local area of the development, with the wind flows in the immediate external environment having a substantial effect on perception and comfort for those outside, and upon entrance doorways. The shapes and groupings of buildings have a great impact here and designers should seek to minimize problems. Wind tunnel testing may be necessary in some cases. Some protection for pedestrians can generally be provided by use of canopies and podiums which reduce downdraught at ground level. Building layout should also avoid creating a tunneling effect between two adjacent buildings, and tall slab buildings should not be pierced with walkways or roadways at ground level since this leads to areas of extreme pressure difference and air flow. Shelterbelts (as described above) can also provide a degree of protection to both buildings and pedestrians, and they are most effective when they are correctly oriented and have a suitable permeability to air flow.

Building openings may be utilized to permit air and heat transfer but they also permit the intrusion of external noise. Their positioning must therefore take account of any sources of environmental noise, such as nearby roads or noise from nearby buildings and processes. City centre locations and even some suburban site locations also provide air pollution difficulties. Such pollution cannot easily be avoided and it may be very difficult to exploit natural ventilation in the detailed building design because of air pollution and, in some situations, noise problems. These problems can be reduced by adopting an appropriate planning strategy early in the design process that can lead to lower ambient noise or pollution levels in critical zones.

Building features

The aim for design at the scale of the individual building should be to combine efficient use of resources, not just in the initial construction but throughout the lifetime of the structure, with comfort and amenity for occupants. It should aim to impose as little burden on the environment as possible. Several authors and researchers have approached the design from the perspective of creating buildings that are effectively *autonomous*. In such designs the flows of energy and other resources are balanced (individually or compensating across the board) and some buildings have been designed to make net resource contributions. Examples are the use of photovoltaic systems integrated into the building envelope and the positioning of wind turbines on buildings to generate electricity, or the collection and use of rainwater. Such buildings are still rather unusual, however, and can sometimes impose on or restrict the lifestyle of their occupants; yet there are many effective measures that can already be taken with more modest effect on lifestyle and at minimal or no net cost.

Building form, layout and appearance

The importance and effect of building appearance has already been mentioned in an earlier discussion; however, some issues deserve explanation at the building scale. Care should be encouraged to optimize the position of each material and its role as a construction element. Consideration should be given to what happens to the buildings within a development when they come to the end of their useful life. Design processes should be encouraged that allow for ease of refurbishment, alteration or demolition, recycling and reuse.

The shape of a building may need to be modified to allow it to operate in an optimum way either for energy/heat transfer issues or to allow for alternative energy generation; this may particularly affect the roof shape and pitch. Colour may also vary according to certain needs, and the more sustainable option may not be the one that most easily blends with the existing surroundings. Care is needed to avoid conflicts over planning decisions.

Environmentally sensitive and energy-efficient buildings should make as much beneficial use of naturally available light as is possible. Until the mid-twentieth century, the use of windows and the plan form of buildings were very much influenced by the limits of natural ventilation and light admission. The development of modern lighting technology and air conditioning, increased external noise levels and poorer air quality all contributed to the expansion of deep-plan, sealed window, artificially lit and air-conditioned environments. Only relatively recently have the advantages of natural daylight and ventilation been recognized once again, but to optimize these advantages will require modification to form and layout.

Beneficial air flow in the interior of buildings may be created by encouraging natural air flow, which can be accomplished by carrying through a series of simple concepts. Plan form should be shallow to encourage single-sided and cross-ventilation potential, and openings should be on opposite walls rather than on one, or adjacent, walls to allow fuller cross-ventilation. Building depth should not be more than about five times the floor-to-ceiling height if cross-ventilation is to be successful; where ventilation uses openings on one side of the building only, depth should be limited to about two and a half times the floor to ceiling height. External shading devices should also be planned carefully since they can reduce wind-induced pressures and air flow. Windows should be openable and designed to provide controlled air flow; however, this is particularly difficult in high-rise buildings and can lead to design conflicts.

If natural ventilation is insufficient to create acceptable comfort levels, then mechanical air flow can be employed. As a first stage, it should be used as a supplement to natural flow and, where possible, air should be drawn from the cool side of the building; alternatively, designers should consider drawing air through cooler pipes or ducts, for instance located underground, to reduce and stabilize its temperature. These options will have an impact on overall building planning.

If the prime concern is to minimize natural ventilation, then different strategies are required. Main entrances should be protected from high wind pressures and the provision of entrance lobbies, bracketed by sets of self-closing or automatic doors, helps reduce air influx.

The frequency with which atria are now included as an integral component of commercial building design has increased tremendously over the last 20–30 years. They appear to provide that most elusive of combinations: an aesthetically pleasing architectural feature, which also has the potential to be environmentally enhancing and energy efficient. Their use as a buffer space, and as a means of providing natural light and ventilation

Figure 4.8 The large and dynamic atrium in The Ark building, London

to the heart of otherwise large, deep and complex buildings, has been an attractive feature exploited by many designers. The shape and form of the atrium has an important effect on the availability of natural lighting in the spaces adjacent to the atrium, and the control of air movement also has significant environmental effects. Their functioning in environmental terms is rarely simple, however, and greater understanding of atrium design is currently needed to optimize performance.

Climate-sensitive building design

The prime need in terms of environmental design of individual buildings is to focus on climate sensitivity, both in terms of reducing impact on global climate and in recognizing the effect of climate on the environments in and around the building.

In practical terms it is necessary to design appropriate building forms, including location, size and type of openings in the building envelope, so as to exploit advantageous solar heat gain. Suitable construction techniques, including the relative positions and thicknesses of insulation and thermal mass (which can be used to modify temperature fluctuations), should also be chosen to maximize benefits. In order to fully exploit the options for use of the thermal mass effect, due consideration is needed in design and in assessment of the consequences for the building appearance and function, which may not be immediately apparent.

Internal layouts should be adapted to climate and building orientation so that rooms or spaces with specific functions are located adjacent to the most appropriate façades. Buildings can be divided into thermal zones with buffer areas such as balconies, verandas, atria, courtyards and arcades, though divisions should avoid providing barriers to cross-flow ventilation if this is required. There also needs to be an understanding that climate-sensitive design requires buildings to withstand wider variations in climate, which may affect such features as foundations (to cope with flood and drought periods) and structure (to cope with higher rainfall and storms/windspeeds).

The building technique that exploits solar heat gain is normally defined as *passive solar design*; this is subdivided into a number of categories depending on how the energy is used. Natural energy flows should be used to distribute heat where possible, augmented with control systems where necessary. Orientation of principal façades should ideally be within ±30 degrees of south, for the northern hemisphere, and internal spaces should be allocated to solar or non-solar façades so as to maximize benefits. All types of passive solar design will thus have some aesthetic and visual consequences associated with optimizing their functional requirements, and this must be taken into account in planning.

Water and wastes

In the previous chapter a case was advanced for the development of different water supply options. If this is to occur there will also need to be an appropriate modification in system design and in policies that affect use. Water storage and treatment on site or within buildings will become more common and perhaps more attention to the active monitoring of consumption through meters will be required. Water usage can be much reduced by inclusion of low water consumption toilet flushes, spray taps and other water-conserving appliances. The information on such devices and their benefits needs to be communicated effectively to building developers, designers and occupants.

Composting toilets are starting to become more common but require different construction techniques and access points within buildings, which affects planning and design. Solid waste collection and disposal systems also need to be designed to allow for appropriate storage and recycling.

Overall, there is likely to be a substantial change in culture with respect to waste disposal. Planning guidance and design will need to incorporate the resultant new technologies and techniques at building scale level.

New technologies

There are many novel technologies that are already being incorporated into building design, but at the moment this tends to be on a piecemeal basis rather than as part of a wider and more comprehensive strategy. As the demand for more environmentally sensitive and energy-efficient design increases, new technologies will become more common and will require different forms of design guidance. Many new technologies attached to sustainable buildings have some effect on appearance and certainly on construction. For successful implementation, understanding is required at all levels from urban planner to site worker. The consequence of a lack of understanding, or of interference with design that leads to a lack of optimization, is that it will result in reduced performance and a potentially poor reputation which can inhibit development of what may be a very worthwhile technology.

In the past, various solar technologies have often been added on to the building after design and construction have been completed, which results in a less pleasing aesthetic product. A more integrated design approach is to be encouraged, to improve benefits and appearance.

The most common type of active solar thermal technology is the flat plate collector. The principal function of such a system is to collect and deliver sufficient heat for domestic hot water, mainly during the summer months. For a family house in the UK, the collector area would need to cover a substantial proportion of the available roof area for full heating and, if heating for all months of the year, a substantial heat store would be required. These factors have an important impact on design and planning not just of the exterior but also the interior of the building. More efficient forms of water collector are now being developed, such as the evacuated tube type (see plate 2).

Energy may be converted directly from sunlight into electricity by using a photovoltaic cell. Such cells have no moving parts, create no noise in operation, and seem attractive from both aesthetic and scientific perspectives. The development is ongoing and there is seen to be great potential for use of photovoltaic arrays as building-integrated cladding materials. Examples of integrated cladding include incorporation into façades, rain screens, shading devices, roof tiles and windows. Advantages of building-integrated systems are: clean generation of electricity; generation close to its point of use within the urban environment; and no additional land requirements. Unanticipated shading of part of an array, say as a result of new development, can cause extreme problems for the operation of the system and must be guarded against.

Photovoltaic cladding materials can now be obtained in different patterns and colours depending upon the nature of the cells and the backing material to which they are applied. This offers an increasing range of façade options that can be exploited by architects to create particular aesthetic effects. Plate 3 shows the Doxford Solar Office in the UK which has a large façade-integrated photovoltaic array and creates a stunning piece of architecture. Plate 4 illustrates something of the range of colours available for photovoltaic cells, which can be used to dramatic design effect.

Another area where there are opportunities to encourage better resource efficiency is in the inclusion of *smart technologies* to improve control over the operation and functioning of the building. When integrated with security or entertainment, these can prove to be elements of design where the client or occupier is prepared to pay additional cost and where greater energy efficiency might be enabled through enhanced control.

Summary

This chapter has attempted to convey information about means to achieve successful environmental design. It is important to recognize the links between scales of operation and the degree of integration that is needed in order to achieve the full benefits.

Whatever design approaches are used, it is necessary to assess the benefits of choosing a particular technology or system and to measure and monitor its performance. The use of simulation, assessment and prediction tools is therefore becoming more widespread, and an outline of those available follows in the next chapter.

Chapter 5

Assessment methodologies

Introduction

Assessment techniques and rating methods are necessary to enable the environmental effects of urban or building schemes to be demonstrated or compared. The use of these techniques permits planning authorities to choose from options, set targets and establish goals; assessment methods and techniques are therefore an essential part of the system that is required to enable sustainable development to take place in a more measured and accurate way.

Assessment and rating systems use diverse indicators of performance, and at urban scale there is a need to integrate a variety of elements, sometimes incompatible in nature. This makes the adoption of any one scheme difficult, as no single one can apply to all circumstances; however, selection from a suite of potential options can be used according to their relevance. Ultimately the means of valuing sustainable design should develop into a more formalized accounting procedure that can be objectively assessed, so that not only are the economic/financial assessments included but also environmental and social issues. There will always be a need for careful interpretation and understanding, however.

Assessment systems and indicators may be used for one or more of the following purposes: to provide a value judgement on a specific programme or project (existing or proposed); to set targets and goals and provide awards and rewards; to monitor trends over a period of time; or to anticipate problems before they arise. The following examples show something of the variety of systems currently available.

SEAs

One methodology that has been proposed, which would support strategic planning, is the use of strategic environmental assessments (SEAs). SEAs use a similar process to environmental impact assessments (EIAs), which have been carried out as an aid to examination of development proposals for a number of years. The difference in using an SEA is that it examines policies (economic, social and environmental), plans (area planning, sector planning or integrated forms) and action programmes. EIAs have often been limited in what they can describe or achieve, whereas an SEA provides a wider view; examines alternatives to the principal proposal; can incorporate a dynamic perspective; and can include a wider environmental focus.

Sustainability checklist for developments

This text-based resource was developed from work at the UK Building Research Establishment. It was designed to be used in relation to development at the scale of urban village or estate and in regeneration projects. The focus is on sustainability relating to the site development, buildings and infrastructure. A scoring system is used to assess performance under the following headings:

- Land use, urban form and design—site criteria, reuse, form, landscape, density, mix and aesthetics.
- Transport—public transport, parking, pedestrians, cyclists, local employment and local facilities.
- Energy—generation and street lighting.
- Buildings—use of BREEAM ratings (see below) and the assessment of other building types.

- Natural resources—local materials, air quality, water, drainage and composting.
- Ecology—conservation, site enhancement and planting.
- Community—involvement and measures to reduce crime.
- Business—enhancing opportunity, employment and training.

The checklists of this method can be used in full or in part and might be useful in some of the following circumstances: to aid in the writing of development briefs or proposals; to demonstrate the sustainability features of a proposal; for authorities to specify standards to be met; or to provide a scoring system for comparison of options. Though the method claims to encompass environmental, social and economic issues, there are some variations in emphasis and there is a need for interpretation both in choosing inputs and in analysing outputs.

BREEAM

BREEAM is the Building Research Establishment Environmental Assessment Method. It consists of a series of rating systems for a range of building types: offices, homes, industrial buildings and supermarkets. The scheme was launched in 1990 in the UK and has been updated several times during the intervening period for the two main categories of building: offices and homes. There are several purposes of the rating system: one is to provide guidance to reduce the effect of buildings on the global and local environment whilst also creating comfortable and healthy indoor environments; a second is to enable developers of buildings who have addressed environmental issues to gain credit for this through the rating of proposals and the award of a certificate. Points or credits are awarded according to criteria specific to the building type and depending on the level attained. Awards are made in the categories of pass, good, very good and excellent. About 500 office buildings in the UK have been assessed by the scheme, and during the most recent years about 32 per cent of buildings have achieved the *excellent* certification.

The dwellings version of BREEAM, EcoHomes, awards credits in seven categories:

- Energy performance, including: CO_2 emissions, improvement over building regulations standards of insulation, and low-energy electrical appliances (maximum 40 credits).
- Transport, including access to public transport and local amenities (maximum 14 credits).

- Pollution reduction, related to ozone depletion and oxides of nitrogen (maximum 28 credits).
- Materials issues, including use of optimum environmental impact materials and recycling (maximum 31 credits).
- Water use (maximum 20 credits).
- Land use and ecological considerations, related to changes to the site (maximum 27 credits).
- Health and well-being, including daylight and noise issues (maximum 28 credits).

The maximum number of credits achievable is 188; a score of 68 is a pass; a score of 90 is good; a score of 113 is very good; and a score of 132 or above is excellent.

In contrast, BREEAM 2002 (previously BREEAM 98 for Offices) scores points in similar categories but with more sub-categories and with further separation within each category according to attributes in the areas of building performance, design and procurement assessment, and management and operation assessment. The 2002 upgrade means that it is more difficult to gain an excellent rating, with the expectation that about 25 per cent of buildings will be so graded in the future. Some obsolete assessment elements were also removed. The main BREEAM office-points awarding categories are:

- Management, which includes operation, environmental policies and systems.
- Health and well-being, which includes a diverse range of factors generally related to systems performance, lighting, ventilation, acoustics and occupant health.
- Energy, which relates to CO_2 emissions, policies, monitoring of performance and maintenance.
- Transport, including relationship to public transport connections and encouragement to use alternative transport.
- Water consumption, including monitoring of use and maintenance procedures.
- Materials, including avoidance of harmful materials, specification of materials with high environmental ratings, and reuse and recycling of materials.
- Land use, with points awarded for reuse of industrial or contaminated sites.
- Ecology, including improvement to the ecological value of the site rated.
- Pollution, which is related to emissions from refrigeration plant, heating system burners and other substances.

Due to the complex nature of the divisions of points-scoring in this scheme, a simple explanation of the assessment is difficult, particularly since there are variations according to whether a new or an existing building is being considered. Buildings must score minimum values in both categories of design and procurement assessment, and in management and operation assessment, to be awarded the specified grade. The individual building performance score indicates an environmental performance index on a scale of one to ten. One of the additional benefits of reference to the BREEAM Offices documentation is the inclusion of useful tabulated checklists that suggest actions for consideration appropriate to the two main elements of design and procurement, and management and operation, according to task or personnel involved and the environmental assessment category.

To be awarded a BREEAM grade, the appraisal must be carried out by a qualified assessor. However, the documentation available for each version of the scheme gives good guidance to potential applicants as to the requirements and it is possible for persons familiar with the content to make reasonable accurate predictions of the score, and further to use these predictions to modify the design to achieve a higher standard.

BREEAM has been used successfully as a marketing tool to attract potential clients and building occupants. Though there are gaps and criticisms that can be made, it has established a wide reputation within the UK and has been emulated elsewhere.

LEED

LEED is the Green Building Council's Leadership in Energy and Environmental Design rating system, designed originally for commercial buildings. Its aim is to provide a US national standard for what a green building should embody. As with BREEAM, the intention is to provide a useful set of design guidelines in combination with a third-party certification procedure. The 2.1 version was released in November 2002 and includes assessment for commercial renovation projects and high-rise residential buildings as well as standard new commercial designs.

The points award system for LEED is simpler than for BREEAM. There is a maximum of 69 points available, but the majority of points are awarded as single units attributed to specific design features; only in the optimization of energy performance is more than one credit available. In addition to the awardable points there are seven prerequisites that must be met. Points are awarded within six categories:

- Sustainable sites, including site selection, transportation, site disturbance, stormwater management and landscape issues (maximum 14 points).
- Water efficiency, including landscape and wastewater issues (maximum 5 points).
- Energy and atmosphere, including energy performance and renewable energy use issues (maximum 17 points, 10 of which are for energy).
- Materials and resources, including reuse of materials, waste management and recycling (maximum 13 points).
- Indoor environmental quality, including air quality, comfort and daylight issues (maximum 15 points).
- Innovation and design process (maximum 5 points).

Standards for LEED awards are set at: certified, 26–32 points; silver, 33–38 points; gold, 39–51 points; platinum, 52–69 points. The number of buildings rated under this scheme is still relatively few compared to the enormous potential, and ratings scored have generally been in the middle categories. Some government agencies have begun to use it as a benchmark for new buildings, which should expand its use. There have been some criticisms that some credits do not relate to a verified measured impact and that there are inconsistencies in value weighting between categories. Despite this, the documentation provided for the scheme is a valuable tool in itself and it is to be hoped that the scheme will expand in use and be further developed in due course.

Green Building Challenge—GBTool

The Green Building Challenge is not a rating or assessment tool in the same way as others mentioned here. Rather, it was an international collaborative effort to develop a tool that confronted some of the more controversial aspects of rating systems in a way that would allow different countries or participants to select the most useful elements. The project was led from Canada, but with input from many countries, and resulted in international conferences and the development of a number of useful outputs. It operated between 1998 and 2002 and was used to compare good practice buildings from different countries. Although the future of the project has not been specified, it is currently managed by the International Initiative for a Sustainable Built Environment (iiSBE).

A spreadsheet-based assessment method, GBTool, has been developed which can be downloaded from its website together with manuals describing its use. The spreadsheet is in fact not intended for end users at present but rather for project collaborators to examine and, if suitable, adapt to local or national circumstances with the adjustment of weightings and categorizations. Judgements are based on a -2 to $+5$ scale, and use of the tool is broken down into a number of levels to enable performance to be assessed.

Australian Building Greenhouse Rating Scheme

This scheme is administered and supported by various government agencies in Australia. Only approved assessors are entitled to provide an official rating; however, a version of the programme is available for initial personal evaluation. The information required is rather simplistic in nature and is mainly aimed at deriving the greenhouse gas emission in terms of normalized carbon dioxide emissions per square metre of building floor area. This is then used to determine the rating on a 1 to 5 star basis. Obviously, the real skill associated with this method is in the choice of modification or improvement to the building project to reduce the emissions. The rating scheme in its bare form does not appear to provide this, though the integration within different government agencies and schemes does mean it has value alongside appropriate advice.

NABERS

NABERS is the project for developing a National Australian Building Environmental Rating System. The aim is for a performance-based rating scheme that will rate the overall environmental performance of a building during operation. A number of academics and consultants have been involved in the project, which commenced in 2001 under Environment Australia leadership. A major component is likely to be based on the Australian Building Greenhouse Rating Scheme (see above).

Green Star

This is the second assessment scheme under development in Australia and was initiated by the Green Building Council of Australia. A commercial consultancy has been involved with finalizing its development and the release of a pilot version in July 2003. Environmental and social dimensions are incorporated under the headings of: energy efficiency; greenhouse gas emission abatement; water conservation; waste avoidance, reuse and recycling; pollution prevention; biodiversity enhancement; reduction of natural resource consumption; productive and healthy environments; useable buildings; social amenity; and transparent reporting.

SAP

SAP is the Standard Assessment Procedure for the energy rating of dwellings, developed in the UK to provide information on performance in terms of energy use and carbon dioxide emissions. It is incorporated into the Building Regulations as a requirement to be carried out to accompany the design of new houses, though it can also be used to assess existing buildings. The methodology is similar to that of a range of housing energy assessment techniques developed in recent years and of similar assessments carried out in other countries. The method of assessment is fairly simple, based on a worksheet that is easily transposed to a computer spreadsheet. Its aim is to allow comparison of options. Though widely used, it is yet to make an impact on the perceptions of the general house-buying public.

Home Energy Rating Systems (HERS) programs

In the USA it is common for individual states to adopt or approve their own particular versions of assessment programmes that are appropriate to local climatic and cultural circumstances. HERS is the generic title under which the various software analysis systems operate, controlled by a non-profit organization, Energy Rated Homes of America (ERHA). These systems represent a broad category of approved methods for the energy analysis of dwellings, and the energy ratings are often used in relation to obtaining loans under an Energy Efficient Mortgage (EEM) programme. The particular advantage that is offered is that the loan amount can be increased since the lender takes account of the lower energy costs likely to be incurred by the building occupant, which increases the proportion of income available for loan repayment.

The analysis techniques are used to rate how well the insulation standards (set by the Model Energy Code of the Council of American Building Officials) are met or exceeded. In the mid-1990s the Residential Energy Services Network (RESNET) was founded to aid in the development of the future market for HERS and EEMs.

NatHERS and FirstRate

These are examples of programmes developed in Australia to analyse the energy performance of dwellings. They include information about the building fabric and the environmental systems installed to provide heating and cooling. Each is a commercially marketed system, and details of their function can be derived from their operators. The methodology seems to be similar to that of energy rating analysis practised in other countries.

Eco-Quantum

Eco-Quantum is available in two forms: one for use as more of a research tool to investigate complex and innovative commercial buildings, and a second for the evaluation of simpler domestic-scale proposals; the latter can be used fairly quickly by architects. The method was developed in the Netherlands and is well established, having gone through several stages of testing. It is basically a life cycle assessment software-based tool which determines the environmental performance of the building in relation to the materials and energy flows. Eleven scores for different effects on the environment are generated, and these are then combined into four principal indicators which match the Dutch environmental rating system.

Green Guide to Specification

The Green Guide to Specification in the UK provides a means to compare the performance of building components and materials by rating each on an *A–B–C* scale: *A* represents options with best performance or least environmental impact; *C* the worst. Each option for a particular facet of building design is scored against thirteen individual criteria, and an overall rating is also provided. Different versions have been produced for housing and for more general use. The criteria can be grouped as:

- Toxic pollutants associated with manufacture or combustion.
- Primary energy required for extraction, production and transport.
- Emissions of carbon dioxide, volatile organic compounds, oxides of nitrogen and sulphur dioxide.
- Resource consumption—mineral, water, oil feedstock.
- Reserves of the raw material.

- Wastes produced.
- Recycling: actual, potential and current UK standard; and energy for recycling.

The guide is relatively easy to use and has been based on sound data. The specification is also used to provide input to other methodologies such as BREEAM.

ENVEST and Ecopoints

ENVEST is a further assessment tool developed by the Building Research Establishment. It is software based and gives the facility to measure impacts per square metre of a building's floor area. In this way it is possible to make comparisons between different versions of the same building and also between different buildings. The method is based on the Ecopoints system, which covers a range of factors similar to those of the American BEES system described below. The latest version of ENVEST is designed to be used in conjunction with a regularly updated website, with a cost for access.

Ecopoints, as defined for this UK system, represent the overall environmental impact of a product or process in the following categories:

- Climate change
- Fossil fuel depletion and extraction
- Acid deposition
- Ozone depletion
- Pollution to air—human toxicity
- Pollution to air—low-level ozone creation—'summer smog'
- Pollution to water—human toxicity
- Pollution to water—ecotoxicity
- Pollution to water—eutrophication
- Minerals extraction
- Water extraction
- Waste disposal

An overall score is created by adding together the score for each issue, which is determined by multiplying its normalized impact by its percentage weighting. As an example, the average annual environmental impact of a citizen in the UK equates to 100 Ecopoints; the higher the score, the larger the environmental impact.

BEES

BEES, the Building for Environmental and Economic Sustainability system, is an interactive computer-based design aid developed in the USA by the National Institute of Standards and Technology. It aims to provide a technique for selecting cost-effective, environmentally preferable building products for commercial and housing projects. Graphical outputs are produced relating to a range of approximately 200 building elements arising from a life cycle assessment approach in the following categories:

Environmental performance:
- Global warming
- Acidification
- Eutrophication
- Fossil fuel depletion
- Indoor air quality
- Habitat alteration
- Water intake
- Air pollutants
- Human health
- Smog
- Ozone depletion
- Ecological toxicity

Economic performance:
- First cost
- Future costs

Version 3.0 of the assessment procedure was issued in October 2002.

Future developments

Obviously, the techniques and methodologies for assessment of sustainability continue to develop. One of the coordinating group activities is the thematic network project 'Construction and City Related Sustainability Indicators' (CRISP) funded by the European Commission. The work of this project is focused principally on the scales of urban blocks, buildings and individual construction products. The European BEQUEST project has also undertaken a comparison of tools as part of a more general investigation, and its website provides useful information. As the systems described above are in a state of constant development with revisions being issued at regular intervals and with new types evolving, a watching brief is required to enable appropriate use.

Assessment techniques should be incorporated to simulate performance at the design stage, but it is also vitally important to monitor performance *in use*, and to feed back results to improve the design stage. At present this post-completion and ideally post-occupancy performance assessment rarely takes place, thus leaving great gaps in knowledge which must be filled.

It seems clear, however, that use of assessment methods is likely to increase and this is to be encouraged as a means to promoting more beneficial environmental design. This encouragement is, however, given with the proviso that those employing such techniques should have sufficient expertise to understand the limitations, interpret the outcomes correctly, and be capable of offering unbiased advice on improvement to the designs submitted.

Part C

Exploiting the potential

Chapter 6

Profiting from sustainable design and development

Introduction

In this third part of the book the focus moves on to how to prosecute sustainable environmental design, how it fits in with social, cultural and economic issues, and how it can become a component of a profitable route to sustainability in a wider context. It must be recognized, however, that the most compelling aspect for both organizations and individuals is the financial element, and whilst some actions to improve sustainability are the result of assessing benefits at environmental or social levels, it is the economic case that is normally most convincing. Of course, it is possible to modify the economic basis upon which decisions are made, and this is one option for aiding the advance of sustainable design and development that needs tackling at national government level. Increasingly wider ranging accounting procedures are also being employed which provide a measure of sustainability that is not just in monetary terms, and this can be used to reveal performance and encourage alternative behaviour from the general public which eventually has an effect, to use accounting parlance, on the bottom line.

In the pursuit of profitable sustainability it is important that factors are considered over a medium to long timescale, and that information and actions at different scales and different levels of responsibility are integrated to give a full picture that can reveal the full benefits. One of the problems encountered in demonstrating the profit is that at the present time the methods of environmental and sustainability accounting are still evolving and the evidence has not yet been fully accumulated or assessed. Nevertheless, some tangible examples are quoted and the reasoning for assuming more benefits is clearly set out.

Accounting for sustainability

Sustainable design is often reduced in financial terms to a couple of very simple and erroneous concepts: firstly that sustainable buildings cost significantly more to design and construct, and secondly that the only savings are reductions in energy consumption, which at current prices are a small fraction of total running costs. These assumptions must be contradicted: design and construction of more sustainable buildings and their associated infrastructure does not necessarily lead to additional cost and can even offer a lower cost option. Also, the benefits of sustainable design and operation are reflected not only in lower energy costs but in lower running costs across many facets of operation, and when this is taken into account such a route can be seen to be more profitable.

There are several ways in which lower running costs result:

- Sustainable buildings are more energy efficient and so have lower energy costs.
- The size and types of building services systems installed are usually smaller and less complex, resulting in lower capital and maintenance costs.
- The design of buildings in a sustainable way, with more focus on structure and fabric, leads to buildings that can be more robust in operation and flexible in use, offering more efficient utilization.

- Well-designed buildings have higher standards of construction and generally the fabric requires less maintenance and refurbishment.
- There are many hidden long-term benefits in terms of the improvements in the built environment that are not often included in analysis.

One of the main issues, of course, is the way in which initial or capital costs of development are compared with longer-term running costs and how this is taken into account by those involved in building development. It is often the case that, in carrying out cost analysis, sustainability must compete with other cost decisions based on traditional assumptions about future impacts and thus the costs, the interest and the discount rates that are applied. In making decisions about investment in sustainability there are valid arguments for modifying these assumptions. Firstly, future energy and environmental costs cannot be predicted accurately; and secondly, because of the long-lasting nature of sustainability issues and activities, it could be suggested that the time periods over which investment is analysed should be longer. There can be capital cost savings too through more efficient use of resources, incurring lower purchase costs and lower costs of waste disposal.

In order to explore opportunities for changes in accounting practice a number of initiatives have been taken. The UK government is funding a partnered programme led by the Building Research Establishment to determine the business benefits from sustainable construction. This is now carrying out a number of case studies, and the initial results show that improvements in performance in energy efficiency can be achieved without significant additional cost, provided that the decisions are taken early enough.

The Forum for the Future has also been very active in developing the economic arguments through its Sustainable Economy Programme. A series of case studies has been collated that show actions that have been taken and their environmental, social and economic benefits. For one building project, for instance, savings in environmental costs of around £180 000 have been predicted as a result of materials reuse and waste management together with the avoidance of landfill taxes. Other projects show avoidance of environmental risk, thus reducing exposure to future costs. Other companies have found improvements as a result of focusing on waste streams and on better tendering procedures for its suppliers. Integration in order to confront environmental issues has also led, in some cases, to better management processes across other areas and reduced wastage of staff time. Financial institutions are beginning to take environmental issues seriously too; some are discussed later that are impacting on financial markets, such as in London.

A number of organizations and assessment methodologies are already initiating changes in the appreciation of the environmental effect on economics by focusing on sustainability and green accounting principles. Triple bottom line accounting is already being practised in a number of organizations; in this a wider range of information is released on the environmental and social benefits and costs and is presented alongside the information of a financial nature, which means that a more complete picture of the operation of an organization and the choices it might make is available.

The Global Reporting Initiative (GRI) is a further methodology that provides globally applicable guidelines for reporting sustainability. It was initiated in 1997 and attempts to bring together economic, environmental and social features to provide a format for reporting the impact of a business. It is working towards the establishment of an independent institution to support its work, but has already made available much practical information.

In the UK there have been initiatives to promote sustainability accounting both in local government and in the construction industry. For local government some authorities have already been utilizing quality of life indicators to measure social, economic and environmental issues, and these can be used as a tool to develop community strategies. This can be linked to *Best Value* approaches that focus on performance indicators and monitoring. Some councils use commitments to reducing greenhouse gas emissions as a tool for promoting sustainable practices, and the Private Finance Initiative (PFI) also gives an opportunity to introduce sustainability accounting. Research is still required in this area, particularly to show the profits that result and in the choice and adoption of common schemes and methods.

Sustainability accounting in the construction sector is seen as a tool to identify, evaluate and manage environmental and social risks. This process functions by considering resource efficiency and cost savings and links to improved social and environmental issues with financial opportunities. Performance assessment and benchmarking for best practice can also be incorporated. A report published for CIRIA included the case study for a hospital project in Swindon; in this over £1.6 million in savings for the construction company were generated, principally through the adoption of energy-efficient design features and efficient use of wall and floor construction resources. Indirect environmental and social benefits also accrued. The financial assessment for this project uses a methodology that operates over a long timescale (27 years in this case) and relates not just to the initial construction costs.

Commercial buildings

In the UK and USA, where commercial development is more speculative in nature, it has been traditional to focus on limiting capital cost as a means to generate profit, though in Europe and elsewhere construction for a specific client with a longer-term interest in a building has meant that the running costs feature more prominently in the financial view. However, even in the UK there have been changes, with periods of low inflation experienced in the speculative commercial sector. This means that the value of investment in buildings can be optimized not by simply building cheaply and relying on asset value growth, but by management to maximize income from rental over the lifetime of the building. At the same time many major companies have been downsizing their central office management and are now interested in renting smaller spaces but of higher quality and with more flexibility. These factors mean that companies involved in development for commercial letting have had to face up to providing what the market needs, not what they want to provide. Clients and tenants now demand better quality spaces and are prepared to pay a premium for this, and such spaces are more easily let in areas or times of oversupply.

There is also now much greater involvement of client groups and future tenants or owners in the development process, and there has been something of a shift in power in influencing design. This has partly been fostered by the greater integration and partnering that now occurs in the construction industry, which enables transmission of information and such influence. There are also several additional factors to consider:

■ Capital costs of sustainable design can be similar or even lower than conventional figures through good design to meet specification; additional design and specialist construction costs can be offset by reduced needs for building services systems and reduced wastage.

■ Higher quality sustainable design is better able to provide the types of buildings that the market desires.

■ The reduction in running costs over a relatively short period can be used to pay for modest additional capital costs.

■ Clients and building-management companies can take a longer-term view, and buildings can also be actively managed to maximize income rather than relying on increase in value of the assets.

- Lend-lease schemes enable a longer-term view of investment and can result in design and use of building assets in a more efficient and ecological way—this can be encouraged by the Private Finance Initiative (PFI) method of procurement.

There is another element of costs in which sustainable design offers advantages and that is in relation to employee satisfaction. For many organizations their greatest asset and their greatest cost is their workforce, and optimizing their satisfaction and function can have substantial financial benefits. Sustainable design, with its focus on quality and more natural environments, has much to commend it; shallower plan, daylit and naturally ventilated spaces are usually preferred by their occupants. Also, in recent years, concerns with 'sick building syndrome' have contributed to a lessening of enthusiasm for sealed, deep plan environments, which are often air conditioned. High quality and pleasant work environments are also factors in the recruitment and retention of high-calibre employees.

There is evidence to show that productivity rises and absenteeism falls in buildings that are well designed from an environmental point of view. The NMB (now ING) Bank saw a dramatic fall in absenteeism of around 15 per cent when it moved to new headquarters buildings in Amsterdam; the new building was designed to be both sustainable and of high environmental quality. Work by Nigel Oseland and information from the Office Productivity Network suggest beneficial increases in performance, perhaps up to 5 per cent. Other information indicates an increase in workforce productivity of about one per cent in environmentally sustainable buildings; but even at the lowest of these values the increase in productivity can pay for very substantial improvements in design and construction. There are also health and safety issues that pertain and, as litigation continues to rise, it is a wise employer who provides working environments of the highest quality.

The final area in which current benefits might be demonstrated is that of the image of the building and the company or organization. Buildings provide potent symbols of the attitudes and attributes of their occupants, and the environmental design quality image is very strong. Companies, organizations and individuals that are prepared to invest to create a strong perception of design quality and interest in sustainability and the future are likely to be more positively viewed by the public and other organizations when choices are made about spending, investment and other activities. Good sustainable design is thus a marketable asset worth promoting. This can be particularly important as more and more groups decide to make financial decisions based on ethical principles.

104

Housing

The preceding sections have been primarily concerned with commercial developments; attention is now focused on housing, where a number of seemingly contradictory situations appear. For commercial buildings and their occupants, decisions are often driven by rather short-term financial concerns linked to business operation; however, in the housing sector one might imagine that owner-occupiers of dwellings would take a longer-term view of the investment decision, and that the managers of social housing in the rented sector would see benefits in investing in quality for long life and robust operation. But in neither case does this seem to be happening, particularly with new-build housing.

Although the energy costs for a home in the UK are still quite low, given the price trends of recent years, the overall cost is still a significant part of the housing budget and even more so for the most disadvantaged on the lowest incomes who often live in the least energy-efficient houses. Investment in high insulation levels, good quality and multiple-layer glazing systems and energy-efficient appliances, heating and distribution systems, would seem an obvious step to take. Most of the additional costs can be recouped within a very short timescale of about four years; given that periods of occupancy average about seven years, the economic case is clearly made. The IPCC obviously agrees with this assertion in its 2001 report on mitigation opportunities. There are, however, perhaps four reasons why the greater use of sustainable design does not occur: firstly, the preoccupation of owners to focus on *location* as the prime, and sometimes the only, relative determinant of value; secondly, the lack of value placed on environmental design quality by purchasers; thirdly, that developers concentrate on providing housing to match an expected price/type combination for an area and thus maximize profit by reducing their costs to the minimum; and finally, the drive by providers of social housing to match cost structures of the owner-occupier market.

These factors might lead one to conclude that there is little profit to be made from sustainable housing solutions; however, the opposite is true. There is great potential if only it can be released, and the keys to this are information provision and market encouragement. Developers say that they simply provide what the consumer asks for; so, if the consumer was made more aware of the benefits and individual profit that could be produced, the situation would change. The situation is improving a little in the UK with the use of the Standard Assessment Procedure (SAP) for the energy rating of new dwellings, but the public needs to be encouraged to use this as a guide to performance in the same way as fuel consumption figures are used for motor cars. The fuel figure for a given size of engine is also an indicator of overall quality in design, yet it is strange to observe that the price increase of the highest over the lowest quality cars in the same mass market category is about 400 per cent, but to get the highest quality environmental design in a house might involve a much more meagre 10 per cent. The architects Brenda and Robert Vale have shown on a number of occasions that it is possible to achieve high-quality and energy-efficient environmental design within the same cost benchmarks that are used for conventional design. Even volume housebuilders have found that incorporating energy efficiency into design only adds about four per cent to costs; this should be compared to the price of a whole project which, at the outset, can only be estimated to within about three per cent anyway. The reason why more energy-efficient houses are not the norm seems to be that buyers do not yet ask for them.

This situation should be contrasted with experience in mainland Europe where, it seems, not only do people ask for higher quality, they also expect to pay for it. Proposals to release the potential profit in the housing sector should therefore include provision of more and better information on the benefits of good sustainable design and environmental performance combined with the introduction and better marketing of schemes to illustrate the potential for increased value. Profits can result, in terms of better financial performance, for the owner-occupiers of houses through reduced running costs and enhanced investment return; for tenants in reducing fuel poverty and release of money for non-energy expenditure; for landlords in improving the quality of their stock and reducing maintenance costs; and for developers who should be able to obtain a higher price for a more valuable asset.

Future profit

Potential benefits have been shown for the existing financial situation, but there are even more to consider in the developing future scenario. Creating the right image, as has been stated above, is important but from more than just the point of view of marketing; investors in a company or enterprise are looking for value and more sustainable practices in the future that accompany that image. This indicates that the business outlook for those prepared to invest in the longer term is likely to be more robust and sustainable too. Being forward looking and sustainable in design and practice means that attention to wastes and inefficiency is probably already occurring, which means future profitability is enhanced. The effect in the building sector is that companies require buildings to match their image and aspirations, and that building developers themselves must consider their portfolio to match future requirements from all tenants and clients.

The Commission for Environmentally Responsible Economies (CERES) is a US-based non-profit organization that promotes sustainable policies that companies can subscribe to and thus gain credit with potential investors. CERES has ten operational principles which it advocates: protection of the biosphere; sustainable use of natural resources; reduction in, and suitable disposal of, wastes; wise use of energy; environmental risk reduction; marketing of safe and environmentally optimal products and services; environmental damage compensation; disclosure of environmental and health and safety information; employment of environmental directors and managers; and public disclosure of assessment and audit reports.

The International Institute for Sustainable Development (IISD) is also active in this area and provides guidelines for sustainable business practice. Also, a recent report for the Corporation of London (*Financing the Future*) examined the role of financial services. Seven principles were drawn up (the London Principles) to encourage institutions to adopt a system that would improve financing of sustainable development.

In addition to the reporting of environmental performance, there are also issues of future development potential to consider such as products and services to enable more sustainability in the company's operation and also for use in the wider community. Consideration of future needs and well-planned development to meet those needs is likely to put a company or organization in a more financially secure position with greater potential for profit in selling those products and services. As an example, a number of major oil companies are already investing heavily in renewable energy sources such as photovoltaics and this is supported by their shareholders, who sometimes prefer such investment over exploratory drilling for new oil reserves. *Smart growth* is a key phrase frequently used to signify the types of development to be pursued in the future; it indicates an approach which permits economic advancement, but in a more sustainable way.

The general public and local communities are also now taking a much more interested and proactive role in future sustainable development. Though not yet fully capitalized upon, the Local Agenda 21 movement has created a number of local networks and organizations that are already primed to help support future development that is more environmentally responsible, and this is bound to be reflected in the response to new, more sustainable initiatives and businesses. The policies and strategies for new development need also to be self-reinforcing, with the creation of local opportunities to bind communities and businesses together.

Neighbourhoods then become more self-sustaining and environmentally sustainable, with better all-round and long-term outlooks.

All of these elements suggest that the built environment sector will have to respond, not only to provide places that match the new, more sustainable economics, but also to maximize their own performance and potential. Unsustainable buildings will not be an asset but a cost, and the pressures from both investors and client groups are beginning to have effects. The range of future profit-related issues can be summarized in the following list:

- Investment is increasingly being influenced by environmental and sustainability concerns.
- Shareholders want to maximize future value and minimize future risk.
- Building location will be less important than the facilities and work environment provided, making some new types of development more cost efficient and profitable.
- There are profits to be made by developing sustainable products and services to meet future needs and business opportunities.
- There are opportunities to initiate new green businesses and consultancy activities, and opportunities will be created in relation to emissions trading and operation of carbon dioxide sequestration in building design and development.
- More efficient design and operation mean lower future resource costs for energy and materials use.
- Sustainable design and operation will result in lower future environmental costs for waste disposal and other environmental taxes or charges.
- There are opportunities to maximize tax breaks, rebates and value from reused or recycled materials.
- There are opportunities to initiate and strengthen local community involvement and support for businesses reinforcing local, more efficient sustainable operation.

Summary

This chapter has demonstrated the potential for sustainable design and development to be profitable, both environmentally and financially. There are some additional perceived risks from employing cutting-edge technologies; however, much can already be achieved by using tried and tested design and construction approaches. The task still remains to make such approaches the common expectation on a large scale. Of course, those prepared to work at the more exciting cutting edge have more to gain from their success and, given the risks taken with architectural aesthetics, there is no reason why more forward-looking environmental design should not be employed.

The following chapter indicates, through the use of case studies, some useful methods that are already being employed and are successful in their own way.

Chapter 7

Case studies

Introduction

The following ten case studies are presented as examples of development that in one way or another embody aspects of sustainability. Some examples are more successful than others and some more sustainable than others; some operate at very different scales. In some cases the outcomes represent the implementation of extensive and coordinated planning at strategic and other levels; in others the outcomes have been arrived at more by chance than by design.

In deciding on the ten choices, one cannot fail to recognize that there are many deserving candidates for inclusion. For example, there are features of other UK urban redevelopments such as at Greenwich, London, and in parts of Manchester, the world's first *industrial city*; and other so-called renaissance cities around the country. There are also many other interesting developments in North America; there are numerous other developments around Europe such as Ecolonia in Holland; and there are cities from the less developed world, such as Kampala in Uganda, Karachi in Pakistan and Curitiba in Brazil, each of which has a claim to showcase some aspect of environmental sustainability.

Unfortunately a choice has had to be made, however, and in making this choice an attempt has been to give some balance in scale and geographical location. On the more positive side, the benefits of the Internet and the willingness to place information on accessible webpages by many cities mean that anyone with a serious interest will be rewarded by finding much further information on many more examples if they so wish.

The sometimes very different examples show a variety of practical approaches to urban-scale sustainable environmental development. No one example is perfect, as all must operate in the real world, but some valuable insights and understandings can be gained from the analysis.

Leicester 'Environment City', UK

Background

Leicester is a multi-cultural city of about 300 000 people situated virtually in the centre of England; household incomes are a little below the national average and unemployment slightly above. It has social and economic problems, in common with many other similar cities, but it has an attitude to environmental matters that is not so frequently replicated. In 1990 Leicester was designated the UK's first so-called *Environment City* in recognition of the commitment and achievements, not only of the local City Council, but also of various other local organizations that had enabled its environmentally sensitive development. In 1992 the success of the Environment City initiative meant that Leicester's profile was high and it was one of only twelve cities worldwide specially invited to be represented at the first Earth Summit in Rio de Janeiro. Three other cities in the UK have since been designated as environment cities: Peterborough, Leeds and Middlesborough, but of the four, it is Leicester that has achieved the highest profile and been the most successful.

From this start point, in 1992 Leicester's City Challenge Programme incorporated a number of environmental issues and by 1995 sustainability was a key component of its Core Area Regeneration proposals. In 1996, following a review of local government in the UK, Leicester City Council became the sole institution in control over municipal affairs, and the following year its reformed programme focused on promoting the integrity and sustainability of the city. The Council's most recent Community Plan aims to bring about new investment through the physical regeneration of the city, and a regeneration company has been established with about £750 000 annual funding. The recent Leicester Local Plan, published in

2001, had as a leading theme the element of sustainability appraisal. The City Council has thus shown continued determination to uphold its environmental tradition and in 2002 representatives of the Council attended and contributed to the Johannesburg Earth Summit.

The establishment and linking of the Council's work to that of other organizations has been a key feature of the successful sustainability focus in its operations. In the following sections, descriptions of what is being done within the council and within other organizations are provided as pointers to successful practice.

Environment, regeneration and development

The body within the Council with responsibility for overseeing or undertaking most of the work in the environmental and sustainable development fields is the Environment, Regeneration and Development Department. It employs approximately 600 staff within four areas of work, and three of these divisions are particularly involved in relevant environmental responsibilities. The City Development Division coordinates activities in support of the physical regeneration of the city; it also aims to enhance quality of life by managing the development of the built and natural environments. Environmental Management and Protection deals with building control and pollution issues. It is also responsible for waste management and provision of energy-efficient services. The Environment Team, which is part of this division, coordinates policy on quality of life and sustainability. Strategic planning and development control are responsibilities of the Plans and Resources Division. Clearly, coordination between these groups is a key to the success of the process.

The Leicester Partnership for the Future, formed in 1998, also brought together diverse groups to further the City Council's aims. It has been a strong supporter of the Community Plan, which was developed on the basis of input and comments from thousands of local people.

The Community Plan

The initial Community Plan developed by the City Council for the period 2000–2003 had six priority areas: diversity; community safety; education; health and social care; environment; and jobs and regeneration. From these a number of *goals* were identified, together with *indicators* to enable measurement of progress, and *targets* to indicate the requirements for successful achievement of the goals. There are a number of important elements within the environment category concerning matters such as energy, traffic and air quality.

In the Community Plan the Council aims to obtain 20 per cent of its energy from renewable sources by the year 2020 and to reduce conventional energy use to 50 per cent of its 1990 value by 2025. A number of measures to reduce traffic volume in the city have been enacted and, at the end of the 1990s, this seemed to be having some small scale of success. Air quality is monitored and the areas that appear unlikely to meet set standards will have sophisticated area traffic management schemes set in place to help with this aim. Waste management and recycling are also addressed. The Community Plan provides the backdrop and strategy to the range of activities being pursued.

Environ

One of the most prominent components of the success of Leicester's environmental and sustainability initiatives has been the Environ Group. Environ was formed in 1993 from the amalgamation of the Leicester Ecology Trust and the Leicester Environment City Trust, both of which had already been active for about ten years. It was established as an independent environmental charity to support and develop community-based practical projects; it now also acts as an information provider and consultancy service and has the overriding aims of improving the environment and supporting sustainable development. Environ works in close collaboration with the City Council in its Environment City initiative, which has also brought together public organizations, businesses, educational institutions, voluntary organizations and individual members of the public. It has a workforce of over 40 professional staff, supported by additional volunteers, and it also works in partnership with other groups.

Environ also participates in several specific schemes such as computer hardware recycling and *Green Accounts*. In the former, redundant computers from businesses are collected and refurbished before being sold on to other users whose needs for less sophisticated systems suit the older machines available. The Green Accounts programme offers recycling options through a *cash-for-trash* approach. Environ has also found itself working in the wider Leicestershire county area outside the city and indeed beyond these boundaries in the East Midlands region as a whole and, on occasion, with international partners.

The EcoHouse

Leicester's EcoHouse is a showhome used to demonstrate numerous environmental design, construction and operational features that can be incorporated into housing and other building types. The House was originally a park keeper's cottage and is located in an easily accessible area of the city on the edge of its Western Park. The cottage was built in the 1920s but substantially modified for its current use when EcoHouse was set up in 1989. It is managed by Environ with support from the City Council, though it recently benefited from a National Lottery grant for its refurbishment and reopened in 2000 after major expansion. Plate 5 shows the south elevation of the EcoHouse.

The displays within the house are visually stimulating and interactive, and demonstrate features associated with use of sustainable timber; energy efficiency; recycled materials; alternative, environmentally friendly materials; water use; wastes and pollution; ecological gardening; and renewable energy. The features on show in the house include: low energy lighting and appliances; high thermal insulation standards in roof and wall and for pipework; a small-scale wind turbine; solar panels on the roof for hot water; heat recovery ventilation; low water use appliances; and recycling of wastes.

The EcoHouse is free to visit and is used often as an educational resource by local schools. It is also used as the venue for a number of environmentally oriented events. It attracts about 10 000 visitors a year and is an important visual exemplar of good ideas for sustainable building. There are other examples of good building practice in Leicester.

The Queen's Building

The city is also home to one of the most notable environmental buildings constructed in the 1990s, the Queen's Building at De Montfort University. It houses a number of facilities but perhaps its most well-known feature is the passive ventilation and heating system used in the main lecture rooms. The architectural expression of the ventilation strategy for the whole building can be seen in the towers on its main roof. The building was also innovative in terms of funding and building practice. Often professionals involved in building and building-services design may be tempted to use specification which maximizes their fee income, which is based on the capital value of work or equipment. In this case the client body was prepared to pay a fee based on an air-conditioning specification but to ask those involved in fact to design a more naturally ventilated and daylit building. Plate 6 shows the main entrance to the building.

The design, construction and operation of the building has been widely reported upon, and though there may have been a few shortcomings inherent in new forms of design, there is no doubt that it acts as a landmark, not just for the University but also for the city.

114

Ashton Green

In the first 15–20 years of the 21st century about 19 000 additional dwellings are expected to be needed in the Leicester area to replace old housing stock and as a result of various demographic and social trends. The primary policy for new housing is to encourage development of previously used brownfield land; however, not all the requirements can be met in this way and some new greenfield sites will need to be developed. Ashton Green is such a site; it covers an area of 230 hectares in the north of the city, 160 hectares of which have been part of its planned expansion since the mid-1970s, and it is designated for mixed-use development over a 15 to 20 year cycle.

The Council owns the whole site and it has decided that projected development must be based on the adoption of best practice in environmental design and sustainable development; the site has been designated a *special policy area* in recognition of the aspirations for its sustainable development. Paradoxically, the fact that the Council owns the land also means it is hampered in development because of guidelines covering disposal of assets at the best price when the specification for sustainability might mean that the development realizes a lower value in cash terms; nevertheless, there seems to be a will to make the Ashton Green development environmentally sound and to adopt higher than normal standards. Plate 7 shows an aerial view of the site.

It is planned eventually to build about 3500 dwellings on the site, which is located between two existing smaller-scale housing developments and close to a business park. Ashton Green will also include a range of new facilities, retail units and new business premises, and a significant fraction of the site (25 per cent) has been designated as open space. It is intended to create a village centre with primary community facilities early in the development so as to encourage local residents to use those local facilities rather than travel by car out of the area. Such facilities, and the provision of additional pupil accommodation at the local school, are planned to be part of the project development conditions. Of the housing to be built, a minimum of about 30 per cent will be required to be affordable housing to match local needs. The first phase of the development, commencing in 2003, has an area of approximately 20 ha and is located on a flat area of what is currently agricultural land. Figure 7.1 shows one of the original outline development schemes.

The development guidelines set quality and sustainability as key features that should be demonstrated, particularly in the design of the focal points around which the community will be built. The aim is also to provide energy from renewable sources and a key advisor on the work

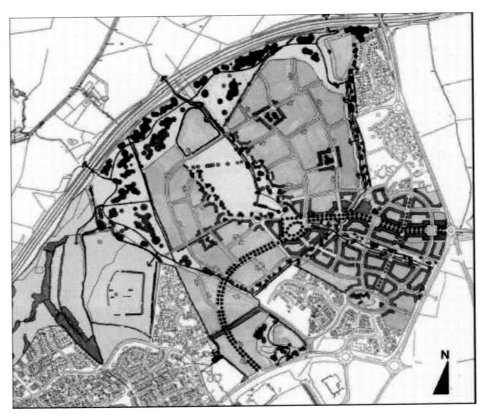

Figure 7.1 Preliminary outline proposals for Ashton Green (Leicester City Council/EDAW)

has been the Institute of Energy and Sustainable Development at the local De Montfort University. Following the award of a grant under the European Union's ALTENER programme in 1998, a feasibility study to examine energy options was carried out and this showed that the site had the potential to derive all of its energy needs from renewable sources. Some issues require particular attention, however: private sector developers often associate innovative projects with increased construction costs and lower land values, and they must be made more convinced of the benefits such schemes will eventually bring. The particular requirements that are set out as part of the Ashton Green scheme will also require modified working relationships to be developed between the public bodies and the private sector developers. It has been important, therefore, for the Council and its advisors to address these issues to ensure the successful execution of the scheme.

Plate 1: Wintergardens create pleasant environmental urban spaces

Plate 2: Solar hot water: high efficiency evacuated tube collectors

Plate 3: The Doxford Solar Office, UK

Plate 4: Photovoltaic cells are available in many colours, offering scope for design

Plate 5: Leicester: Ecohouse

Plate 6: Leicester: Queen's Building, De Montfort University

Plate 7: Leicester: Aerial view of Ashton Green development area (Leicester City Council)

Plate 8: Newark and Sherwood: Autonomous House

Plate 9: Newark and Sherwood: Hockerton Housing Project

Plate 10: Newark and Sherwood: Hockerton wind turbine

Plate 11: Newark and Sherwood: Boughton Pumping Station

Plate 12: BedZED: High density terraces with solar access

Plate 13: BedZED: Aerial walkways connect roof gardens on adjacent terraces

Plate 14: BedZED: Interior view out through sunspace

Plate 15: BedZED: South-facing façade showing photovoltaics and ventilation cowls

Plate 16: Austin: Casa Verde house (Austin Energy Green Building Program)

Plate 17: Austin: The Gables housing project with integrated water treatment (Austin Energy Green Building Program)

Plate 18: Portland: The Jean Vollum Natural Capital Center (Clive Knights)

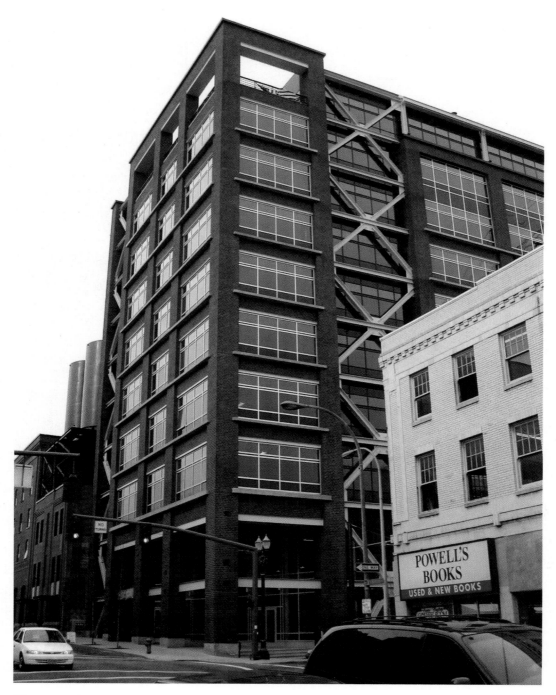

Plate 19: Portland: View of the Brewery Blocks redevelopment (Clive Knights)

Plate 20: Melbourne: Aerial view of Federation Square site during development

Plate 21: Melbourne: Federation Square site nearing completion

Plate 22: Melbourne: Queen Victoria Market—the roof is being used to mount a large photo-voltaic array

Plate 23: Sydney: Water control and treatment systems on the Olympic Parklands

Plate 24: Sydney: Stadium Australia—designed for environmental comfort and a variety of uses

Plate 25: Sydney: Water is collected for use from the roof of Stadium Australia

Plate 26: Sydney: The photovoltaic *Towers of Power* at Homebush Bay

Plate 27: Sydney: Houses at the Athletes' Village

Bo01
Site

Malmo City Centre

Plate 28: Bo01: Aerial view of Malmö showing the site (Göran Rosberg/Ronny Bergström, Malmö City Planning Offices)

Plate 29: Bo01: View along western edge of the development (Jan-Erik Anderson/Eva Dalman)

Plate 30: Bo01: View of colourful façade

Plate 31: Bo01: Green public circulation route (Jan-Erik Anderson/Eva Dalman)

Plate 32: Bo01: Green roof

Plate 33: Hong Kong: City of contrasts—apartments and green hillsides (Edward Ng)

Plate 34: Hong Kong: Three-dimensional walkway systems for pedestrian movement (Edward Ng)

Plate 35: Hong Kong: Verbena Heights development (Edward Ng)

Development codes have been prepared that set out a range of targets including those for energy use in the housing, and a number of unconventional approaches are set for inclusion in the energy infrastructure for the development. The first step is to reduce energy requirements for both heating and cooling by taking advantage of good site design, which includes planting to modify local microclimate. Energy demand can be further reduced by specification of insulation levels in excess of regulatory standards and by orientation of the buildings to optimize passive solar benefits. Appliances for use in the buildings (so-called *white goods* used in the kitchen, for instance) could be required to meet low energy-use standards. The residual primary energy demand (for heating and electricity) is planned to be met by a combined heat and power (CHP) system utilizing a biomass energy source. Solar hot-water collectors have been proposed for integration into the buildings as it has been estimated that they would be able to supply 65 per cent of domestic needs. Photovoltaic panels may also be used to demonstrate the benefits of solar electricity in a number of key buildings such as the community centre and school. The aim of these combined measures is that the development is designed to have a net carbon dioxide emission of zero.

In terms of transport policy, public transport links to the area of the site will be enhanced as part of the initial development; low speed limits for private vehicles will be imposed and, additionally, the layout will incorporate footpath and cycle routes; all of which should encourage alternative transport and a healthier lifestyle as well as lower pollution emissions. The housing density is expected to vary across the development with the aim of ensuring most residents have short-distance access to the public transport routes. The variety of the proposed scheme is also designed to emphasize design quality and reduce the bland appearance often characteristic of new housing development.

As the site contains many trees and hedgerows, the development will also involve an ecological survey with the aim of subsequently minimizing the adverse effect on wildlife in the area. A sustainable urban drainage system will also be required to be designed as part of the first phase of the development, which is due to deliver about 700 housing units between 2003 and 2006. Means to reduce water consumption within the dwellings by up to 30 per cent will also need to be provided.

Although an existing development framework diagram exists, prior to construction a new full masterplan will have to be produced to define the overall scheme and the implementation of its various sustainability features.

Energy

As well as an interest in environmental issues, Leicester has long been committed to supporting energy efficiency measures and its current policies are focused on reducing energy use by improving efficiency and energy conservation; developing environmentally friendly renewable energy technologies; and use of forward planning to reduce energy requirements.

In the 1990s the City Council adopted an energy action plan and supported over 1700 home energy efficiency surveys for local householders, and it also set up the Energy Sense Project. This scheme offers free advice to all local residents, distributes information packs and helps locals to understand and optimize their choices of improved energy efficiency measures. A local Energy Efficiency Advice Centre serving homes and businesses can also be found in the city, funded by a national body, the Energy Saving Trust, and a Home Energy Efficiency Scheme (HEES) has also operated since 2000.

The Council's Community Plan already commits it to targets for increased use of renewables and energy conservation. Its local support for the use of solar water heating for the canteen in one of its main buildings and the initiation of a solar hot water rental scheme in 2000 has also helped encourage a number of other schemes within the city. The rental scheme means that ten systems per year will be installed and rented to the building occupiers so that the cost is spread rather than causing a large initial capital outlay. A solar hot water heating system has also been placed on the roof of a local primary school as an exemplar of the technology. Five Leicester schools have also benefited from the installation of photovoltaics technology. The arrays were originally part of a set for a national television programme and were installed with support from a national government funding programme. Additional educational spin-offs came from the educational materials provided along with the arrays and the ability of the schools to monitor performance and use this in lessons.

Many of the energy-related schemes in the city are rightly oriented to the alleviation of fuel poverty. As part of this, the HEES offers help to low-income families with young children and also to older people in poor housing; in both cases grants can be awarded to help install additional insulation and improve the energy efficiency of appliances. Approximately 1000 households per year in Leicester receive help under this scheme.

Environmental issues

The Council has adopted the Europe-wide Eco-Management and Audit Scheme (EMAS) as a means to focus on monitoring, maintaining and improving environmental standards within the city. Many organizations and businesses underestimate the cost of waste by a significant margin.

EMAS provides a way to examine resource use, waste and pollution and the Council has eight targets: reduce Council use of energy and fuel; reduce Council air pollution emissions; reduce Council waste; reduce household waste; reduce Council use of water; reduce Council use of paper; improve the quality of the natural environment on Council-owned land; and improve the quality of open space on Council-owned land. Since signing up to this scheme in 1999, the Council has also tried to promote good environmental practice to local businesses and encourage sustainable business practices in the workplace.

The Council has ambitious targets for increasing recycling of household waste to 40 per cent and thereby reducing the amounts of wastes currently being sent to landfill sites. Almost 100 recycling points are provided around the city, and there are schemes for recycling a range of materials: aluminium, paper, glass, steel and plastics. One of the materials that has received particular attention is paint. Paint can contain a number of toxic substances and, when dumped at landfill sites, can leak out, causing environmental damage. Since the average household has around 17 tins of partially used paint there is a large potential problem. In Leicester, under the *Community Re>Paint* scheme, the paint is collected, graded and, where possible, redistributed for use. The Council also offers an office recycling service to collect materials such as office-grade paper, printer cartridges, drinks containers and other valuable office supplies. Computer recycling is also undertaken as part of the Environ organization's work.

Environmental education and general awareness-raising has also featured in the range of activities supported by the City Council. A series of Eco Schools has been founded in the city's educational establishments with the aim of involving children in environmental projects and encouraging them to help in ways that protect the local environment. There has also been a series of successful campaigns under the general title of *Turning the Tide* across the region. These campaigns have both increased awareness of environmental issues and acted as a stimulus for behavioural change. The concept behind these initiatives is that even small changes can lead to a more sustainable future.

The Council also has a purchasing policy that favours environmentally friendly products. It has produced a guide that helps local individuals and organizations to purchase goods which maximize recycling potential whilst minimizing resource depletion and pollution.

Leicester Environment Partnership

The Leicester Environment Partnership was formed in mid-2001 with two main spheres of operation: firstly to improve coordination in the work and activities of the various organizations already involved in environmental matters; and secondly to stimulate environmental awareness in new bodies and organizations. In 2002, 15 organizations were represented in the partnership, including several Council departments, the Environment Agency, the water company serving the area, a wildlife trust, a residents' association, De Montfort University, Friends of the Earth and Environ.

Though the partnership has been in existence a relatively short time, it already has a work programme that includes several important areas and has started the task of producing an environmental vision for Leicester. The large amount of redevelopment and regeneration within Leicester has prompted the partnership to encourage the adoption by developers and builders of high environmental standards and specification in the buildings being designed and constructed. A further task is the assessment of the city's overall environmental impact by means of assessing its environmental footprint. It has also been able to influence and direct £800 000 of funding which is being used to support environmental initiatives in deprived areas of the city.

The main role of the partnership is likely to be an enabling one as there is limited direct funding available which could be used to initiate or substantially modify urban scale development; however, the partnership is able to exert influence in certain areas and to mobilize support for particular themes.

Discussion

Leicester has been very successful in promoting sustainability and environmental issues over a long period of time, and there is no doubt that Leicester deserves praise for its attempts to focus on, and improve, sustainable development within the city. This has been recognized by a number of external awards, including being one of only five winners of the European Sustainable City award in 1996. In 2001 the Council received *Beacon Status* as an exemplar of national good practice in the UK for 'maintaining a quality environment'. Despite this, many commentators draw attention to the difficulties in establishing and maintaining the focus and commitment to environmental matters and the ongoing need to continually emphasize and develop environmental policy. Some other cities are now also beginning to show strong environmental leadership, but this should not detract from the achievements of this city.

In Leicester, a strong corporate policy framework with widespread community involvement to support sustainability has been put in place and seems to be working effectively. It has enabled the city to establish a high UK profile in environmental matters. The integration that has been achieved between businesses and traditional areas of environmental work (waste, recycling, energy and related topics) marks Leicester out as both innovative and the propagator of good practice. In order for it to continue, the various individuals, groups and organizations within the city will need to continue working together in support of evolving environmental and sustainability initiatives, and to support the Community Plan.

Newark and Sherwood District, UK

Background

Newark and Sherwood District Council covers an area of 650 square kilometers in the East Midlands region of the UK. It includes contrasting zones such as former coal-mining communities and the more rural Trent River valley. The area has two main towns, Newark and Southwell (each with rich historical pasts), and about ninety villages and hamlets; it also includes part of Sherwood Forest, which is known around the world for its association with Robin Hood. The district is somewhat different to the other case studies presented here, for it has a much more rural character with no large urban areas; it covers approximately one-third of the county area but has only 10 per cent of its population. There are cities nearby, however, within short travelling distances, and transport links are also very good with major road and rail routes passing through or close to the area. The population of the area is a modest 100 000 and the reason for its inclusion is not that it can act as an exemplar of new *city* development but rather that it has the potential to show an alternative lifestyle and options, and also because within its boundaries it includes several notable environmentally focused developments.

The District Council

Newark and Sherwood District Council has been a strong supporter and advocate for sustainable development since the 1980s. As part of its Chief Executive's Department it has an Environmental Stewardship Team, a major component of which is the Newark and Sherwood Energy Agency. The public aim of the team is 'to engage local people on Local Agenda 21 activity that locally implements the agreements made at the Rio Earth Summit, 1992; to develop effective environmental management systems within the Council and raise the national reputation of the Council as a leader in the field of environmental stewardship'. Its policy aims are to help develop an energy-sustainable district Council area and promote and support activities that lead to reduction in pollution, combat global warming, improve resource efficiency and create employment.

The Energy Agency was formed in 1996, but the Council's work in dealing positively with energy issues dates back to 1985 when local tenants of pre-Second World War housing demanded action to alleviate problems of damp; poor insulation standards and ineffective and inefficient heating systems were to blame. The Council reacted well to the challenge and, working with tenants, it developed a 20-year strategy for improvement. The strategy initially targeted the worst properties and evaluated the most cost-effective solutions that could be employed before moving on to other targets. The programme was very pragmatic and recognized the budget limitations and was one in which the outcome of satisfying occupants' need for affordable heating was ranked higher than improvement targets based on simple modernization issues such as numbers of refurbished kitchens or bathrooms. Members of the Council's teams have also been very active in developing a systematic approach to measuring and monitoring as a means for target setting. In 1985 only 6 per cent of the Council's houses were capable of delivering affordable warmth; by 2001 that figure had risen to 93 per cent. Along with this impressive change, energy efficiency had also improved by almost 40 per cent and carbon dioxide emissions reduced by about 20 per cent. The benefits have not only been in improved consumption figures but also in better fabric maintenance (good for the Council as the owner) and better health for building occupants. The economic assessment shows that in Council housing an investment of £5.3m would yield almost £1m savings per year in fuel charges (which would be available for spending on other items, thus improving the general economic wellbeing of the area); plus over £1m saving in healthcare costs; and also a number of job creation opportunities. Overall, the payback period for such investment was calculated at 2.2 years. The Council has also been active in promoting better housing in the privately rented and owner-occupied sectors, and has been collating a database that enables targeted actions and advice.

The current approach adopted by the Council has three elements: identification of householders at risk of fuel poverty; identification of dwellings at risk of fuel poverty; and provision of ongoing advice, education and guidance. Where appropriate, grants are made available to help with upgrading and there are links to third parties for funding options. Awareness-raising throughout the district has also been a major task and this has utilized press articles, environmental calendars and a mobile energy advice bus. It also has extensive web-based advice and information sources.

The Council has also been involved in supporting development of renewable energy technologies and businesses. There are already examples of use of biomass energy (some of which are described below) and this, it is hoped, can be further expanded. The proposed Council strategy shows a potential to meet a target of 20 per cent emissions reduction from 1990 levels by 2010 if all sectors are included, and the potential to provide 12 per cent of local electricity from local renewable resources.

As a result of its efforts it has been awarded Beacon Council status by the UK national government for its work in tackling fuel poverty, enabling it rightly to claim to be a national exemplar of good practice.

The Autonomous House

Architects Robert and Brenda Vale have been leading international lights in the movement for environmentally sensitive and energy-efficient building design for many years. In the Newark and Sherwood district town of Southwell, close to a medieval minster, they were given the opportunity to build a house for their own occupation that could embody their advanced ecological design concepts and autonomous operation. The location set them a challenge since the area was subject to rigorous planning constraints, and the building has been designed to be free of reliance on almost all mains services. The exception to this is the fact that the house is connected to the electricity grid, but the claim is that the photovoltaic system installed makes a net contribution to grid power supplies. A view of the photovoltaic array, garden and house is shown in plate 8.

From the outside the house reflects the character of the town in its form and materials, though it has a basement, which is rare in contemporary UK housing. Its first and second floors are made of concrete to provide thermal mass. Most striking is the level of insulation achieved in all the elements. External walls are of clay bricks with a concrete block inner leaf, accommodating 250 mm of mineral fibre insulation in the cavity. The architects were fortunate in having a local authority that sympathized with their aims; in many other localities their departures from normal building practice would have been unacceptable or difficult to carry through.

The roof is another feature that externally hides the fact that its structure is far from conventional; it includes 500 mm of cellulose fibre insulation. The clay pantile finish gives the illusion of normal design despite an exceptional insulation value. Windows are triple glazed, krypton filled with low emissivity coatings, all within timber frames. The west-facing garden elevation is dominated by a double-height, double-glazed conservatory with windows opening into the upper floor rooms (see figure 7.2).

Figure 7.2 Autonomous House conservatory

In terms of services, the house uses tried and tested technologies to produce a package that is unusual for the UK. A mechanical ventilation system with heat recovery connects the conservatory, the kitchen and the two bathrooms to provide recirculated heat. Domestic hot water is mainly provided by a heat pump using warm exhaust air from the composting toilet. Space heating is provided from the passive solar source of the conservatory and this is supplemented by a wood stove. Electricity is supplied by a 2.2 kW photovoltaic system mounted on a pergola in the garden that is connected to the grid. The grid connection evens out the peaks and troughs of supply from the intermittent system. Perhaps the most adventurous feature of the house is the water supply, which relies on rainwater collected from the roof which is then fed into 30 cubic metres of storage tanks in the basement. After treatment it is pumped to a tank in the loft to be available as required for general purposes, though drinking and cooking water passes through a further ceramic/carbon filter. Similarly, the sewage system is also independent of external services. A composting toilet serves the house, with a holding compartment in the basement; it is vented by a small fan and the by-product is a permanent supply of garden fertilizer. Greywater enters a soakaway through a grease trap.

The ecological theme is maintained in the choice of materials. For example, the bricks were fired by landfill methane at a works 60 km from Southwell. The hard core for the slab consists of demolition rubble from the building previously located on the site. Internal finishes, furnishings and fittings were selected with a view to keeping to a minimum the production of organic chemical gases. Despite the radical methods and technologies, the overall building costs were very similar to conventional construction costs.

The success of the Autonomous House encouraged the local authority to follow a policy for more ecological housing such as that at Hockerton and Sherwood Energy Village, which are described below.

The Hockerton Housing Project

The Hockerton Housing Project is another scheme associated with the architects Robert and Brenda Vale. The original concept had been to create a housing development for five families where the occupants could follow an ecologically sensitive lifestyle and in which they would be self-sufficient in food, water and energy; it has thus been promoted as a model for sustainable living. The development is unusual in that it would not normally have been permitted in the area because of planning restrictions; however, Newark and Sherwood Council granted permission under a special agreement in 1994 that allowed the construction of this radical new development to go ahead. The Hockerton scheme consists of five largely self-built, earth-covered houses running east to west in a 60 m long terrace. The properties have extremely low conventional energy requirements (overall energy consumption is 75 per cent less than for a conventional house) whilst still affording the occupants most, if not all, of the facilities and amenities associated with modern life. Plate 9 gives a panoramic view of the terrace of properties.

The 10 ha site is rural in character and lies close to the village of Hockerton but also close to the main town of Newark. Parts of the site are set aside for specific functions associated with the ecological mode of living. A substantial area is used for sheep grazing and poultry whilst another is used for crop cultivation. A further major feature of the site is a lake, which was constructed in front of the dwellings. The main feature of the dwelling units, however, is their earth-sheltered construction, combined with large conservatories that together run the whole length of the terrace.

Materials used have low embodied energy content and were sourced from the local area wherever possible. Manufactured materials had also to be of low environmental impact and meet specified functional standards. Construction took approximately 18 months between 1996 and 1998 and building costs were comparable with those of conventional design and construction, though the self-build element distorts the comparison.

The houses have no need for a normal space-heating system and this is a result of the solar orientation and the extremely high insulation standards. The roof of the terrace consists of 300 mm of concrete, 300 mm of insulation and approximately 400 mm of earth covering; the rear and side walls are also well insulated and have even greater depths of earth covering. The high thermal capacity of the concrete and earth enables a stable temperature to be maintained on a daily and seasonal basis, and also acts to protect the fabric of the structure. All five properties have their main living spaces regularly arranged behind the wide conservatory in six standard three-metre wide bays. The south-facing aspect and high thermal capacity surfaces enable solar heat gain to be absorbed during the day and re-emitted to the dwellings later. The windows from the rooms in five of the six bays open onto the conservatories and are triple glazed with low emissivity coatings; the external conservatory windows are double glazed. The sixth bay acts as an entrance and lobby area for each dwelling unit. A heat recovery ventilation system is used to extract stale air from certain rooms such as bathrooms and kitchens and return the heat to fresh incoming air in other rooms. Analysis by the occupants has shown that it is possible to maintain internal winter temperatures at the relatively stable level of 18–20°C and summer temperatures between about 22 and 23°C, though the conservatories do reach a few degrees higher.

Rainwater that falls on the conservatory roofs is collected and filtered so that it can be used for drinking after suitable treatment, and water storage sufficient for 250 days is available on site. Water consumption is minimized in the dwellings by use of low water use appliances, toilets and taps. Waste water and sewage are treated on site by means of a floating reed bed system located at one end of the lake. This must be periodically cleaned and maintained but produces water that meets international standards and is suitable for discharge into the remainder of the lake, which can be used for swimming and which is also home to a substantial fish population.

Electrical power is supplied from solar photovoltaic collectors along the ridge of the terrace of houses and from a small 6 kW wind generator also situated on site (see plate 10). The electrical system is connected to the national power grid. Initially there had been some difficulties in getting permission for the erection of the wind generator as it was an unknown technology in the local area. Three applications were made before a Council policy was formulated that allowed the generator to be built.

Figure 7.3 Hockerton reed bed system

Typical electrical energy usage by each dwelling is 6–12 kWh per day, which is substantially lower than that of a normal household. Hot water is provided by air-to-air heat pumps connected to storage cylinders, and though back-up immersion heaters are available they are rarely used.

A number of television and radio programmes, as well as numerous press articles, have established a strong public image for the project. This has had a spin-off in a demand for on-site visitor tours and lectures off-site; these, together with the sale of a range of publications and the provision of consultancy advice, have been a valuable additional income source for the occupants through a not-for-profit company, limited by guarantee, Hockerton Housing Project Trading Limited. Each household is expected to commit a certain amount of time to the support of the project for such activities as giving tours, crop cultivation, animal care, community duties and other maintenance needs. Members of the households have also agreed to a covenant that limits their ownership to one private vehicle, though an additional communal electrically powered car is available for local short journey needs (and which is charged from on-site renewable electrical energy supplies). The Sustainable Community Project established

Figure 7.4 View from roof of Hockerton Housing Project site

at Hockerton has been devised to provide a coordinated package of services to help others initiate, plan and establish further sustainable communities.

Overall, the Hockerton Housing Project has been a very successful experiment, providing attractive and comfortable low energy and low environmental impact dwellings. It has been particularly successful in demonstrating that a number of features could be replicated in other designs and also in disseminating information and advice on how this can be done. Though rural in character, many of the ideas could be incorporated into urban projects and indeed some of those designers involved in such projects have visited and benefited from Hockerton's example; there is no reason why such examples should not become more common in the future.

Sherwood Energy Village

As previously stated, the largely rural Newark and Sherwood district also contains areas of industrial activity, one of the most prominent of which (at least until the early 1990s) was the coal mining industry. Political conflicts between national government and mining unions, economic pressures due to availability of cheap imported coal, and the availability of cheaper and cleaner alternative fuels, particularly natural gas, all played a part in the dramatic reduction in demand for UK-sourced coal and the subsequent decimation of the industry. Where once there were scores of coal mines there are now only a few left; and this reduction happened in the space of little more than a decade. Some of the communities severely affected were in the Newark and Sherwood region; one in particular was Ollerton. It had initially been extended and developed as a town in the 1920s to provide housing for a workforce and their families in an area with a number of local coal mines; however, the last remaining local colliery, in the town itself, closed in March 1994.

In the immediate aftermath unemployment in parts of the town rose to 35 per cent and there was enormous social, economic and cultural upheaval. Also left behind was an environmental problem with fears over soil and groundwater pollution, derelict land, subsidence and poor environmental quality of life. The clearance of the colliery site left behind about 40 ha of brownfield land around the pit itself and a further surrounding area of about 60 ha of spoil tips. Having seen what had happened in other former coalfield communities, the reaction of the local people was to stay in the area and fight for new economic development with diversification, and to create a type of community in which they would have more control over the future and which could develop sustainable and less polluting employment and infrastructure.

Following the closure of the pit, a two-year debate and consultation period took place, led by the Ollerton and District Economic Forum, and various concepts and schemes were put forward. The option chosen was to redevelop the coal mine site as a new mixed-use area to contain housing, industry (with a focus on renewable energy technologies) and recreation facilities; the project became known as Sherwood Energy Village. Local professionals such as architects (Benoy Architect and Masterplanning Ltd) and solicitors provided help in visualizing and setting up the scheme, and the example of another local project, Boughton Pumping Station (described later), also served to stimulate ideas in the local community.

A novel method was used to set up control over the development. Sherwood Energy Village was registered as an Industrial and Provident Society, which is a form of cooperative very different to a limited company with a focus on people rather than capital. The legal structure allows the organization to seek and utilize external funding but it does not pay dividends and any profits are reinvested. This form of organization allows for democratic control and local involvement, but it also has some drawbacks in that it is more costly and complex to set up and operate. Sherwood Energy Village bought the site from the previous owners, British Coal, for £50 000 and obtained around £4m in funding from a variety of sources including local agencies, national government and the European Union to cover the basic reclamation and infrastructure costs. Ongoing costs are being met from a number of funding agencies at local and national level.

The aim for the village is to embody principles of sustainable development that integrate economic, environmental and social needs. The development is planned to have zero net carbon dioxide emission in construction and use; materials are to come from sustainable sources, and energy efficiency and environmental sensitivity are key design parameters. Another interesting feature of the site development is the planned use of a sustainable urban drainage system that will be the largest in the UK. The system is designed to reduce the risk of flooding and provide storm water management. It uses a combination of features: permeable surfaces, filter drains, swales, basins and ponds. This series of measures, particularly the swales, helps to collect water runoff and clean it of pollutants, using suitable planted vegetation.

Land reclamation on the pit site began in 2000, following landscaping and planting on the surrounding tips. Outline planning permission for the site was obtained in 2002 and work on installing the infrastructure for the site was begun; many of the other aspects of the site have already been planned, however. An area immediately adjacent to the site has been developed as a large supermarket.

The designated housing area covers about three hectares and, when complete, is expected to number about 110 units; it will aim to showcase green technology with special building regulations devised by Robert and Brenda Vale, which improved on the existing national standards, to guide design. Twenty-four self-build houses have been planned along with twelve self-sufficient autonomous houses and three demonstration eco-homes. The other housing will also be expected to adhere to high energy-efficiency standards. Walking and cycling around the redeveloped site are being encouraged by planned boulevards and cycle routes.

Approximately 16 ha have been set aside for light to medium industry and commerce with the aim of attracting inward investment and job creation. Industrial units have been planned of various sizes but particularly to fill a gap in existing markets for premises between about 500 and 1000 square metres. Companies with ethical and environmental attitudes in keeping with the concept of the village are being particularly encouraged. Retail- and craft-oriented activities are also planned. A special form of lease is being developed for the industrial and commercial development, aimed at benefiting both the local community and the businesses. Sherwood Energy Village also operates its own advice service (Sherwood Environmental Exchange Bureau) to assist local community enterprises and regeneration initiatives with a sustainability focus.

A major element of the site will be a 20 MW renewable energy power plant using oil derived from forestry biomass material as its fuel source. It is symbolic that the site, once the source of a non-renewable fossil fuel, will be used for a low-pollution renewable energy supply. The forestry material will be sourced off-site, with the conversion to oil fuel-stock also taking place off-site, which will reduce pollution and transport costs. Though the power plant is relatively small, it is at such a scale that biomass technology seems to be most successful and is probably one of the most economically viable means of carbon-neutral heat and power generation. Planting of trees to enhance carbon sequestration as part of the development will also take place.

The location of Ollerton close to existing tourist sites facilities means that it has the potential to expand into a leisure and recreation area. There is to be an exhibition and conference facility that will act as a landmark building, and also hotel accommodation. Eight hectares of the site are set aside for a sports arena which is to be located in a part of the site with a natural amphitheatre. There are also areas for wildlife parks, and an energy trail.

It is difficult to know how successful the Sherwood Energy Village will become; it has a long way to go and former coalfield communities often have a poor public image outside the area, which can inhibit new investment. The location of the development is good, however, and there are a number of local attractions that might encourage movement of people and businesses into the area. Perhaps as important is the local community's strong resolve, enthusiasm and ideas, which ought to help it succeed in its ambitions.

Other projects

Several other small-scale projects exhibiting a focus on sustainable energy or environmental design can be found in the Newark and Sherwood area. One of the inspirations for the Sherwood Energy Village was the nearby redevelopment of the Boughton Pumping Station. The building was originally constructed as part of the local water supply system, providing water to the City of Nottingham, and was built in the early part of the twentieth century. In 1991, after the building had been derelict for almost 20 years, a local group purchased it from its former owners, the Severn Trent Water Company, for a nominal sum of £1. The group reformed as a charitable trust and managed to obtain funding from a variety of sources to renovate it. The pumping station (see plate 11) now houses over 20 businesses, IT training, a restaurant, and exhibition and conference facilities. The building is served by a combined heat and power plant fuelled by woodchip biomass.

At Collingham two projects have been undertaken. In Millennium Green, 24 environmental houses have been constructed which have only 50 per cent of the normal utility requirements for gas, electricity and water. Roof-mounted solar panels are used in conjunction with efficient heating boilers for well-insulated dwellings using low-energy lighting and rain-water collection systems. Also in Collingham is the Geothermal House, which is heated from a 110 m underground source via a heat pump.

Discussion

The examples of development in the Newark and Sherwood area show that even in adverse economic conditions, or ones that do not provide the large-scale investment available in major urban areas, environmentally sensitive yet economically sound changes can be enacted. It is true that in urban areas, schemes such as Hockerton could not easily be accommodated because of the land requirements, though as an example of community living it acts as a good exemplar, and as a showcase of ecological design it is excellent. Many of the technologies and techniques utilized in

Newark and Sherwood have shown what can be done, and have been taken up in other projects. The role of the local council has been crucially important in permitting and encouraging such examples, and ultimately its aim has been to help revitalize the local economy whilst following good environmental principles. It has acted as a successful pathfinder in pursuing sustainable and energy-efficient design in the built environment; the cluster of organizations that has developed in the local area bears testament to the council's success. Other councils, both large and small, could learn something from the example it has set.

BedZED, the Beddington Zero Energy Development, UK

Background

Beddington Zero Energy Development (BedZED) has helped define the concept of a *green urban village* and has become widely known as an example of sustainable development because of its technical features, its aesthetic impact and its approach to ownership. As well as being a commercially oriented development it aims to be environmentally sensitive and energy efficient in both design and operation. It is also designed to be carbon neutral, with on-site energy production from renewable sources. In summary, the scheme is a mixed-use suburban development of 82 flats and houses together with a number of workspace units. The project is situated on a 1.4 ha brownfield site, this being the location of a former sewage works at Hackbridge within the London Borough of Sutton.

The partners

In order to develop the scheme and to put into practice its pioneering principles, a number of organizations have collaborated in the venture; these are the Peabody Trust, the BioRegional Development Group and Bill Dunster Architects, and they have been supported by the enthusiasm of the local council and the various building professionals and consultants involved in its construction.

Peabody is London's largest housing association and is involved in providing social housing stretching across many areas of the UK's capital city. The Trust was set up with an initial sum of half a million pounds in 1862 by George Peabody, an American who founded the Morgan Grenfell Bank. The Trust's original work was to improve the lot of London's poor, and it did this by supporting the provision of well-designed housing to replace the slums prevalent in the late nineteenth and first half of the twentieth centuries. Besides the relief of poverty, it has acted as a catalyst to trigger economic and social regeneration; its substantial asset base means that it can help raise private finance for social housing and other opportunities. It has a strong reputation for encouraging quality design and technical innovation, yet still aims to provide affordable homes.

BioRegional is an environmental development charity founded in 1994, with offices in Sutton. Its normal work has been involved in linking practical sustainability for business and industry with the ideal of local production for local needs. In this it supports the idea of developing businesses based on sustainable land-use, thus providing employment without reducing biodiversity; it also has a market-led approach and promotes the use of suitable advanced technologies. Though it had no previous experience in building construction it was instrumental in devising and instigating the BedZED project. The group's primary role in the eventual delivery of the BedZED scheme was concerned with defining the ground rules for a green construction site, integrating transport and energy issues, managing and sourcing the materials used in construction, reducing and dealing with wastes, and ethical financing. BioRegional is also concerned with helping the occupants to ensure the development operates in an environmentally sensitive way.

Bill Dunster Architects have an international reputation for development of sustainable architectural solutions and are one of the UK's leading architectural practices in this field. They hold an underlying belief that, even with the tight market constraints prevalent in the UK building industry, sustainable development is both possible and affordable. Environmental and energy issues (including use of renewable energy) form a significant part of their portfolio of design solutions under the banner of ZEDFactory, which focuses on Zero Emission Development. A feature of their designs is the careful integration of required features into the design of each component so as to reduce waste and provide multi-functionality. The aim is to create excellence in environmental performance within the normal cost constraints. A number of the technologies and techniques utilized at BedZED had already been tested through a range of previous design ideas and competition schemes, and in a more practical way at the principal architect's home, Hope House in Surrey.

The London Borough of Sutton had been active for many years in promoting sustainable practices even before the BedZED proposal took shape, and had an existing record in environmental fields such as recycling. Its Local Agenda 21 stance is strong and well developed. Transport issues also have a high profile, with initiatives to support the use of public transport and alternative vehicles such as those powered by gas or electricity.

134

The development

Peabody, acting as the developer, bought the site from the local council even though it did not submit the highest cash bid; what won it was the added value that the scheme was able to deliver. The BedZED development consists of 82 homes in one, two, three and four bedroom configurations, giving a total of 272 habitable rooms. The accommodation is provided in the form of terraces of town houses, maisonettes and apartments that are laid out in five rows, each 6 m from its neighbour, separated in mews style to allow space for ground-level access routes and gardens. Aerial walkways span the gaps between the terraces to allow occupants from upper-storey units to reach garden areas on adjoining roofs. The general arrangement can be seen in plate 12 and the linking aerial walkways are shown in plate 13.

The basic dwelling building module is a three-storey town house that can be used as a single residence or can be subdivided into flats and maisonettes. All dwellings have some garden space, either on the ground or as roof gardens. This gives a sense of space and place sadly lacking in many similar dense developments. The principal orientation is to the south and this, together with the profiled shape of the terrace roofs, allows maximum passive solar benefits to be gained from the windows and sunspace conservatories.

Figure 7.5 BedZED façade, showing main features

The housing units are linked in the development to about $1600\,m^2$ of flexible workspace subdivided into approximately 23 units with mezzanine levels, which can be interconnected to be more flexible in arrangement. A range of community facilities is also designated at the site including a village green, café, shop, and a sports club. There is very little in terms of technology in the scheme that has not been used previously and been shown to work; what is novel is the overall integrated approach to delivering the design in the development constructed.

Energy-efficient design

One of the principal features of the scheme is its claim to have zero energy requirements in terms of energy derived from conventional fossil fuels. This is a key feature of Bill Dunster's Practice work where there is an aim to reduce energy demand to a level where renewables can be employed as the principal energy source. The first step in this design approach has been to utilize very high levels of insulation: at BedZED 300 mm of fibre insulation is used in the roof and walls, 300 mm of polystyrene insulation is positioned in the floor, and windows are triple glazed. The design allows much of the thermal capacity of the building structure to be exposed to the sun, including exposed ceilings and tiled uncarpeted flooring. This has the effect of introducing thermal mass into the natural heat flow pattern and thus reducing temperature fluctuations.

An airtight construction technique has also been used to reduce unwanted infiltration (air leakage) and this has been combined with a heat recovery ventilation system that aims to recycle up to 75 per cent of the heat that would otherwise be lost in the exhausted stale air. This ventilation system uses wind cowls that have been installed on the roof to operate in a two-sided mode (fresh air in one side and used stale air out the other) with the heat exchanger integrated into the design. These cowls act to aid natural ventilation and provide night-time cross-ventilation for summer cooling. The main façades of the dwellings themselves face south to maximize controlled passive solar gain, which plays a major role in providing heating for the dwellings. Besides the southerly orientation, each unit is provided with some form of sunspace to trap the solar heat (see plate 14). The heating requirements are estimated to be only 10 per cent of those for a conventional dwelling built to the Building Regulations minimum standard, and the performance is so good that typically only one or two small radiators are required for conventional heating purposes. Office areas that are part of the development are located in shaded zones to avoid excessive daytime solar heat gain and thus the need for air conditioning.

The facades of the housing incorporates 109 kW of photovoltaic modules, which allow the generation of solar electricity (see plate 15). This electricity can be used in a variety of ways, though the developers are keen to suggest the potential for it to be used to power electric vehicles, which are planned to be part of the communal shared transport strategy.

The main source of energy for the development is an on-site 135 kW combined heat and power (CHP) unit. This is matched to the predicted energy demands arising from the housing in conjunction with the workplace units. The CHP unit uses as its fuel a waste timber product arising from a tree surgeon, from woodlands under BioRegional's stewardship and from other local sources; waste that might otherwise be dumped at landfill. The CHP unit takes the waste timber and processes it through a woodchip gasifier. The process is claimed to be carbon neutral because of the nature of the waste, though it still results in carbon dioxide production. Perhaps the details of this require some clarification and further justification to ensure tree planting to match the use.

The CHP unit is connected to the electricity grid so that surplus power generation can be fed into the national network and payment received as a result. The unit also provides hot water for the site and, to even out demand, extra-large hot water cylinders are installed in each dwelling to act as thermal stores. Low-energy white goods are installed in the properties to further reduce energy demand. Overall, the development is predicted to use 60 per cent less energy than an equivalent non-energy-efficient scheme.

Environmental features

Some of the main additional environmental features of the development relate to transportation issues. A part of the development agreement has been the commitment to a legally binding green transport plan. The provision of some on-site workplace units means the need to travel to work has been reduced. Public transport is also a good option as the site is near to rail, bus and tram links. Parking at the site for private cars has been reduced and alternatives to motor vehicles have been promoted, with enhanced bicycle storage and the commitment to electric cars and communal pool cars. Overall there is a *pedestrians first* approach at the site, with cars generally excluded except at the perimeter. The density of occupation is also important in supporting transport infrastructure; average density is 47 units per hectare, but when communal facilities and the sports area are excluded the remainder of the development has a density of approximately 100 units per hectare.

Water is another important environmental consideration—both in its supply and in the disposal of waste. An average household uses about 150 litres of water each day and approximately one-third of that is simply for flushing toilets. Low-water-use wcs are installed with alternative flushing options, and spray-type taps which deliver lower volumes for hand-washing are also specified. Water-efficient washing machines have been installed and water meters are located in prominent positions so as to guide the occupants in controlling use. Water recycling and the use of rainwater collected from the roofs (to supply about one-fifth of demand) will also be utilized. This water can be stored in foundation-level tanks and used for flushing toilets. Overall, the scheme aims for a reduction of one-third to one-half in water demand. On-site water treatment has been planned with the use of a small-scale sewage plant, a so-called *living machine*. Measures have also been taken in the design to reduce problems of surface water run-off, with porous surfaces laid over gravel and a drainage pond, which could be a wildlife feature.

The choice and sourcing of materials of construction were carefully considered; wherever possible, materials were provided from within a 56 km radius of the site. Materials included reclaimed steel (sandblasted and then repainted) and recycled timber cladding; the aim was to use natural materials that were renewable or recycled. One of the few exceptions to the materials sourcing guidelines was the windows; the low U-value (0.6 W/m^2 per °C) triple glazed types could not be produced at reasonable cost within the UK and were imported from Denmark. Extensive recycling facilities are also available for day-to-day waste use, with the aim of reducing material for landfill by 80 per cent by comparison with conventional dwellings.

Finance

The total project costs have been stated as £15.7m, though full details are not available. In any case the costs of some measures can be offset by the subsequently reduced need for other systems; for instance, at BedZED the estimated 10–15 per cent additional building costs for the environmental features can be offset against the reduced heating system cost and the efficient centrally planned and operated CHP scheme. The pricing of the housing units that were for sale was set against strict budget guidelines and initially ranged from £102 500 for a one-bed unit to £238 500 for a four-bed unit. In order to encourage other types of occupiers, especially workers on low incomes, alternative finance options included shared ownership (in which the occupiers take out a loan to purchase only part of the property), *at-cost* rent schemes, and an *affordable rent* scheme. The project has been very successful in attracting demand for all types of dwelling.

Discussion

The BedZED development has achieved a high public profile in the UK, where it represents not just an alternative sustainable and energy-efficient housing option but also one that responds to the need for high design quality and the provision of affordable accommodation in the nation's capital. To be completely successful, its occupants will also need to adapt their behaviour to fit in with a more sustainable lifestyle, but certainly the facilities provided should enable such a transition to be more easily accomplished.

The scheme shows a high degree of integrated thinking with its many features that were well designed and planned before incorporation into the basic building elements. This has led to a substantial and successful passive approach which makes the building work to provide energy-efficient base-line comfort, rather than relying on expensive addition of servicing systems. In fact there are very few add-ons in this scheme, due to the success of its initial design and planning.

The project has very effectively produced a good mixed development solution in which the housing density, approaching 50 dwellings per hectare (even taking into account ancillary areas), achieves the concentration levels necessary for sustainable urban design. Despite the density, the scheme still provides a sense of openness with the workspace roofs being used as gardens and the provision for all dwellings to have some private garden space; normally, at these densities, the only private external space one might expect would be a balcony.

Only time will tell if the scheme will be completely successful as the occupants, and their lifestyles, settle into a longer-term pattern, but it has already played a significant role in redefining city living. Technically, the scheme could certainly be replicated but requires substantial commitment and expertise by all partners which it may not yet be possible to find at all locations.

BedZED recently won the accolade of the Royal Institute of British Architects when it was chosen as the best example of sustainable construction. The project shows that sustainable living is affordable, technically possible and comfortable, even in the demanding market of suburban London.

Austin, Texas, USA

Background

The City of Austin has a strong claim to be used as an exemplar of best practice in sustainable development because of its history of green building and energy efficiency going back to the early 1980s. Its efforts have evolved in recent years into more sophisticated programmes with an emphasis not just on environmental principles, but also on sustainable communities and smart growth.

Austin is a city in the centre of the state of Texas. After a decline in the 1970s, its population rose during the 1980s and 1990s to over 650 000 in April 2000, with a further 160 000 residing in the surrounding areas of Travis County. The city's population is expected to continue its upward trend, reaching 800 000 by 2010. As a result of this changing demography the city has been in the position of having to deal with the need for new building and with the increasing demand for other services. Over this period of time the local community-owned utility company, Austin Energy, has also been trying to moderate increasing demand for energy. The means by which the City Council chose to tackle these issues was not purely regulatory, but rather by a process of market encouragement. Over the years there has been a number of initiatives and this approach continues to be pursued vigorously in its most recent programmes.

Austin Energy Star Program

In the 1980s the City Council became interested in promoting energy conservation measures for the practical reason of avoiding or delaying the need for the construction of a new electrical power plant. Since the electrical utility was community owned, local people were obliged to take an interest in the process and several initiatives were conceived, including the Austin Energy Star Program. This was introduced in 1985 to enable the energy rating of new homes to be performed, and of the original initiatives it has become the most well known and publicized. The purpose of the original programme was to encourage local designers and builders to produce homes that exceeded the minimum requirements of the City Energy Code. A further aspect of the scheme was to educate builders into new ways of working, and to encourage local citizens to take notice of the energy efficiency ratings in making decisions about housing purchase.

140

The Austin Energy Star Program provided standardized ways of comparing new homes in which one, two or three stars could be awarded. The number of stars indicated the level of energy cost savings by comparison with a home built to the city's Energy Code. Factors that were included were: insulation levels; glazing effects; use of shading; heating, ventilation and air conditioning system efficiency; heat pump use; and fuel source. This rating system was backed up by an effective publicity machine that was set up by the local Environmental and Conservation Services Department, and as part of the exercise extensive information was made available to the local population through newspapers, through real-estate agents and through the builders themselves. The programme was designed to enable those homes that were improved beyond the standard to achieve some level of marketing and sales advantage, and in this it was successful. All types of builders seem to have accepted the scheme and regularly used the rating to advertise their houses (for instance Casa Verde builders—see plate 16); the scheme was also readily accepted by the public. Most of the builders active in the Austin area participated in assessment because of the advantages it offered, and about 75 per cent of new homes were rated by the scheme.

The success of the original Energy Star Program showed an alternative way to achieve higher standards than by the imposition and enforcement of stricter regulations. A better mechanism, it would seem from the evidence of Austin, is to encourage a demand from the public for more energy- and resource-efficient buildings, which in turn encourages the designers and builders to meet that demand in a more wholehearted way rather than simply providing the minimum to achieve a regulated value.

The Green Building Program

By the early 1990s protection of the natural environment and enhancement of quality of life became issues of public concern and, as a result of this and the success of the Energy Star scheme, there was a drive to develop the range of the assessment and thus the Green Building Program was born. The Green Building Program is a more comprehensive sustainable systems approach that incorporates water resource efficiency, environmental impacts of use of building materials, and waste reduction, as well as energy efficiency. In addition, economic sustainability and social issues are taken into account by incorporation of factors relating to job creation, local resources and healthy living environments.

The expansion of the energy rating programme was initially developed by the Austin-based Center for Maximum Potential Building Systems and was later supported by a US Department of Energy grant made in 1990. One of the main advances was the expansion not only to deal with a wider range of issues but also a wider range of building types. The importance of having an impact at the earliest stages of building design and construction was recognized, and so technical and design assistance has been one of the areas heavily promoted under the scheme. The expansion of the scheme now means that the Green Building Program awards up to five stars for proposals meeting various degrees of commitment to green building; at each star level the four resource areas are addressed (energy, water, building materials, solid waste). When launched, it met with immediate success and its impact was further enhanced when it was selected at the 1992 Rio Earth Summit as a finalist for a United Nations award. Plate 17 shows The Gables, a successful development with reed bed water treatment ponds. Though the original focus of the Green Building Program had been the single family dwelling unit, it has expanded to deal with multi-occupancy buildings, commercial properties and also the City Council's own municipal building programme; it can also be applied to the renovation of existing properties.

The Green Building Program is funded primarily from electrical utility revenues; this is justified from the capital cost savings made as a result of lower energy demand. It also receives contributions from the local water utility, environmental and solid waste departments, again because of the savings encouraged by its use.

The programme has supported and funded the production of many useful guides and other technical resources. The most substantial is the Sustainable Building SourceBook, which, at almost 300 pages in length, contains a wealth of information in the form of a technical and reference manual. Details are provided to explain the basic operation of a range of technologies; information is provided as to the technical state of development and also on practical implementation.

A second element is the publication of a series of Factsheets that provide information in concise form on a range of topics regularly featuring in enquiries to the programme staff. These cover issues such as materials, cooling systems, indoor pollution, air quality and window choice, and these can also be accessed over the internet. Case studies of good projects are also publicized, with examples available in which images are combined with information on the particular green building features incorporated into each project; examples are shown in figures 7.6 and 7.7.

An interactive CD-ROM *Green by Design* has been developed that provides details of a seven-step process for green building, as well as case studies of projects and the Sustainable Building SourceBook in a convenient form.

142

Figure 7.6 American Youthworks Building (Austin Energy Green Building Program)

The Green Building Program has an easily identifiable logo used on its own marketing information, that is also available for use by building professionals who have joined the programme. It can also be used on buildings that have been rated under the scheme together with information about the level attained, which is displayed on a plaque, thus enabling potential purchasers to be aware of the green value of a building almost immediately. The clear marketing, not just of the programme but also of the concepts it stands for, is perhaps the single most important facet of the scheme that underpins its success.

Figure 7.7 300 West 6th Street building in Austin (Austin Energy Green Building Program)

Austin Energy

The Star Rating and Green Building programmes are only part of the story of how Austin controls its energy demand. As already stated, funding for these initiatives has largely been provided by the local electrical utility, Austin Energy. The utility is also involved in many more schemes, however, including residential and commercial energy efficiency programmes.

The residential programme provides for loans (at low interest rates) and rebates to pay for the cost of home energy improvements. The types of

144

improvement that qualify include installation of high efficiency air conditioning/heat pumps and heating systems. For electricity customers with low household incomes, or for older residents, a sliding scale is used to assess whether such customers might qualify for free improvements such as installation of loft or attic insulation, repair or sealing of ductwork and pipework, weather-stripping and installation of solar shading. For business customers the utility provides help and advice on energy use and costs, including advice on alternative energy sources, energy-efficient products and assessment tools.

The utility claims to have accumulated savings that would now equate to the operation of an additional 280 MW of generating plant; this would seem to be clear proof of the success of the schemes.

Sustainable Communities Initiative (SCI)

In Austin, the local politicians and community leaders recognized some years ago that the city's increasing population and their demands for housing and services was putting pressure on financial and natural resources, and that care would be needed to allow growth and development that would not impact adversely on their quality of life. In 1996 the Sustainable Communities Initiative (SCI) was formulated, following work carried out by a task force of the Austin Citizens' Planning Committee, and the SCI is now an integral part of the city government. Its purpose has been to bring together diverse views on how to plan and develop the city, and also to act as an umbrella organization for coordinating existing practices and for developing new initiatives that require support. Its stated aim is to provide a framework for economic prosperity, social justice and ecological health in the Austin region.

The SCI's work is concerned with integrating a number of factors that it defines as aiding sustainable development. These are: a long-range outlook; equity; stewardship of the natural environment; economic, human and biological diversity; community self-reliance; recognition of social, environmental and economic interdependence. It has a community responsibility and reports each year to the City Manager and to the City Council. Its publications show the importance attached to the development of green businesses and resource conservation; it also supports a regional approach to sustainability planning. In its work, the SCI embodies a multidisciplinary approach and one that responds to the local situation in terms of local natural resources, local business and local public concerns. As with many of Austin's schemes, the preferred changes are not pushed by regulation but, rather, encouraged by market development.

One of the most significant developments coming from the work of the Sustainable Communities Initiative is a sustainability evaluation matrix, which can be applied in the assessment of capital development plans (it is known as the Capital Improvements Plan or CIP matrix). The City Council is the largest single investor in community infrastructure, and the use of the evaluation matrix enables the making of better decisions with regard to investment by presenting a systematic basis for reviewing the social, economic and environmental implications of individual schemes and their alternatives. Table 7.1 indicates the relative weighting attached to categories within the matrix in its 2002 format, and some of the impact indicators. The matrix spreadsheet itself gives guidance as to a value (from 0 to 10) that should be used to rate each criterion for a project; thus the total score is a combination of the weighting and the value given for a particular project.

Constituent departments of the City Council have seen use of the matrix as a positive addition to the selection process, as a good score makes it more likely a project will be funded. The matrix is still only part of the process and undoubtedly other pressures and political issues have an impact; nevertheless, its use is a major step forward. Its use has also aided understanding of project costs, benefits and impacts from a sustainability perspective and has allowed some long-term community viability issues to be better understood.

The SCI has been involved in a number of other projects besides the CIP matrix development. In 1997 a group of experts was used to form the Sustainable Energy Task Force with twin aims of developing a plan for transition to renewable energy sources and identifying opportunities for distributed electricity generation. Some of the outcomes have been proposals to install up to 100 MW of generation plant utilizing renewable energy sources and to establish a green pricing plan. In 1997 and 1998 the SCI also helped to instigate an examination and assessment procedure for the sustainability implications of day-to-day and long-term activities of all the City Council's departments.

The SCI is also assisting with a sustainable communities indicators project, established in 1999, that involves the three local counties around Austin of Hays, Travis and Williamson (and also relating to the adjacent counties of Bastop and Caldwell). This project is aiming to increase regional awareness and commitment to sustainable community development by better defining the vision and attitude of local citizens to sustainability and by creating a set of quality-of-life indicators.

The SCI has had an important role in providing help and information for local planning activities and also in providing information on good practice and new techniques used in other communities and cities. Overall,

Table 7.1 Austin Sustainable Communities Initiative: weighting of factors in analysis

Criteria	Description—impact indicators	Weighting (%)
Public health/ safety	Public health; Safety; Crime prevention	13
Maintenance	Maintenance; Protection of assets	13
Socio economic impact	Local job creation—considers long-term (not construction) and spin-off (not city jobs); Job training; Public–private partnerships	10
Neighbourhood impact	Preserves or adds heritage value; Adds or increases utilization or access; Increases property values; Adds/increases recreational opportunities; Adds/increases educational opportunities	11
Social justice	Equity; Diversity (consider who is being served by project mission and location)	12
Alternative funding	Grants; Aid; Bond alternatives	5
Coordination with other projects	Coordination with other departments and services; Consolidation of services; Synergy (interconnect/ nexus); Shared operating systems benefits	6
Land use	Regional sustainability; Preservation of sensitive lands; Adds new asset in nodal area; Transit or pedestrian oriented development; Improves/ increases carrying capacity of existing infrastructure in nodal area; Does the above in area slated for nodal development	10
Air impact	Zero pollution; Optimization	4
Water impact	Zero pollution; Optimization; Conservation	4
Energy impact	Conservation; Optimization; Renewables	4
Biota impact	Diversity; Preservation; Restoration; Location	4
Other environmental	Design; Materials; Adaptive reuse	4

the Sustainable Communities Initiative must be considered a successful programme, given its modest resources. It has had a significant impact in a number of important areas but, in addition, has been able to engage in holistic thinking and to bring a more connected approach to aspects of the decision-making process linking urban sustainability considerations through to individual building construction.

Smart Growth Initiative

Smart growth in the Austin context is its plan to preserve and enhance the city's quality of life by managing its future growth and minimizing negative impacts on the environment. This is particularly important given the recent population growth (predicted to continue) in Austin and its surrounding area.

The main components of the Smart Growth Initiative are related to issues of new building development and water use. These factors have resulted in the designation of the Desired Development Zone (DDZ) and the Drinking Water Protection Zone (DWPZ), which are represented graphically on the smart growth map produced by the City of Austin. The goals of the scheme are threefold: firstly, to define and control where growth should occur, taking account of traditional neighbourhood development and transport/transit development; secondly, to improve quality of life by consideration of neighbourhood and environmental issues, accessibility and mobility, and of the local economy; and thirdly, to enhance the tax base by incorporating strategic investment, efficient use of funds and regional partnerships.

The Desired Development Zone covers an area that envelops the eastern two-thirds of the city and includes the most urbanized areas (the downtown area and the area around the University of Texas). It is in this zone where the City Council wishes future growth to focus, though not uniformly, and there are priority areas.

The Drinking Water Protection Zone includes restrictions arising from the need to maintain the watersheds that supply some of the city's drinking water. It also includes restrictions designed to support endangered species habitat, provide protection for an aquifer that feeds local springs, and avoid development on shallow soil and steep slopes in the countryside that are not suitable for intensive development.

In addition to the restrictions applying to the specified zones, detailed guidance is provided as to the nature of neighbourhood and transit-oriented development that the City Council wishes to see promoted. In order to support the preferred development, regulations have been revised to make it easier to gain approval, and financial incentives are also offered. The principal means of ensuring the City Council's preferences are followed is by assessment using a smart growth matrix. This measures how well a proposed development meets certain aims such as: suitable location of the development; proximity to mass transit; urban design characteristics; compliance with local neighbourhood plans; and potential increases in tax revenue. A scheme that scores sufficiently high ratings in the matrix assessment may qualify for incentives in the form of full or partial waiver of city development fees (up to certain limits) and a waiver of the need to invest in certain associated public amenities or infrastructure. This is again another example of a successful attempt to develop the market by making the more sustainable options the more attractive ones from a financial point of view.

Planning and neighbourhoods

The City of Austin has allowed issues of sustainability to permeate many areas of operation. There is active encouragement to apply principles of good practice for sustainable development, and those working with the City Council are able to access a database giving details of codes, ordinances and specifications produced by both governmental and non-governmental organizations, which can act as models for operation.

The City Council also has a nine-member panel to advise on long-range planning issues: the Planning Commission. It deals with issues relating to neighbourhood and master plans, land development codes, zoning and site planning, and the capital improvement programme. It has 18 goals, based in two main groupings: sustainability and quality of life, and growth management. The establishment of this panel indicates the seriousness with which the Council takes these issues.

One of the major local developments currently underway is at the former Robert Mueller Airport. The airport has now been replaced by the larger Austin–Bergstrom International Airport, itself a redevelopment of a disused airforce base. The Robert Mueller site of over 250 ha, which is relatively close to the city, is being redeveloped in a more sustainable way with a focus on quality of life. It includes mixed-use building schemes, green space and neighbourhood-based public transport.

There is in fact a strong focus on neighbourhoods in Austin, with neighbourhood planning given a high profile. A useful support publication is the Neighborhood Resource Guide, which covers such topics as organizing a neighbourhood association, traffic and transportation, safety, environment, planning and zoning. It is available to support local citizen activities.

Discussion

One of the reasons behind the success of the programmes that have been introduced, developed and used in Austin must be the connectivity between local citizens and local issues. The initial driving force was the need for the community-owned electrical utility to find a means to deal with increased energy demand other than the immediate (and costly) building of new power plant. There seems to have been a good common-sensical approach, which has now spanned a period of about 20 years. It has also been commercially beneficial.

Architects, builders and developers based in and around Austin know that the local people have an energetic interest in environmental matters, and they have responded to the challenge. Representatives of some of these groups have also been involved in the formulation of the codes, and a group, the Sustainable Building Coalition, which includes strong representation of building professionals, has been set up to enable business networking and meetings centred on topics of interest and value.

The process of stimulating demand for the use of the various programmes and ratings has also been very effective and local officials must take some credit for this. Their marketing of the schemes has produced good consumer awareness, which in turn has enabled others to capitalize in marketing their own systems and products.

The decision to establish the Sustainable Communities Initiative has been a strong commitment by the City Council to promote the concept of sustainability. The various programmes and environmental initiatives now under its umbrella, covering areas such as green building, water conservation, air quality, waste and recycling, mean that Austin is one of the leading cities in the US in terms of resource conservation and environmental sustainability. Sustainability considerations are increasingly being used to guide decision-making in the city. A further sign of the important link between Austin and sustainability was the choice of the city by the Green Building Council to host the first international Green Building Conference in late 2002 (this follows the award of the 'Green Building Program of the Year' to Austin Energy's Green Building Program earlier in 2002, at the national conference).

Though there is undoubtedly more to achieve, the City of Austin must rank as one of the more successful examples in the United States of incorporation of sustainable development principles into all levels of activity ranging through regional, urban, neighbourhood and building scales.

Chattanooga, Tennessee, USA

Background

The name of Chattanooga is probably best known around the world from the song made famous by Glenn Miller in the 1940s: 'The Chattanooga

Choo Choo'. The train no longer stops in Chattanooga but transport continues to play an important role in its redevelopment as an example of a sustainable city, and it remains an important transport connection point linking the North and South of the United States. Indeed, these days the city is becoming better known for its environmental credentials than for the aging tune, with visitors from around the world coming to examine the changes it has achieved.

Chattanooga is a modest-sized city on the southern border of the State of Tennessee where it meets the State of Georgia; its population is about 150 000 and has grown in recent years, in part due to its revitalization and regeneration. This population is augmented by the adjacent Hamilton County with a further 300 000 people. The city has undergone much change in recent years as it has coped with pollution, unemployment and major change to traditional industries.

Most of the city's development came about during the 20th century, though the first settlements were established over 200 years ago on the Tennessee River, which provides the northern and western limits to modern Chattanooga. During the second half of the nineteenth century industrial development gathered pace and by the 1860s Chattanooga was a rail transport hub and by the 1880s a major industrial centre. It was also the site of the first Coca-Cola bottling plant. In 1909 the city's Terminal Station (with a dome roof and an elegant interior) was opened, and for the next 60 years it served as the centre of a prominent rail and transport interchange. In the 1930s the Tennessee Valley Authority was created in the region, forming one of the major electricity generation sources in the southern United States and providing a driving power source for a number of other industries. By the mid-1960s the city was a major manufacturing centre, but the prevalence of heavy industries led to environmental problems and in 1969 the city was assessed to have the worst air pollution in the country, according to the US Department of Health, Education and Welfare.

Both industry and rail transport were in sharp decline at this point, however, and the late 1960s and the 1970s saw a period of rapid change. The city's downtown area was experiencing degeneration in its prime retail and residential developments; many traditional jobs in the manufacturing sector had been lost to overseas competition, with consequent increase in unemployment; and there were concerns over racial conflict, schools and poor infrastructure. The main station was closed to the public in 1970, but was fortunately saved from demolition and later reopened as a vacation centre. One major benefit of this otherwise unhappy period was the adoption of an Air Pollution Control Ordinance, which later became a model of good practice both in the state and in the country at large.

The city also had an image problem, or rather a lack-of-image problem (it had been described as 'the invisible city'), which was hindering its attempts at self-promotion and regeneration. However, in the late 1970s and early 1980s the city began to revitalize and, whether by chance, design, force of circumstance, or will and commitment of its citizens (possibly a combination of all four), it has managed to focus attention and investment on the environmental aspects of its redevelopment. Over a period of approximately 20 years it has repositioned itself as one of the exemplars of what can be achieved both in terms of post-industrial urban regeneration and of sustainable environmental initiatives.

Chattanooga regenerated

The process of regeneration was most helpfully enabled and directed by the results of a study carried out in 1983, which expressed the feelings of isolation and powerlessness felt by local people. This prompted the City Council to start a process of community meetings called *Vision 2000* during 1984 in which eventually over 1700 local citizens participated. The outcome was a portfolio of aims and commitments with 40 community goals for the year 2000 and, alongside this, the establishment of the Chattanooga Venture partnership to support the process.

Chattanooga Venture was created as a non-profit organization by bringing together community leaders, members of the local Chamber of Commerce, the City Council's Planning Commission and the Lyndhurst Foundation. It had a triple focus: environmental, social and economic; and this might be seen as a precursor of the approach of triple bottom line accounting favoured in more recent times. The organization aimed to generate positive change with citizen involvement and to provide incubation for, and facilitation of, task forces, projects and other organizations working within its remit. Its first task was to attempt to create and implement the methods of achieving the goals set out by the Vision 2000 exercise; the goals were set under headings of *future alternatives*, *places*, *people*, *work*, *play* and *government*. Over 200 projects or programmes were instigated, and the process was so successful that it has been used as a model of community activity in other cities, and Chattanooga Venture has compiled a step-by-step guide to aid other communities in pursuit of similar aims.

Part of the programme that was instigated involved creating the *Environmental City* project, which successfully worked towards the expansion, or relocation into the area, of clean industries. The Chattanooga Environmental Initiative has also exploited public–private partnerships, which have been used on a number of occasions.

152

Electric transport initiative

One of the most prominent and successful achievements of the revitalized Chattanooga has been its investment in electric transport and its associated development of a local industry. This was initiated when the city's then Mayor, Gene Roberts, requested that alternative transport strategies be found to avoid traffic congestion. Chattanooga's downtown area was overly stretched out, consisting of three main components: a south-end shopping area, a central business zone, and a north-end entertainment and recreation district near the riverfront. All this made it difficult to traverse on foot and required people to drive between separate distinct areas. When regeneration, particularly at the northern end of the town, was proposed it was seen that the areas needed better linkage and a means of reducing reliance on car transport. Another benefit that could be seen of new development and improved transport was the replacement of low-tax-value parking space with high-value commercial development. The result of this exercise was a decision to invest in a free shuttle bus service to bring together the major zones of the downtown area.

Various stakeholders were invited to be involved in the planning process, and as a result, the proposal was enabled to take account of relevant concerns but also to get a mandate to follow sustainable development principles and attempt to use emerging technologies. An electrically powered shuttle system was subsequently chosen as the most suitable option. Initially, no supplier for the proposed electric buses could be found and a private company, Advanced Vehicle Systems (AVS), was formed. When this was followed by the privatization of Electrotek (a vehicle testing facility formerly owned by the Tennessee Valley Authority) in 1988, two of the major components were in place for development. The Electric Transit Vehicle Institute (ETVI) was then established as a non-profit organization, and ETVI purchased the buses manufactured by AVS and leased them to the local Chattanooga Regional Transit Authority (CARTA), which in turn operated the shuttle bus service. ETVI was reconstituted in 2003 to reflect a revised role and function and became the Advanced Transportation Technology Institute (ATTI). The first shuttle bus ran in 1992 and linked the new Tennessee Aquarium at the north end of town with other destinations. Figure 7.8 shows the shuttle bus in operation.

The buses run frequently and have no charge; two main routes are in use and are linked to CARTA-owned parking areas. These park-and-ride garages are located at each end of the downtown zone. The shuttle bus system has also helped to support the regeneration in the area,

Figure 7.8 Chattanooga's shuttle bus by the Children's Museum (Electric Transit Vehicle Institute/ATTI, Chattanooga)

providing a more sustainable, clean, practical and convenient alternative to the motor car. Local businesses have also reported improvements in sales, partly due to the shuttle operation. It has also improved further the quality of life by alleviating congestion and significantly reducing the high pollutant emissions associated with short car journeys in the downtown area.

The close relationship between the companies and organizations involved in the shuttle bus project meant that each was able to respond quickly to need and also to be aware of, and involved with, the ongoing

154

development process. As a result of the focus on electric transport the city became a so-called *Living Laboratory* for battery-powered bus development and electric vehicle mass-transit; the ATTI operates one of only a few electric vehicle test facilities in the world. AVS has since manufactured buses used in many other US cities and also overseas; the purchase price for the buses is now comparable with that of diesel-powered alternatives, and their life-cycle costs are much lower.

The annual running costs of the system have been funded through the City of Chattanooga and through the use of parking revenues. The Department of Transportation Federal Transit Administration, the State of Tennessee and the City of Chattanooga contributed to the initial costs of the system, which totaled $22 million (80 per cent coming from federal sources).

Taken together with the impact of the changed transport pattern, the reduced pollution, the establishment and growth of new local industry and the revitalization of some of the downtown areas, the electric transport initiative must be viewed as one of the most noticeable sustainable developments made to date in the city. Despite this, the number of electrically powered vehicles is still very small and the number of jobs created is measured in tens and hundreds rather than thousands, but the city is well placed to capitalize on the initiatives in the future.

Parks and green areas

The local citizens identified the natural landscape as one of the most important resources in the Chattanooga area. Rivers, creeks, forests, mountains, valleys and the parks and greenways of the city are all seen as important, not just for the need for environmental protection but also as an economic resource attractive to visitors and local citizens alike. In 1986 the Tennessee River Gorge Trust was set up with the aim of protecting over 10 000 hectares of the river gorge. Control over areas of the gorge has been achieved, using a variety of measures including direct purchase, easement and lease agreements. This project has been very successful, with over half the area now within its control. Besides these more wilderness areas there are many opportunities within the city, which have been taken, to develop new green areas or to make them available to the public. The Chattanooga Greenways Program has a projected network of 120 km of parks and tracks linked to the central Riverpark. The aim is to protect local creeks and other green areas in a way that also provides recreation opportunities for local people. There are also more specific sites of an educational nature such as the Greenway Farm, and nature *preserves* such as at Maclellan Island in the downtown area.

Riverfront redevelopment

One of the most important areas of change has been the zones located to the north of the downtown area along the Riverfront. The major redevelopment was launched in 1986 and the plan included promotion of mixed development and a parallel parkland and trail network stretching for over 30 km, including a 13 km riverwalk. Since renovation the most popular segment of the Riverpark has been a former patch of wasteland previously used for illegal dumping; this area has become transformed and shows the

Figure 7.9 The Tennessee Aquarium with shuttle bus in foreground (Electric Transit Vehicle Institute/ATTI, Chattanooga)

double benefit of removing an eyesore and replacing it with something of benefit to the community as well as improving the environment. Currently over a million people a year visit the park.

Perhaps the most important single element of the Riverfront re-development has been the building of the Tennessee Aquarium. This was constructed with $45 million of private funding and, since it opened in 1992, it has had over 10 million visitors and has produced more than $130 million in additional investment. The aquarium's displays focus on the region's river systems and freshwater flora and fauna; it also serves as an education centre and illustrates the local area's dependence on its natural systems and bioregion. The aquarium has been a great success, not just in terms of visitor numbers but also because of its association with additional, well-documented local economic investment following from its construction. More recent nearby developments have been an IMAX 3D Theater and a Creative Discovery Museum.

Another significant part of the river development is the Walnut Street Bridge. The bridge was originally built in 1891 to meet the needs of the then growing city. It was the first multiple-use bridge to span the river and is of an interesting truss design (the oldest of its size in the southern United States), but by 1987 it had fallen into disrepair and was due for demolition. Following a public outcry and the intervention of Chattanooga Venture, the City Council was persuaded to spend the money set aside for demolition on its renovation. It was reopened as the largest pedestrian walkway in the United States in 1993 and connects the downtown area to the north shore of the Tennessee River.

Taking the Walnut Street Bridge and other pedestrian bridges, the greenways and many other parkland features together with the shuttle bus link means that Chattanooga is a very walkable and pedestrian-friendly city, further enhancing environmental benefits.

Eco-industrial parks

Eco-industrial parks are areas in which manufacturing and service businesses cooperate closely to enhance and exploit both environmental and economic performance in conjunction with reduced waste production and efficient resource use. Businesses are encouraged to collaborate to improve performance by sharing resources such as land, water, energy and wastes. One is located in the South Central Business District of Chattanooga (formerly the site for metal foundries and other industries, railroad tracks and warehousing), and another on the site of a former munitions dump. Reclamation of the South Central site was chosen because it allowed land close to the city centre to be used for economic regeneration;

the City Council however, wanted to go further and proposed a zero-emissions zone in which the wastes of one business could be the feedstock of others. The redevelopment plan includes an ecological centre and environmental conference and training facility as well as provision of a sports stadium and opportunities for environmentally sound businesses to establish or develop.

The second eco-park at the former ammunition plant (known as the Volunteer Site) has been designated as the Strategic Defense Environmental Center for the US Army. This site of about 3000 ha is intended to be used for environmental research and for recycling industries but only the brownfield portion of the site is set aside for redevelopment. One of the industries to be located there is a test facility for soil and groundwater remediation technology that can develop methods to clean up chemical contamination. Over half the site will be left as forested greenfield area in which natural flora and fauna can flourish. Over $3 million in initial grants has been awarded.

Housing

One of the goals from Vision 2000 had been the improvement of sub-standard housing and the reinvigoration of local neighbourhoods. Chattanooga Neighborhood Enterprise (CNE) was created as a result to bring together public and private interests with the aim of delivering affordable housing in Chattanooga and Hamilton County. CNE used private sector approaches in order to redevelop poor quality inner-city residential areas and to create new options for low- to moderate-income families to achieve home ownership through targeted lending initiatives. The process also gained a number of associated benefits by capitalizing on the interest and enthusiasm of local residents to be involved in projects that also improved the appearance and safety of their localities. In the late 1980s and 1990s over 4200 housing units were rehabilitated, with investment of over $600 million. Investment of private funds enabled leverage of more substantial public funding. CNE's lending arrangements, which include sale of loans on to a secondary market to release more capital, have been seen as innovative models for community financing for affordable homes.

Though these programmes have addressed the need for improved housing, there is also the need for step changes in housing design and in occupant attitude to energy use to reduce emissions related to construction and building as part of an overall sustainability regime. This needs to apply to new build as well as renovation projects.

Maintaining regeneration and sustainable development

In 1992 a review of the original Vision 2000 initiatives found that over 220 projects had been devised, meeting approximately 85 per cent of the original goals and aims of that programme. Almost $800 million had been invested and 1300 direct new jobs had been created, as well as many construction jobs. It was seen as a time to revitalize the process to carry it forward, and a second community visioning activity was carried out in 1993, *ReVision 2000*. This exercise produced 27 new goals along with 122 recommendations and Chattanooga was to be promoted as a centre for environmental initiatives. 1994 saw the establishment of the Vision Committee, which included political, civic, business and neighbourhood representation; its aim was to ensure the successful outcome of ReVision 2000 goals with community participation. This programme is currently underway and a number of successful projects (some described in this section) have been carried out.

The Chattanooga Institute was formed in 1997 to advance the process already begun and maintained by the developments since the forming of Chattanooga Venture, the Vision 2000 exercise in 1984 and ReVision 2000 in 1993. The main impetus for its formation came from the Chattanooga Chamber of Commerce. The Institute has a vision centred on enabling sustainability in a way that embraces the parallel needs of economic growth, social equity, environmental stewardship and quality of life. Put bluntly, it aims for sustainability with profitability.

The Institute has three main areas of work: corporate and community development; the Living Laboratory Exchange Program; and the production of publications and audiovisual material. The views promoted include the need for collaboration and integration between business, community and the environment. The continuing involvement of local citizens has been stressed as a crucial element of this work. The Institute is also very useful in providing another focus of attention and promotion of activities to enable the regeneration process to continue.

Accolades and awards

In 1990 the US Environmental Protection Agency (EPA) awarded a clean air standard to the city, which was highly regarded in reports to President Clinton's Council on Sustainable Development and mentioned for 'citizen collaboration in cleaning up the environment, rebuilding the economy and revitalizing a city in decline'.

In 1996, Chattanooga was selected as the first North American Best Practice City for sustainable development by the UN Conference on

Human Settlements (UN Habitat II Conference in Istanbul, Turkey); it was also identified as one of the twelve best practice examples worldwide. The Tennessee River Gorge Trust has also received a national award for environmental sustainability.

As an indication of the change in perception of the city and its claim to be a sustainable environmental city, it was chosen to be the venue for an important conference in 1998. Over ninety key participants attended the Tools for Community Design and Decision Making event held in the city. The conference theme was the presentation and evaluation of a number of design aids (mainly software based), which might enable cities and communities to move in an effective and calculated way towards sustainable development.

Discussion

In the past some criticisms were made of the local government in the Chattanooga area, not because of any obstruction caused but rather that the government was not leading the way. Support had normally been provided for initiatives set up, but usually as a partner. In 1991 plans were made by the mayor and county executive to make Chattanooga both a model and a laboratory for sustainable development. With that in mind, local officials appointed a task force to represent the community to develop policy recommendations. An initial plan, *Target 96*, included 94 recommendations dealing with economic, environmental, educational and community issues which were to be implemented over a 10-year cycle.

One of the main results of the plan was to encourage the development of public–private partnerships. The Chamber of Commerce adopted *the business of the environment* as one of its main themes. The urban Design Studio has also been working to turn concepts and ideas into reality.

It must be stated that the involvement of local government supported, but did not particularly initiate, sustainability projects in the way that might be done in mainland Europe (where local government is responsible for integrating sustainability across all areas and for avoiding conflicts, also for monitoring and regulating). In many countries the involvement of both national and, particularly, local government in coordinating and implementing sustainability is seen as essential. The level of strategic planning has thus been somewhat removed from its expected resting place, though utilizing local enthusiasm and interest in the way Chattanooga has done is also a productive way forward.

The City of Chattanooga has been successful in carrying out regeneration with a sustainability focus. It has capitalized on its cultural heritage and its local natural features to make it a good place to visit; a place which is also accessible to a large fraction of the US population. However, what has been achieved cannot really be said to have occurred because of a green sustainable development plan, though, taken together, the components almost add up to one. One of the most positive features of Chattanooga's regeneration is the level of participation and collaboration involving a wide range of stakeholders from the general public, government, business and community groups. This also resulted in aggressive marketing and re-imaging of the city.

There have been increased costs, some provided from federal and state funds but also borne by local citizens, and this seems to have had collective support. As part of the process, public–private partnerships have been a particularly successful element. The inward financial investment totals about $1 billion over the period.

The City of Chattanooga has achieved much. What began as a need to address a number of specific and seemingly independent economic, environmental and social problems evolved into a process that saw the issues as interdependent and interlinked, and with a focus on solutions based in the local community and on improving the quality of life. It would be fair to claim that sustainable development has been carried out in a way that implements the necessary economic development whilst also conserving natural resources, reducing pollution and respecting environmental needs. In this respect one should look to what has been achieved and seek to use this to inform and optimize models of sustainable regeneration. Chattanooga is a good example of what a modest-sized city can achieve if certain key stakeholders work together in a flexible and focused way.

Portland, Oregon, USA

Background

Portland is located on the west coast of the United States. The city is home to a population of about 450 000, the area being supplemented by a further 220 000 citizens in its county area of Multnomah. As well as fostering environmental and sustainability policies within its own city and county boundaries, the city's activities are also linked to a number of regional, national and international programmes and initiatives. Portland is often held to be home to the best examples of sustainable urban policies and green building in the United States and there are many noteworthy schemes and developments, only some of which is there space to describe here.

Interest in energy and environmental matters began in the late 1970s, following from the OPEC oil price increases and their consequent effects. In 1979 Portland developed its first version of an energy policy (the first such local policy in the USA) and the main focus of the first plan was to improve home insulation standards. Though interest in energy matters waned in the 1980s, environmental and energy matters re-emerged onto the public stage in the 1990s with concerns about global climate and pollution issues, and this resulted in a revised energy policy with a variety of aims and scales of working.

On a broader scale, the City Council's Comprehensive Plan has systematically addressed environmental, energy and sustainable development issues in some detail, and such a plan is an important aspect of establishing these issues as elements of the city's future development. A community energy efficiency plan has been produced, and a Local Action Plan on Global Warming has been adopted which sets out more than 150 strategies to help reduce carbon dioxide emissions to 10 per cent below 1990 levels by 2010. This target is more strict than that agreed in the Kyoto Protocol (even though the latter was not ratified in the US). At the present time it seems unlikely that the ambitious target will be achieved, but that has not stopped the City Council from attempting a number of good measures.

The City Council has also been a strong advocate for the use of the Green Building Council's LEED (Leadership in Energy and Environmental Design) environmental assessment and rating system, which it has helped to apply to a number of buildings in its area. Also, a green policy aimed at designing and constructing new, and retrofitting older, city buildings using only resource-efficient practices was unanimously approved.

The sustainability initiatives taken within the city mean that it has much recent work to showcase, though it should also be observed that a number of the environmental initiatives in the Portland area pre-date the international interest in sustainability and also the most recent local legislative and other policy changes; this demonstrates the long-term interest of the community in such issues and also its determination to carry on with such policies.

City Energy Challenge

The City Energy Challenge (CEC), one of the city's first major successful schemes, was created in 1991 to promote reductions in energy use in the city's facilities and operations, and followed as a result of the previous year's modified energy policy. The 1990 plan was a much broader version of the first version developed over a decade earlier, and led to the formulation of 89 targets and goals.

The initial aim of CEC had been to improve energy efficiency by 10 per cent by the year 2000 and to reduce annual energy costs for the City Council by $1 million by 2000. As a result of over 100 projects being enacted over a ten-year period, both targets were surpassed and a revised goal of $1.5 million savings was set, and subsequently passed, part way through the period; annual savings now exceed $2 million. The types of projects undertaken have included improved energy design in new construction, energy-efficient retrofitting and negotiation of reduced tariffs from energy utilities.

As a means to encourage renewable energy sources the City Council agreed a contract in 1995 (revised in 2000) with a local supplier to purchase a proportion of its needs as green energy (mainly from wind power sources). The contract enabled the City Council to offset the marginal additional cost of the renewable energy source against savings on the conventional energy supplied under the remainder of the contract. The slightly negative feature of this was the small percentage of renewables initially contracted for, at only 5 per cent of the total, but this is still a valuable contribution and in 2002 the City Council's use of green electricity amounted to 600 000 kWh. Mobile solar photovoltaic electricity generators have also been used on Council maintenance vehicles which were otherwise required to keep their engines running to power external equipment.

Several other projects have been enacted, such as the use of a novel technology in the form of a methane-powered fuel cell (200 kW) that was installed in 1999 at a wastewater treatment plant. The system operates to convert the gas produced as a by-product of the sewage treatment process into electricity. Substantial support was obtained from the US Department of Defense and State tax credits, as well as from the local utility company, to finance the initial costs of the project. By 2001 almost all of the city's red/green traffic signal equipment, which had previously used incandescent lamps, had been converted to the more efficient light emitting diodes (LEDs). Also, as part of the work of the CEC scheme, a series of bi-monthly e-mail circulations is sent out entitled *Green Tips*, giving advice on energy efficiency strategies for both office and home use.

The CEC scheme is now managed by the Energy Division of the Office of Sustainable Development. Looking forward, the staff of the scheme have identified the potential to save a further $3.8 million per year from the City Council's annual energy costs of $11 million and the potential to save on energy use and carbon dioxide emissions, especially if the advantages of emerging new technologies can be utilized.

BEST Program

The Businesses for an Environmentally Sustainable Tomorrow (BEST) programme was established in 1992 by the Portland Energy Office with the aim of promoting businesses that created economic benefits without adversely affecting the natural environment. The programme helped to provide technical and financial assistance relating to the use of energy and water, transport systems and reduction of wastes. The information, which had formerly been available from a diverse range of sources, was brought together under this programme into a more convenient and comprehensive one-stop-shop service.

BEST works in partnership with utility companies, private and public bodies to ensure that businesses in the Portland area can have access to information about best practice, design options, grants and incentive schemes, educational information and workshops. In effect it acts as a broker between those offering information and financial assistance and those who wish to benefit from them, and it produces easy-to-read and persuasive factsheets giving the required details.

The majority of businesses signing up to the scheme seem to have been initially interested in energy efficiency design advice that was available from local energy suppliers. As a means to further promote the programme, BEST awards are made each year to businesses that have made significant progress in individual sectors and also across all four areas of energy, water, transport and waste.

The operating costs of the programme office, which are typically $40–70 000 per year, have been sourced largely from a mixture of public grants and contracts with local utilities. The claimed successes of the programme include $3.5 million saved for businesses through cost-avoidance measures; almost 13 million kWh of electrical energy saved; savings of over 15 000 tonnes of carbon dioxide emissions; and avoidance of almost 50 000 tonnes of solid waste disposal.

Oregon Office of Energy

At State level, the Oregon Office of Energy is very active in promoting efficient use of energy and alternative energy supply options. It is based at Salem, approximately 80 km south of Portland. In 2002 its website won an award for Best Energy Education Promotion and its work cuts across all sectors by providing information for residential, business, institutional, industrial and educational organizations and individuals.

State involvement in environmental and energy matters is important in order to stimulate the market by tax and other incentives and also to set a policy framework within which cities and counties operate.

Without guidance and interest at such a level, city innovations can be lost since some activities simply transfer to adjacent areas. The Oregon Department of Environmental Quality (DEQ) has also had influences over associated environmental issues, including transport and transport-related pollution.

The Climate Trust

One of the most important initiatives in the Portland region came about as a result of radical legislation enacted in the State of Oregon that obliged new energy facilities to reduce their carbon dioxide emissions. The energy businesses can choose to offset the required reductions by supporting projects to sequester the additional carbon dioxide emissions or to reduce emissions elsewhere. This works in practice through the business or the developer paying mitigation funds as a penalty, and these funds help to finance the projects that reduce or sequester the required emissions. The Climate Trust was established in 1997 as a means to provide the necessary framework and organizational structure for the operation of the scheme.

The Trust receives several millions of dollars each year as a result of the legislation and uses this money to pay qualified organizations to carry out the projects that counteract the carbon emissions. These funds have allowed a number of important schemes to be initiated and, in mid-2002, the Climate Trust awarded a $1 million contract to Portland City Council to reduce the effects of carbon dioxide emissions by improving the energy efficiency of residential and commercial buildings in the city.

Office of Sustainable Development

The City of Portland's Office of Sustainable Development (OSD) came into being in late 2000 as a means to coordinate activities to promote the economic, environmental and social health of the city. It acts as a bridge between the work of the Sustainable Development Commission, the Energy Division, the Green Building Division and the Solid Waste and Recycling Division of the City Council.

The functions of the Office are defined in three main areas: to create policies and programmes that help integrate effort related to energy, resources, waste, sustainability and education; to give leadership and promote good practice in sustainability related to all sectors of the community; and to provide a means for information exchange through workshops, conferences, training programmes and technical group meetings.

Sustainable Development Commission

In 1994 the City of Portland adopted a set of sustainable city principles that have since helped to guide its policies and practice. In connection with these principles, Portland has established a panel of local citizens, the Sustainable Development Commission (SDC), which has the task of developing and encouraging strategies that ensure natural resources for future generations and promoting present-day fairness and quality of life. It has a strong impact on the attitude and functions of the city's elected officials and staff, though it has no powers to change regulatory processes or legislation; it must act through advice and persuasion. Project areas in which the Commission has been active include: sustainability benchmarking; economic development; government operation; global warming; and green building.

The Benchmarking Sustainability project compared Portland to nine other US cities. Six of the cities were selected because they had similar populations, densities and costs of living, and a further three because they were thought to exhibit well-managed features. Portland showed to be better than average in a number of categories such as air quality, carbon dioxide emissions, personal vehicle use, urban greening (tree canopy) and recycling, and was one of the best performers overall. There were some areas for concern, however, one of which was the rate of increase of vehicle mileage and of congestion; this may be as a result of the urban sprawl of the city and its planning policies that may have led to reduced population densities and which could also limit the viability of public transport.

In terms of economic development, the SDC helps to advise on and to promote sustainable industries and business practices. In 1999 a report was published that investigated the potential to grow environmental services and technologies industries in Portland; such industries already employed over 13 000 people in 700 firms at the time of the report. It was concluded that, with suitable support, an opportunity for the region to capitalize on its reputation as a leader in environmental technology existed; areas such as sustainable cities and green building, and environmental systems in manufacturing and distribution, all offered markets for development.

These ideas have been reinforced by a further report published in 2002 by Climate Solutions. Climate Solutions is a not-for-profit organization set up to support the development of clean energy solutions and high technology industries, which can go on to create employment. Its work has dealt with a range of new and renewable energy options such as fuel cells, photovoltaics, advanced power systems, wind energy, geothermal power, small-scale hydroelectric schemes and biomass. It is also keen to incorporate energy efficiency techniques. Its report developed the argument that, within

166

about 20 years, between 12 000 and 32 000 jobs could be created by expansion of such industries, the higher figure of job creation being dependent on public policies being created to support the developments needed.

The SDC has also taken an interest in reviewing the city's environmental performance and the impacts of its various spheres of operation, and several reports have been produced. It also liaises with the City Council's *Green Team*, a group of employees who help to initiate workforce-led projects. Projects relating to battery recycling, green fairs and transport have been promoted.

A particularly successful element of the SDC's work has been its interaction with architects, builders, local government and the community to produce the Green Building Initiative, which was adopted by the City Council in 1999 and led to the formation of the Green Building Division within the Council.

The Energy Division

The Energy Division of OSD has several programmes aimed at residential and commercial sectors and their energy and resource usage. It has won several awards for the programmes and techniques it has helped to develop. It provides help on commercial energy costs and usage, which can be reduced through taking advantage of advice available on technical and financial matters related to upgrading equipment and improving systems. The substantial *Green Office Guide* document, which the Division has coordinated, gives advice on greening a company's bottom line through design and operation of more resource-efficient office environments. The guide lists opportunities and examples related to specification and use of lighting; office equipment; paper products; heating and cooling; water; and cars and parking. The Guide also includes notes and contact details for a wide range of organizations that might provide assistance in carrying out the recommendations it contains. The BEST programme (see above) acts as a means to recognize good energy performance by businesses that have taken advantage of the advice by making public awards under its scheme.

Teleworking is being promoted in Portland as a way to reduce the energy and pollution costs associated with commuters travelling to and from the workplace, normally by private car. Telework guidelines were introduced in 1995 to help local businesses manage the issue. There is also a link to the State Employee Commute Options rule that requires businesses to help reduce the number of employee commuter trips by 10 per cent.

OSD's Energy Division is also active in the residential sector and has promoted a series of schemes all focused on reducing energy consumption and improving comfort. As part of one programme it is possible to arrange for a free energy audit through utility companies to get advice on problems and improvements. The Energy Division has also acted as a link between building occupants and utilities in the promotion of weatherization insulation schemes; depending on household size and income, the installation of the insulation may be free as part of a county-wide block-by-block improvement scheme. The various energy utility companies also offer financial incentives, including cash rebates and low interest rate loans; the incentive for the utility company is both to secure customers and to reduce the peak demand for its supplies, which incurs higher infrastructure investment costs. Over 20 000 apartments and 2000 low-income houses have been weatherized over a ten-year period.

Help with the costs of higher efficiency appliances and more efficient heating systems can also be obtained through programmes such as the Oregon Residential Tax Credit (tax relief) scheme. This relates to particular items of equipment that qualify under the terms of the scheme. Workshops are also offered to residents under the Energy Division's umbrella to help with water and energy conservation and a variety of other related topics, and a number of advice and financial schemes also operate to support water conservation measures. An online resource, *Green Pages*, has been developed by OSD to help provide information on reducing waste and pollution and increasing recycling.

The Multi-family Assistance Program (MAP), under the guidance of OSD, enables owners of rental properties to make improvements that save energy, water and other resources, reduce maintenance costs and increase recycling. MAP operates as a one-stop-shop to provide advice on technological and financial issues as well as providing an auditing service to identify options for improvement.

The Green Building Division

The Green Building Division of the Council develops green building policies for city facilities and city-funded projects. It also provides awards, incentives and grants, design and construction advice, workshops and resource information for both residential and commercial sectors. This all helps to promote resource-efficient building in Portland, following the City Council's adoption of the Green Building Initiative in 1999. The division focuses on the concept of *G/Rated* (green rated) building. Within the city's buildings, municipal projects must meet the standards laid down in the US Green Building Council's LEED scheme that provides project checklists under which credits can be awarded; the Council has in fact adopted a modified version of the LEED rating system which incorporates local codes and environmental conditions.

In 2002, the City Council produced its latest version of a 97-page resource guide *Greening Portland's Affordable Housing* for the residential sector. Its aim is to help improve the environmental performance, occupant health and easy maintenance of affordable housing. In addition to guiding principles the document also provides a valuable checklist, similar to that of the LEED scheme, which is cross-referenced to information and local sources of materials and expertise. A further element of the approach in this sector is the G/Rated Residential Incentive Program, which encourages innovation in residential design and construction. House owners who wish to execute projects that can demonstrate resource conservation, energy saving, better health and safety, and environmental protection or restoration, are eligible to apply for an award of up to $3000. A jury of green building experts selects schemes so as to support a variety of housing types in a variety of locations that use a range of green features. Owners must agree to verification of the completion of the work and the option for the Council to publicize the scheme before they receive payment.

A Commercial Incentive Program also exists under the G/Rated banner to encourage design and construction of green buildings. The main thrust of the support available is to provide funding to aid the additional costs of professional consultancy and advice services that would enable a more environmentally responsive project to be procured. There are two schemes in operation: the Portland LEED Track and the Innovation Track. Owners and developers of commercial, institutional and mixed-use projects in Portland are eligible. For the Portland LEED Track up to $15 000 can be awarded for projects meeting the Portland LEED *certified* rating and up to $20 000 for those achieving *silver* rating; for the Innovation Track the focus is more on use of emerging and transferable green technologies and up to $5000 can be awarded. In order to apply for the money there is a straightforward and well-documented procedure to be followed. A number of projects have so far benefited from the scheme.

Jean Vollum Natural Capital Center

One of the recent landmark buildings to be completed in Portland is the Jean Vollum Natural Capital Center; a $12 million redevelopment of an 1895 warehouse building in the historic Pearl District. This district was a reminder of the city's industrial past but has begun to be revitalized and is in the process of being transformed into an urban village. The project was led by Ecotrust, a non-profit organization with a focus on environmental matters, and the building is named after its founding member and the person responsible for funding the purchase of the site. The resulting scheme covers an area of 7000 m^2 on three floors which provides space for retail, office and conference facilities. The building, completed in 2001, is also located close to a number of public transport links and services and can be seen in plate 18.

One of the most important features of the project has been the management of construction waste, with over 97 per cent reclamation being achieved. Seventy-five per cent of the existing envelope was retained in the redevelopment and many of the new materials were sourced locally and/or contained a high recycled content.

The building incorporates rainwater management into its landscaping and internally uses one-third less water than a conventional building. Though the building is air conditioned, it operates at over 20 per cent better efficiency than current codes and was designed with good indoor air quality in mind. Daylight design has also been employed to give 90 per cent of the space an outside view, with daylight reaching 75 per cent of occupied areas.

The LEED version 2.0 analysis of the building yielded 41 credit points out of a maximum of 69 and the subsequent award of a Gold standard; it has also been the recipient of several other awards. But the building has been successful not only in assessment grades but also in its revitalization role and as a piece of architecture, having been described as a 'landmark of national significance' by the President of the US Green Building Council.

The Brewery Blocks

The Brewery Blocks are another redevelopment scheme taking shape in Portland's Pearl District on a former brewery site, but it is a redevelopment that incorporates both renovation and new build. This major scheme, costing some $200 million, will eventually create five blocks of retail and office space together with residential development covering a total of 170 000 m^2. The aim is to transform the industrial site into a new urban centre while preserving the worthy historical elements and retaining the character of the area.

Energy-saving features should result in a reduction of 20–30 per cent over conventional design and include both novel artificial lighting systems and controllers, and also good use of daylight. Air conditioning uses a more efficient chiller system, and almost 400 photovoltaic solar panels

Figure 7.10 View of the Brewery Blocks redevelopment in Portland (Clive Knights)

should provide an on-site electrical energy source. Domestic hot water will be supplied for its condominium tower from 54 solar collectors. A more immediate financial reward, on top of the long-term energy costs, is the eligibility for tax credits from the state Energy Office programme, which are worth 35 per cent of the green building investment.

Besides the focus on preservation and renovation, a high percentage (96 per cent) of site wastes have also been reclaimed, recycled, or otherwise diverted from landfill disposal. A view of part of the development is shown in plate 19.

Swindells Hall

This building cost $8.6 million and was completed in 1999. It is located at the North Portland campus of the University of Portland and provides over 4000 m² of laboratory and office space. Life-cycle analysis was used to help make decisions about the building materials, and other materials were chosen with regard for their toxicity and transportation impacts. Recycled materials are widely used, including over 200 tonnes of reclaimed steel. Energy efficiency strategies such as condensing boilers, indirect evaporative cooling systems and energy-efficient lighting and control systems have been used and, as a result, energy use shows a 50 per cent saving by comparison with the benchmark of the state energy code.

Viridian Place

Viridian Place is located in a commercial district to the south of Portland at Lake Oswego. Its original budget was $2 million and it provides over 1500 m² of office space designed in an environmentally sensitive manner. It was a ground-breaking project and an exemplar of new techniques; the developers estimated that it cost approximately 15 per cent more than a conventional design. As technologies and techniques become more widely used and understood, one could expect such cost variations to reduce. There have also been benefits to offset the costs in any case, not just from energy and other savings and from tax credits available, but in the form of attention and publicity drawn to the scheme, which has resulted in increased business activity for the building owners and its tenants.

Other environmental initiatives

As a means to help visualize the physical location and interaction of aspects of the built and natural environment and both beneficial and problematic features of the city, a Green Map has been constructed. The goal of the map is to show the pattern of places that exist within the city and to use this to help define ideas and concepts in a more visual way, and to aid in decision-making.

In a further initiative, officials from the City of Portland and Multnomah County have been developing a sustainable procurement strategy that recognizes not just the price of particular products, but also public values and longer term interests and how these impact on purchasing. In order to bring more information to the marketplace a Sustainable Products Purchasers Coalition (SPPC) has been established; this works to elicit and disseminate life-cycle data for a range of items so that buyers and organizations wishing to specify more sustainable products are in a position to do this.

The City of Portland has provided the focus for development work on so-called *Ecoroofs*. Ecoroofs are, in effect, roof gardens which have thin soil layers that support plant species adapted to rooftop environments. The benefits from such roofs are: roof protection from extreme weather; higher insulation and thermal capacity; capture and filtering of rainwater (improving stormwater protection); and improved aesthetics. Such roofs are being tested on three existing and a number of potential projects.

Another environmental initiative is that which deals with recycled paint. Since paint requires careful disposal as a waste material, recycling offers many benefits and the latex paint recycling facility in the area is the only municipally owned plant in the US. Eighty-three per cent of the paint can be recycled and, once harmful or unsuitable materials have been screened out, the remainder is sorted into nine basic colour categories which are then sold in sealed buckets for reuse.

Discussion

The City of Portland has an international reputation for the environmental schemes it has initiated and for the way in which it seems to have balanced community needs, economic development and environmental requirements. Its emphasis on environmental matters appears to have a number of economic paybacks that are not just listed on the balance sheet. As examples, it has been voted by *Money Magazine* as the best place to live in the USA and has been noted as 'San Francisco without the hassle and the expense', is widely regarded as a walkable and child-friendly city, and has also become popular as a place of study. Its free city-centre transport system is highly esteemed, and cycling is a joy.

Though it has achieved much, there is still plenty of potential to be fulfilled. It has been a pioneer in the use of the LEED rating system, yet still relatively few buildings have achieved high scores under the system. The city has also tended toward urban sprawl, which seems to account for the increased vehicle mileage being noted in surveys. Though this is still not as high as in some comparable cities, it does show some potentially negative change. The city is certainly a pleasant place to live but it must continue to develop and to build upon its environmental reputation to act as an exemplar to the rest of the nation.

Melbourne, Australia

Background

Australia is a land of contradictions: its citizens seem generally environmentally aware; it has abundant supplies of renewable energy available over most of the country, including its main urban areas; and national, state and local governments seem to have a genuine interest in environmental sustainability; yet, for all this, Australia has the highest per capita energy usage in the world (on a par with North America) and many citizens do not yet recognize the need to change their approach. Part of the reason is the size of the country and the less immediate apparent impact of environmental pollution issues; a second factor is the general availability of relatively cheap energy sources; a third contribution is the sprawling nature of the principal urban areas, which increases typical journey distances; and finally, the distances between major urban cities encourage long-distance transport by surface vehicle or air, with associated energy use and pollution.

Despite these issues, there are reasons to be positive about a number of activities being undertaken in the country. In 1997 a five-year government-funded package of measures totalling $180m Australian dollars, aimed at reducing greenhouse gas emission, was initiated. Australia also offers examples of sustainable development that do have potential both to improve the environment and to be economically and socially acceptable. One of the cities in which a number of initiatives have been undertaken is Melbourne. The *City of Melbourne* is in fact just the core business and commercial zone of a much larger metropolitan area and it is also the capital and focus of the Australian State of Victoria. The city is claimed to be one of the most livable in the world; a city of culture and fine lifestyle rather than of tourist sights and views, though with the continuing development taking place it is not short of impressive architecture and environmental features. In 2000 it became only the third major city in the world to achieve the World Health Organisation's Safe Community Accreditation.

The area of the City of Melbourne is a modest 36.5 square kilometres and it has a growing residential population of about 60 000. The typical daytime population is ten times higher than this, however, as it is the main focus of a metropolitan area of over 8800 square kilometres and a population of three and a half million. The city is also the transport hub and the main business and commercial centre for the state. It also works in collaboration with its surrounding municipalities in addressing environmental and sustainability issues where a broader geographical approach is essential. Despite its small size, the city contains about 500 hectares of green space embodied in about 60 parks, gardens and other open areas.

Since the mid-1990s the City Council and its representatives have taken an increasingly proactive attitude in regard to environmental sustainability, but this has also been a multi-faceted stance that encourages business development. Since 1998 there have been a number of programmes and strategies set in place, and several of the key features of the approaches taken in Melbourne are discussed below.

Developing sustainability attitudes

During 1999 a series of workshops was held on the topic of ecological sustainability in which a key group of councillors, Council staff and experts collaborated to generate new ideas for Melbourne. These arose from the recognition of the generally poor performance of Australian cities in terms of sustainability and the particular need to address associated environmental problems. The environmental problems have a disproportionate effect due to the number of the country's inhabitants that live in its main cities. The aim was to examine how the City of Melbourne could develop its programmes and policies in relation to the sustainability issues identified in its City Plan (a forward looking ten-year document produced on a regular cyclic basis as part of normal strategic planning activities). The main themes of the workshops were: *sustainable building practices*; *transport*; *other energy-related opportunities*; *biodiversity*; *water*; and *materials flows and wastes*; and as a result a series of recommendations was brought forward under each theme.

The recommended initiatives for sustainable building can be categorized under the following themes: to report on case studies of environmental management and to develop data from a benchmark project; to develop performance criteria in relation to green building; to develop and monitor pilot projects, such as for greenhouse gas sequestration and use of environmental assessment as a part of Council reports; to establish contact and working relationships with energy and environmental organizations in the city and state; to encourage the state government to improve building regulations; and to establish an environmental fund for sustainable development initiatives and promotion of green investment.

A number of the wide-ranging recommendations covering various areas already came under the responsibility of existing task groups, committees or departments, but additionally, and subsequent to the meetings, an Environment Development Unit was formed out of that branch of the

Council dealing with economic and strategy planning. It had four main concerns:

- Monitoring and development of the Council's greenhouse strategy.
- Facilitating and encouraging energy conservation and renewable energy use by the city's business community.
- Development of policy in relation to the Council's investments in sustainable business opportunities.
- Introduction of *triple bottom line* concepts into the city's corporate management.

The unit took these four areas and has developed umbrella projects to address issues raised by the reports; these dealt with such areas as life-cycle analysis for the building and construction industry.

City Plan 2010

The strategic planning document, City Plan 2010, takes environment and sustainability as cornerstone issues. It has four main themes: connection and accessibility; innovation and business vitality; inclusiveness and engagement; and environmental responsibility. The Council also took an important decision several years ago to monitor and track the city's economic, social and environmental performance through a triple bottom line (TBL) accounting procedure. Indicators produced as a result of the City Plan are also reported in a transparent way, using this methodology, and are used as a measure of performance. The aim is to optimize social equity, environmental quality and economic prosperity. The Council's successful employment of TBL has allowed it to encourage wider use of the method and it has developed a range of toolkit resources, available over the internet, that relate to different sectors: business; corporate planning; councils' sustainability reporting; and capital works items.

Under its commitments towards Melbourne being an environmentally responsible city, the Council has set out a number of key strategic directions. These are:

To reduce greenhouse emissions generated in the City of Melbourne. This includes a commitment to reduce emissions by 20 per cent by the year 2010, based on 1996 values, and to achieve a net zero greenhouse gas emission target by 2020. Supporting measures include the encouragement of renewable energy generation, energy efficiency, and the promotion of carbon sequestration techniques.

To encourage efficiencies in resource use and waste reduction within the city. This includes promotion of reuse and recycling and of better use of resources. Water, food waste and general waste materials are areas of focus.

To protect and enhance the city's biodiversity. This involves promoting the city's parklands and natural features and protecting important habitats. It also links to needs to reduce harmful pollution and waste.

To enhance environmental leadership opportunities for Melbourne's business community. The city aims to maximize awareness of good business practice and to disseminate information. Businesses concerned with environmental management and other green topics are being encouraged as part of the city's development. It also aims to host important national conferences and exhibitions and to make an impact by showcasing the city's activities at international level.

To create a sustainable built form for the city. The city aims to take a lead role in developing the built infrastructure of the city in a sustainable and energy-efficient form. This strategy has many cross-links to areas of resources use, wastes, planting and landscape as well as ecologically sustainable building design.

In order to monitor its environmental performance, the Council has identified a number of indicators within the broad categories of: business commitment to environmental improvement; community uptake of environmental initiatives; changes to greenhouse gas emissions; and the city's natural environment.

Melbourne principles for sustainable cities

An international workshop on building urban ecosystems was held in Melbourne in April 2002, organized by the United Nations Environment Programme International Environmental Technology Centre in collaboration with the Environment Protection Authority, Victoria. An output of the meeting was a set of principles provided to act as a thought-provoking guide and a framework for strategic action. As an indication of the City Council's continuing focus on sustainability for the future, the following month it adopted the principles as part of its initiatives towards making Melbourne an environmentally healthy, vibrant and sustainable city. There were ten basic principles:

1. Provide a long-term vision for cities, based on: sustainability; intergenerational, social, economic and political equity; and their individuality.
2. Achieve long-term economic and social security.
3. Recognize the intrinsic value of biodiversity and natural ecosystems, and protect and restore them.
4. Enable communities to minimize their ecological footprint.
5. Build on the characteristics of ecosystems in the development of nurturing of healthy and sustainable cities.

6. Recognize and build on the distinctive characteristics of cities, including their human and cultural values, history and natural systems.

7. Empower people and foster participation.

8. Expand and enable cooperative networks to work towards a common, sustainable future.

9. Promote sustainable production and consumption through appropriate use of environmentally sound technologies and effective demand management.

10. Enable continual improvement, based on accountability, transparency and good governance.

Sustainable business development

Encouraging and supporting business development is a normal role for a local council and in Melbourne there has been no shortage of development in recent years, with growth in the City Centre and Southbank, along the Yarra River and in the entertainment precinct. The Port area is undergoing redevelopment and there have been major projects at Federation Square and the adjacent Birrarung Marr Park. Plate 20 shows an aerial overview of this development, close to the city's centre, and plate 21 a view of this dynamic piece of architecture at ground level.

However, whilst an important aspect of the City Council's activity has been to encourage a vibrant economy, it has also taken a view to encourage businesses with a green and environmentally sound focus, not just to improve current environmental performance but also to secure the longer-term viability of the city's economy. The Council aims to be a major centre for sustainability-oriented businesses in the Asia–Pacific region. It has tried to avoid the trade-offs that often occur between each component (economic, environmental and social) of sustainability, by promoting an attitude that shifts focus from provision of a product to provision of a function. In this way attention can be paid to the best and most sustainable method of delivering a service to meet a need. The encouragement of good business practice is also valuable since it limits a company's exposure to future risk that comes about because of rising environmental costs and liabilities, as well as giving the company a head start in research and development; it is a commonly held opinion that processes producing waste and pollution are inefficient processes.

The Council has also tried to work towards more sustainable practice within its own operations and, by publicizing its achievements, it acts to encourage others. It has established a *Sustainable Business Directory* and provides resources and advice that can lead to better environmental performance in the commercial and industrial sectors; it has also set up a small business development fund that can provide low-rate loans to encourage green enterprises. This forward-looking view means it has tried to set itself up as a natural home for green businesses of the future.

Sustainable energy and greenhouse strategy

In 1998 Melbourne joined the Cities for Climate Protection (CCP) programme and, as part of its ongoing commitments, it has developed a sustainable energy and greenhouse strategy that aims to stabilize and reduce emissions of greenhouse-effect gases. Information on the energy use and emissions resulting directly from the Council's operations has been collated, together with the wider data that quantify the emissions from the city as a result of all activity within the municipality (though Council emissions are less than one per cent of the total). The Council adopted the aim of reducing its own emissions by 30 per cent, compared to 1996 levels, by 2010, and the plans indicate that it can achieve the majority of that reduction (25 per cent) from strategies already in place. A much more difficult target will be that set for the municipality as a whole (a 20 per cent decrease by 2010), as stated earlier. To achieve this target the Council aims to encourage reduction and to build partnerships that set emissions reduction targets as part of their key aims and policies. The strategies already in place and planned to take place suggest a decrease of up to 12 per cent will be achieved, so there is still some way to go. Despite this, there are new opportunities arising and it is hoped that these will be capitalized upon.

In 2000 the Council joined the Greenhouse Challenge programme as part of its aim to achieve net zero emissions. It has committed itself to develop abatement opportunities over a ten-year cycle and will work with other members of the programme. Some of the specific aims are:

- A doubling in the efficiency of power generators using conventional energy.
- A 50 per cent decrease in demand through efficiency improvement and design changes in the commercial sector.
- A 15 per cent reduction in demand due to improved efficiency in the industrial sector.
- By the end of the planning period, the Council to purchase 100 per cent renewable energy and the commercial sector to purchase 40 per cent renewables.
- Carbon sequestration projects to offset remaining emissions.

Outside the Council's operations, and as part of its greenhouse strategy, rebates of up to A$1500 dollars have been available for residents changing to solar energy use.

As part of the Cities for Climate Protection programme, which is integrated with the Council's greenhouse strategy, a series of five milestones is prescribed to be identified and met. Melbourne was the first local council in Australia to achieve all five milestones of the programme and to report progress against its 2010 targets; further, within the system, the Council adopted some of the most stringent reductions in the country. The improvements in the 2001–2003 plan set important targets for the Council's operations in the building, public lighting and vehicle fleet sectors. There are also many strategic initiatives beginning to be used to encourage improvements, such as incorporating sustainability assessments as part of Council reports, promotion of *environmental champions* within the workforce, and encouraging use of environmentally responsible procurement.

Environmental indicators

Since 1998 a bulletin, *Environmental Indicators for Metropolitan Melbourne*, has been produced on an annual basis. The indicators are derived from analysis of the status of the municipalities that constitute the wider city and are evaluated under seven categorizations in the most recent document, these being: air emissions; beach quality; open space; water quality; urban waste; greenhouse gas emissions; and triple bottom line. In previous reports transport, litter and biodiversity were also major categories.

The report shows that in most categories there seems to have been satisfactory progress or achievement of standards. However, in water quality and urban waste there is some cause for concern (including increased pollution from heavy metals in some waterways and excessive use of water for gardens at 35 per cent of the total, and unfulfilled potential to compost or recycle greater proportions of wastes). The availability and publication of the data act to spur effort in particular areas and allow measurement of improvement over a period of time.

Energy

Several of the Council's plans and targets rely on energy supply and use patterns changing quite substantially. The organization with responsibility for providing alternative energy supply opportunities is Sustainable Energy Authority Victoria (SEAV). SEAV helps councils and local residents in choosing green energy and power options. One of its relevant initiatives has been the production of the *Energy Smart Housing Manual*; it is available to builders, designers and homeowners and, in the course of eleven chapters, covers all the major topics necessary to procure an energy-efficient home.

180

The organization also promotes itself strongly to the commercial sector through its 'energy smart' business approach. The 250 000 businesses in the state are responsible for 56 per cent of its greenhouse gas emissions and the aim is to help obtain the 15–25 per cent savings which can normally be achieved through use of good practice. A greenhouse rating scheme was also constructed to help assessment of commercial buildings.

Some of the initiatives with regard to energy have the opportunity to become attention-grabbing focus points such as the plans to install photovoltaic solar panels on the roof of the renowned, and heritage listed, Queen Victoria Market in the centre of Melbourne (see plate 22). In the first phase of the project (completed during 2003) approximately $2000\,m^2$ of the roof have been covered with 1382 solar panels, funded in part by a grant of one million Australian dollars from the Australian Greenhouse Office's Renewable Energy Commercialisation Programme. Assuming the project to be successful, an even larger fraction of the roof's total area of about $10\,000\,m^2$ may be covered. Other initiatives have seen the installation of a further 182 photovoltaic solar power systems and 799 solar hot water systems.

A new venture is the Community Power not-for-profit organization, which enables businesses and local residents to purchase renewable energy and green power from accredited sources. Thirty per cent of the city's street lighting and 20 per cent of Council building energy use is already supplied from renewable energy sources.

Transport

The key to improving the environmental performance of most of Australia's cities is the reduction of private vehicle use. The urban sprawl common to most of its cities is particularly pronounced in Melbourne, and so the provision and encouragement to use public transport systems is an important feature. Melbourne already has an extensive tram network serving the main urban hub and there is also an extensive suburban train network, yet there is more that can still be achieved. The growing outer suburbs are in most need of development and this is beginning to take place. New lines, stations and network facilities have been built, along with new trams and trains. The bundle of activities aimed to encourage more use of public transport is called *TravelSMART* and has been in operation since 2001. In 2002 a major redevelopment of one of the city's main rail interchanges was announced as part of a public–private partnership agreement. In another initiative, bicycle use is being encouraged through the city's Bike Plan (2002–2007), which aims to further integrate and develop the cycle network in the city.

Figure 7.11 Symbols of sustainability: Melbourne's tram network and the Town Hall's focus on sustainability

Hundreds of millions of dollars have been committed to the various transport improvement strategies and building projects at both city and state level.

Materials and wastes

In 1999, the City of Melbourne enacted an Environmental Local Law that embodied the city's Environment Management Plan (EMP), which sets out the requirements for properties in the city, and their owners and occupiers, relating to waste disposal and environmental practices. The aim is to provide a safer, cleaner and more pleasant environment through responsible land management and dealing with wastes in an appropriate manner. A checklist is available to help and ensure compliance with the plan, and its operation helps to underpin the status and importance of a number of environmental policies.

In another development, the City Council has instigated a *Waste Wise* programme, which comprises a detailed system for waste collection and processing, and particularly for recycling. The main focus is on the residential sector, but commercial recycling opportunities are also being developed. One of the reasons prompting these actions was the realization that a large fraction of wastes that were being sent to landfill sites could be recycled or, particularly in the case of food and garden wastes, composted.

Discussion

Melbourne has had a number of successes in its approach to sustainability. However, the starting point was at a level of quite poor performance, in common with other Australian cities. The Council itself is making substantial improvements to its performance, but the overall success relies on other, private sector, businesses to follow suit. There have been definite improvements in provision of renewable sourced energy and in control of wastes and pollution, but the impact on the wider level has not yet kicked in. The majority of the carbon emissions reduction has been achieved by the planting of trees which act to sequester the emitted gases.

The built environment has also had a relatively small part to play thus far, which is somewhat disappointing given the large energy use and emissions, particularly from the commercial sector, which provides great potential for savings. The workshops held in 1999 in fact delivered a good range of recommendations related to green building, but these have yet to bear full fruit. The targets for improvement in the 2001–2003 Greenhouse Action Plan do, however, start to make buildings a more important target, with planned emissions reductions being almost half of the total. Building energy auditing and retrofitting of energy efficiency measures are set to increase, as is the use of renewable energy sources.

Overall, the Council has set itself some ambitious but necessary targets and has put in place action plans and policies across a range of sectors; it has also made a clear start in developing itself as a 21st century ecological city; its citizens and business leaders must now begin to more fully subscribe to the same philosophy if the process is to be completely successful.

The Green Olympics, Sydney 2000, Australia

Hanwen Liao, Researcher, University of Sheffield

Background

The Olympic movement undoubtedly provides one of the most influential events in modern human society. There are no other activities that can draw so much world attention as the Olympic Games. Past experience has shown, however, that hosting an Olympic Games might leave negative environmental consequences if no actions were taken to prevent or minimize the harm. However, in more recent Games a series of steps has been taken to establish a more healthy relationship between sports and environment. In 1992, the International Olympic Committee (IOC), together with many international sports federations and national Olympic committees, signed the Earth Pledge, formally confirming their commitment to environmental protection and enhancement. In 1994, the IOC signed a cooperation agreement with the United Nations Environment Programme (UNEP) to develop joint initiatives. In the same year, at the IOC's Centennial Olympic Congress, *environment* was approved as the third pillar of Olympism after *sport* and *culture*. In 1996, the Olympic Charter was modified to refer to the environment, recognizing 'the urgent need for people to preserve and respect the environment in which they live'. Besides the intrinsic benefits that an Olympic Games project can bring to a particular city and its hinterland, the Games are also important as they provide a world stage to show that the theories can be put into practice.

Historical development

The modern Olympic Games event is not only a sports event, but a veritable microcosm of society and the problems that trouble it. It involves a significant capital investment to stimulate economic growth; it also involves a huge amount of purchasing, distribution and ultimately disposal of products; the movement of goods and people; administration and management of human resources; and is nowadays accompanied by large urban-scale construction activities. It clearly has a significant impact on the built and natural environment. During the early stage of the Olympic history, building activities were quite limited because of the difficulties faced by incipient Olympism; however, the trend of Olympic urbanism has gradually appeared. The first Olympic village was built in 1932 for the Los Angeles Games and symbolized the beginning of Olympic intervention into urban development. Thereafter, with only a few exceptions, the degree and scope of this kind of urban-level intervention has generally increased for every Olympic event: from building a few essential competition stadia and an athletes' village in 1936 (Berlin), 1952 (Helsinki) and 1956 (Melbourne); to the creation of a concentrated Olympic site as a major urban programme in the 1960's and 1970's Games (e.g. 1960 Rome, 1968 Mexico City and 1976 Montreal); to finally being integrated into the city's long-term planning and urban regeneration strategy in the 1980's and 1990's Games (e.g. 1980 Moscow, 1988 Seoul and 1992 Barcelona). This process culminated in Sydney for the 2000 Olympic Games.

The impact of each Olympic Games on the host city's facilities, environment and infrastructure has grown stronger and stronger and the Olympics have become a catalyst for urban change. The award of the Olympics usually initiates major new developments and enables a *fast-track* procedure to be adopted, thus enabling quicker passage through the planning and development stages.

Sustainable development issues were rarely addressed by event planners or venue designers in any organized manner prior to the 1990s, however. In a few cases, a lack of careful planning created Olympic development that overshadowed and marginalized the local people's needs, and even left a negative legacy for the hosts.

Since 1994, candidate cities for both Summer and Winter Olympic Games have been evaluated on their environment plans. The IOC's bidding procedure includes requirements in terms of environmental protection, environmental measurement and compulsory ecological studies. These now occupy an increasingly large fraction of the candidature file and are of importance in the choice process. In 1994, the Winter Games in Lillehammer became the first Olympics to address consciously environmental issues and publicize their efforts. Thereafter, the Olympic organizing committees of Atlanta 1996, Nagano 1998, Sydney 2000 and Salt Lake City 2002 have all launched and implemented their own environmental sustainable development guidelines. Three future Olympic cities, Athens (2004), Turin (2006) and Beijing (2008), have also released their own environment improvement plan to address existing urban problems.

The main environmental design features of these plans can be summarized as follows.

Establish Environment Management Systems (EMS), including the creation of planning tools or environmental guidelines for large building projects; the development of new green building standards, purchasing guidelines and products lists; the creation of special departments to coordinate the environmental issues; and the conduction of environmental audits at various stages of design and construction.

Apply environmental protection and enhancement measures, including the creation of Olympic parkland by remediation of contaminated and degraded land; the protection of natural habitat and threatened native species; and the carrying out of regular environmental impact assessments.

Establish a resources management system, including the promotion of the application of energy-efficient facilities; maximization of use of green power and renewable energy; acting as a showcase of natural lighting, cooling and ventilation strategies; the use of water conservation, treatment and recycling techniques.

Instigate a waste management system, including promotion of reduction, reuse and recycling of waste materials, and reuse of existing facilities and recycling of building materials.

Other features, including the construction of environmentally friendly transport systems (providing public transport to reduce the use of private cars); the use of temporary facilities and structures to reduce the environmental impact; the promotion of innovative building technology to achieve sustainable objectives; the management of the venues' reuse after the Games to match local long-term requirements; and the promotion of public environmental education programmes, encouraging the involvement of local stakeholders.

Homebush Bay

On 23 September 1993, the 101st IOC session was held in Monte Carlo; there Sydney beat four other cities, Istanbul, Berlin, Manchester and Beijing, to be chosen to stage the 2000 Games. In fact Sydney's bid for the Olympic Games can be dated back to the 1970s when an investigation was made by the then New South Wales (NSW) State Government about what to do with the government-owned land at Homebush Bay approximately 15 km west of Sydney's city centre. Homebush Bay had a varied past and had most recently been home to the city's abattoirs and brickworks; before that it had acted as a military armaments depot and as a site for a variety of industrial processes. It was also used as a landfill site for chemical and other industrial waste as well as household rubbish.

The growing environmental awareness of the late 1960s led such areas to become the targets for remediation. In February 1973, the report of the investigation proposed the possibility that Homebush Bay could be rehabilitated by planning to host a future Olympic Games. In 1980, the Government assessed the possibility of bidding to hold the 1988 Olympic Games in Sydney. The assessment included the examination of sites throughout Sydney, and also led to the building of the State Sports Centre in 1984; this was the first step towards the redevelopment of Homebush Bay, and towards a future Sydney Olympic Games. However, the Government decided not to proceed with a formal Olympic bid at that stage. Then, in the middle of the 1980s, the State Government had to tackle another problem: the Royal Agricultural Society (RAS)'s Sydney Showground at Moore Park lost its viability and needed to be moved. Thus, in 1988, all three matters were put on the Government's agenda, resulting in the turning of a nagging problem into an economic opportunity by moving the showground, addressing the critical environmental issues at Homebush Bay, and bidding for the Olympic Games, all integrated into one solution.

Before Sydney was granted the 2000 Games by the IOC, the development work at Homebush Bay had already been in progress. The State Government closed both the brickworks and the abattoirs at Homebush in 1988. Tighter controls on dumping of industrial and household waste had been in place for over a decade and finally, when all the dumpsites were closed, a large area of rehabilitated land, the Bicentennial Park, was opened in 1988. Sydney's sports facilities were gradually planned at Homebush, and the decision to locate most Olympic venues on one concentrated site would play a key role in shaping the physical development of Sydney in general. Sydney Olympic Park is the largest concentration of venues in Olympic history; it also integrated the main Press Centre and Olympic Village for the first time. In addition, Sydney's bid committee broke new ground in promising the most *environmentally friendly* Olympic Games ever. Sydney developed environmental guidelines which were later adopted by the IOC as the standard for environmental policies for Summer Olympic Games.

As the Games planning progressed, Sydney made a series of efforts to implement their environmental sustainable development commitments. This included a law in 1993 that required Olympic development applications to be consistent with environmental guidelines. Matters that were considered under the law included: water and energy conservation; waste minimization; protection of natural environments; planning and construction; biodiversity; ozone depletion; and pollution and resource consumption. Several other planning documents were released to guide the Olympic development. All these documents fitted in with the principles of ecologically sustainable development (ESD), in particular the conservation of species and natural resources, and the control of pollution.

A commitment was made to a number of environmental principles:

- Protect and enhance remnant natural ecosystems on Olympic development sites.
- Improve the quality of water entering waterways from Olympic sites.
- Remediate the legacy of past pollution to ensure land is suitable for use.
- Protect soil and sediments within areas for which the Olympic authority is responsible.
- Encourage the use of recycled materials and reduce waste generation.
- Minimize the demand for potable water from the city's main supply.
- Minimize the use of energy from non-renewable sources.
- Minimize emissions of greenhouse gases and minimize the use of ozone-depleting substances.
- Minimize the use of materials that deplete natural resources or create toxic pollution.
- Minimize the impacts of noise and night lighting on environmental conservation and neighbouring residential areas.
- Minimize impacts on air quality.

These commitments have been implemented in the design and construction process of all Olympic venues in Sydney.

All the construction projects in Sydney Olympic Park at Homebush Bay were finished before the end of 1999. The new venues included Stadium Australia, the Archery Centre, the Hockey Centre, the SuperDome Multi-Use Arena, the Sydney International Aquatic Centre, the Tennis Centre and the Sydney Showgrounds. Other facilities such as Athletes' Village, Media Village, Olympic hotels and railway station were also built at the same time. Darling Harbour, situated much closer to the city centre, was the second largest of the Olympic precincts; an entertainment centre and exhibition halls hosted wrestling, weightlifting, volleyball, judo and boxing. Besides these two main precincts, a number of other sites were established to host specialist sports that were unable to be accommodated at the main Homebush Bay or Darling Harbour sites.

The XXVII Olympic Games was held from 13 September to 1 October 2000. Sydney won popular acclaim for the organizational staging of the Games and, among all the Olympic cities, it must be regarded as the host of the most successful Green Olympic Games thus far. It achieved a number of environmental successes and showcased several new approaches and technologies; in the following sections some of these principal features are described.

Olympic Parklands

One of the most significant elements of the Sydney Olympics environmental strategy has been the extensive renovation and rehabilitation of the land on the Homebush Bay site. Part of the site was redeveloped to accommodate the main Olympic sports facilities and athletes' village, but work has continued on much of the surrounding area in a programme that will not be complete until 2010. The overall site was 760 ha in area, and over 430 ha was designated to form parkland around the venue as a recreational space. Over 100 000 trees have been planted, and 180 ha has been returned to a variety of specialized habitats including wetlands, wood-

Figure 7.12 Water management in the Olympic Parklands area is a critical and continuing feature of its sustainability

lands, grasslands and saltmarshes. There has been great emphasis on adapting the land towards its original flora and fauna, and an ecological databank linked to a geographical information system (GIS) has been created.

The site had become badly polluted due to the range of industrial activities that had taken place over a period lasting more than 100 years. Over 160 ha of land was contaminated with a range of substances such as asbestos, heavy metals, DDT and dioxins, resulting in the need to treat or contain over nine million tonnes of soil. An early decision had been taken to treat the material on-site rather than transfer the problem to a dump elsewhere. Chemical and particularly biological treatment processes were used. Hills of earth were sometimes sealed and have become part of a process of *mound management*. The materials that can leach out of the wastes have been a particular problem and control of water-borne material was a priority, particularly since water management for the site was an important component of the environmental development (see plate 23). Indeed, the Parklands development was designed to be independent of the city's main water supply.

The improvement on the site was dramatic and has been characterized by the changes embodied in the phrase *Wetlands to wastelands 1894–1989/Wastelands to wetlands 1989–1999*. It is certainly one of the most important long-term environmental legacies of the Games in Sydney.

Olympic buildings and projects

Numerous building and refurbishment schemes were undertaken as part of the provision of facilities for the Games. The landmark projects of the Homebush Bay site included the main arena, Stadium Australia; the multi-functional SuperDome; the Aquatic Centre; and the Athletes' Village. Space does not permit descriptions of all projects but several key developments are included below.

Even before the Games were awarded to Sydney, preparations to build the main athletics and sports arena, later to be known as Stadium Australia, were underway (see plate 24). The stadium embraces a number of environmental principles in terms of its materials and construction and has been designed to operate using 30 per cent less energy than conventional benchmarks. The energy modelling carried out was very sophisticated, and novel passive ventilation strategies were investigated as part of the scheme to help ensure comfort. Use of artificial lighting was reduced by an estimated 17 per cent as a result of computer-based techniques to maximize daylight in the design. Rainwater collected on the roof of the structures is used to irrigate the pitch, and recycled water is used in the toilets (see plate 25). Together with other water-conserving measures, this means that water consumption is lower by about 14 per cent, with about half the remainder being supplied by recycled or collected water.

The stadium also embodies a degree of flexibility, firstly from the choice to use temporary stands at either end of the stadium for the period of the Olympics in order to maximize spectator seating (up to 115 000); these are being replaced by smaller, more sustainable units suited to subsequent likely crowd numbers (80 000). Secondly, retractable banks of seating at the lowest level of the side stands can move on rails so that the shape of the arena can be modified and used for a variety of different sporting and non-sporting events.

Alongside Stadium Australia and stretching along the site's main boulevard are 19 *Towers of Power*, so-called because they house over 1500 photovoltaic solar panels for electricity production (see plate 26). They are also multi-functional in that they serve as lighting gantries, provide shelter, and display signage for visitors. The use of renewable energy

Figure 7.13 Retractable seats at Stadium Australia offer additional flexibility and more profitable use

to power the venues and also the inclusion of renewable energy generation capacity around and on a number of the buildings at Homebush was also a feature of the Games. The concept was that the specification of green power sources would help create a demand and develop local renewable energy companies and businesses. The supply from the major electrical utility company, Energy Australia, goes under the banner of *PureEnergy* and utilizes a variety of sources including solar power, wind power, hydropower and landfill gas.

Also close to Stadium Australia is the SuperDome, a flexible multi-use space that can be used for sports, exhibitions and indoor concerts, seating up to 20 000 spectators. Its event area, measuring 47×77 m, is large enough to accommodate a number of uses. The SuperDome also embodies a range of energy and environmental design components:

- A model environmental management system was used during construction.
- Waste management strategies were used during construction.
- Over 1000 amorphous silicon solar cells are accommodated on the building's roof, with capacity to supply 70 kW of electrical energy.
- High efficiency lighting is used to reduce energy use, and maximum use of daylight is made.
- A microclimate control system was installed to limit air conditioning to specific areas.
- All electrical power is to be sourced from green energy.
- A dual water system is used to maximize use of recycled water, with about 30 per cent grey-water use.

The Sydney Aquatic Centre, providing the main swimming facilities, has been described as one of the best and most advanced in the world, and reflects Australia's interest and success in the associated events. The Centre itself has a reduced visual impact as a result of the surrounding landscaping and is also very flexible in use so as to maximize potential future events, with moveable floors and moveable bulkheads. A variety of lighting configurations is possible and the zoned air conditioning (to keep swimmers warm and spectators cool) helps to reduce energy use.

The Athletes' Village was constructed adjacent to the main Olympic site at Newington. It has been claimed to be the first predominantly solar-powered suburb in the world. It has 665 permanent houses, and a lend-lease scheme operated in which buyers purchased the property before the Games with a guaranteed income during the interim period until they were released after the Games, having been refurbished. Photovoltaic panels on each roof generate over 1 million kWh of electricity each year and solar hot water is also generated, boosted when necessary by a gas back-up system. The design of the houses was also low energy, with use of wall and roof insulation together with thermal mass flooring, producing a predicted 50 per cent saving in energy use. Ninety per cent of the properties were oriented so that the main living spaces could benefit from passive solar gain whilst pergolas and planting were placed so as to reduce the risk of overheating during summer. Cross-ventilation strategies were also employed to improve occupant comfort, and low-energy appliances were installed to further reduce energy demand. A life-cycle assessment procedure was employed to provide eco-rating of materials considered for use in the development. Non-toxic and low pollutant generating materials were favoured, along with sustainable timber products. There is a slight downside to the village and that is due, perhaps, to the need to make the properties attractive to middle income buyers. The units, as well as being of a high standard, also contained some features associated with high energy lifestyles such as air conditioning units, and their size is commensurate with Australian standards which seem to encourage urban sprawl. Plate 27 illustrates part of the athletes' village development.

The two connected hotels, which contain over 300 rooms and suites and were built at the heart of the Homebush site, are also designed to include environmental features. They are committed to purchasing 100 per cent green power, and over $400\,m^2$ of roof-mounted hot water collectors produce a 40 per cent saving in energy for this use. A novel system of window opening and ventilation is also installed which acts to reduce air-conditioning load, and the windows themselves are made from recycled glass.

Impacts at urban and district level

Olympic interventions have impacted on the local urban development since as far back as Rome in 1960, which represented a clear break with previous Games in the style and nature of urban development. It was the first time that a stadium was built as an element of urban intervention; this linked to a whole urban development programme at varying scales. The athletes' village was designed as a city residential zone rather than a temporary solution viable only for the time of the Games themselves. Olympic urbanism since then has been incorporated on many occasions with ambitious urban development, either by consolidating the existing fabric or by expanding the new territory of the city. From Rome to Sydney, the Olympic interventions in cities came in two main ways, which largely depended on the local conditions and the development mode expected by the local people. One mode was to create a single major grouping of venues, usually strategically positioned in an area deficient in amenities and development. The self-enclosed Olympic site has relatively clear boundaries with the rest of the city, and has a road infrastructure that defines it. The Munich Games in 1972 and Montreal Games in 1976 took this approach. The concentrated Olympic site can promote either the regeneration of the city centre if it is located around that area, or the expansion of a new city sub-centre if it is located in a peripheral area. The opposite mode places venues throughout the city region and helps therefore in spreading the benefits and also perhaps the difficulties throughout a larger area. But, no matter which mode is adopted, the development of Olympic facilities is based on attempts to redress urban or civic deficiencies. The Seoul Games in 1988 and the Barcelona Games in 1992 are good examples of using the Olympic events to recover an urban area in crisis.

The Sydney 2000 Games drew from both models to some extent. Some of the existing infrastructure in the city was used and new venues were created, scattered throughout Sydney's larger metropolitan area within a 44 km radius. Homebush Bay was the prime site, however, with twelve individual venues hosting 22 sports and 500 000 people visiting each day during the Games. Sydney was successful in that the Olympic events were fully used to promote the city's transformation and remediation. Sites all over the metropolitan area were carefully chosen so that the whole urban tissue was reinvigorated. The Games redevelopment also fitted in with the city's westward-focused strategy for development. Homebush Bay, which is halfway between the Central Business District (CBD) of Sydney and its western suburb of Paramatta, has been transformed by the Olympics into one of the largest and best serviced new residential communities in the state. The Olympics gave the chance for Sydney to realize its westward strategy, which will benefit the city's development in the 21st century. The Games have resulted in the linking of Sydney's two CBDs more organically, with better access to sporting and recreational facilities for the metropolitan population in the long term.

Most recent host cities have sought to minimize investment in temporary facilities for the Games themselves whilst maximizing investment in the integration of the Olympics into their city's longer-term development strategy. The major benefit to Sydney is not the new sports facilities, but the additional investment in the city's buildings, transport and telecommunications infrastructure. Besides the sporting facilities, the major projects brought forward by the Sydney Olympics include: a new airport rail-link at a cost of US$ 500 million, the completion of the Eastern Distributor Road linking the airport to the CBD, the US$ 350 million expansion of

Sydney airport and another US$ 220 million in smartening up the city centre. Sydney also enhanced the city's fibre-optic network, with 4800 km of cable linking 105 locations but focused on a ring between the Sydney CBD and the Olympic Park area. All these Olympic legacies provide Sydney with a significant boost to the international credibility and quality of life.

Impacts at building and systems level

The Olympic Games provide a significant opportunity as well as a challenge to combine the best architectural design with state-of-the-art environmentally friendly technologies and innovations. This trend can be dated back to the early stage of Olympic urbanism, and although it is difficult to measure the success in design practice given different cities' situations, there is little doubt that the Olympics have had international impacts in design and innovation. In Sydney's case, a crucial factor in achieving the environmental promise of the bid was the environmentally sustainable design features of all major venues and arenas, the Athletes Village, and other Olympic facilities at Homebush Bay. The main design approaches applied in Sydney's Olympic Park to improve the building's environmental performance can be summarized in ten principles, listed as follows:

1. To use natural lighting, natural ventilation and passive cooling technology as much as possible (this is the primary strategy in Sydney's Ecologically Sustainable Design proposals).
2. To use innovative and lightweight structural systems to save use of building materials and to contribute to architectural flexibility (examples include the roofs of the Sydney Tennis Centre and the NSW Hockey Centre).
3. To use innovative, environmentally friendly and energy-efficient technologies in the artificial lighting and control systems; cooling, heating and ventilation systems; and water systems used in the buildings (applied in indoor arenas such as the Sydney Aquatic Centre and the Sydney SuperDome).
4. To use green and renewable energy sources in the sports venues and Athletes Village.
5. To develop and install systems for collection and recycling of water and use of dual water systems so as to minimize the consumption of potable water.
6. To utilize recycled materials where possible and suitable.
7. To eliminate use of harmful materials in all Olympic projects.

8. To establish a waste management system to minimize the waste production from the construction process and from daily operation of the site (including the introduction of life cycle assessment, waste audits and environment impact assessment).
9. To encourage the use of natural and renewable building materials in place of other materials where appropriate, and the establishment of a green material products list and guidance.
10. To reduce the parking space in order to control the use of private cars as part of the Olympic park traffic control strategy.

Among the ten strategies listed above, many of them need to be applied in association with each other to create energy-efficient and environment-friendly architecture.

Discussion

World sporting events such as the Olympic Games have emerged as a significant catalyst of urban change in recent decades. By presenting the host city with a world focus opportunity in front of a huge global audience, the Olympics attract considerable capital investment that acts to accelerate urban development and renewal. The Olympic legacies include a broad spectrum of factors associated with urban regeneration, infrastructure improvement, growth in real estate markets, and heightened awareness of environmental and sustainable development issues. Although Olympic urbanism does not have a very long history compared to the Olympic movement, it does have an increasingly significant impact in attracting global attention.

A recent evaluation carried out by the consultants PriceWaterhouse Coopers has documented the economic benefits of the Games, which can be summarized as:

■ A$3 billion in business outcomes (A$600 million in business investment; A$288 million in new business under the Australian Technology Showcase scheme; A$2 billion in post-games sports infrastructure and service contracts).
■ Over A$6 billion in infrastructure developments in the state of New South Wales.
■ Over A$1.2 billion projected additional convention business for the state over a 15-year period.
■ Over A$6 billion in in-bound tourism spending in the year following the Games.

196

■ Enhanced business exposure and development of greater expertise for tendering for large-scale projects in Australia and overseas, including for the 2008 Games in Beijing.

In addition to the economic benefits for Sydney, the Olympic environmental legacies continue to be enjoyed by the local people and can be seen at several levels: global, urban and district, individual building, sub-building system, and construction materials. By most standards the Games were an environmental success; however, some notable international environmental pressure groups still perceive that more can be done, having awarded ratings of six or seven out of ten for the Games' overall environmental performance. Part of the reason for this is that the major organizations involved in the Games and the multinational sponsoring companies still use the same business practices with the same negative environmental effects, and, in themselves, have a long way to go to achieve environmental sustainability.

To improve the quality of life is a long-term target of human activities, but, in so doing, there can often be adverse impacts on ecological integrity. However, the Sydney Olympics seem to have achieved a good balance of environmental design and operation, combined with economic success and good awareness of social and community issues. The whole design represents a high level of achievement in environmentally sustainable architecture, encompassing numerous state-of-the-art technologies and design innovations. It is a milestone of Olympic building history and sets a benchmark for hosts in the future.

Bo01—the 'City of Tomorrow', Malmö, Sweden

Background

Public awareness and concern for environmental matters seem to be more deeply ingrained into the minds of the population of the Nordic/Scandinavian countries than most others. It is difficult to know why, but when it comes to building design, their practices have often been well ahead of those of other nations. It was only in the 1990s that thermal performance standards in England's building regulations caught up with those prevalent in Sweden some 50 years previously. Even in the present day there seems to be a more accepting attitude to the need to build sustainably and to high standards, so as to minimize energy use and reduce environmental impacts. In 1996, for instance, the Swedish government stated its aim to act as an international leader in promoting ecological sustainable development.

The City of Malmö is the third largest in Sweden and is situated in the south-western corner of the country; though it has a population of only 250 000, it is a multicultural city. Traditionally, Malmö was an industrial city based on shipyards and textile industries but over a period of 50 years it has suffered decline and is in the process of trying to transform itself into a high technology centre through a process of sustained strategic planning. It hopes to be seen as a city at the northern edge of Central Europe rather than at the southern edge of Northern Europe.

The form of strategic planning it has chosen is not that of top-down but rather bottom-up, and it has modelled itself on the approach of Bilbao in Spain but with its own different priorities. Its masterplan is ambitious and attempts to encompass physical, economic, social and ecological issues. Though the city is still in a process of evolving its planning approach and there are concerns that the right type of new housing should be available, it was ready and enthusiastic to take advantage of the opportunity to host an international exhibition for European city district development.

Project development

In 2001 the first international European housing exhibition, Bo01, subtitled *The City of Tomorrow*, was held. It showcased not only energy-efficient and environmentally sensitive design but also the latest ideas from a range of contemporary architects and developers of how people should live in cities of the future. Buildings for the site were designed not only by a range of good Nordic architects but also by those with wider international reputations such as Ralph Erskine and Santiago Calatrava. The exhibition was supported by the Swedish Government, the City of Malmö, various finance and developer organizations and the European Commission.

The new housing district was built on a waterfront area at Västra Hamnen with views over the Öresund stretching towards Copenhagen. The 18 ha site is also within walking distance of Malmö city centre as well as local beaches. A hundred years ago the site had been below sea level, but after a process of landfill it became used as an extension of the port facilities and for shipbuilding, particularly in the period following the Second World War. In the 1970s the area was redeveloped into a car factory and exhibition fair halls though, due to economic problems, the factory was closed down quite shortly afterwards. In the 1990s the site was chosen to host the City of Tomorrow Expo, which aimed to focus on ecologically sustainable living in the developing information and welfare society. It was an attempt to marry ideas of ecological, social, technical and human sustainability in a high quality development. Plate 28 shows an aerial view of the site and the city, and figure 7.14 a site plan.

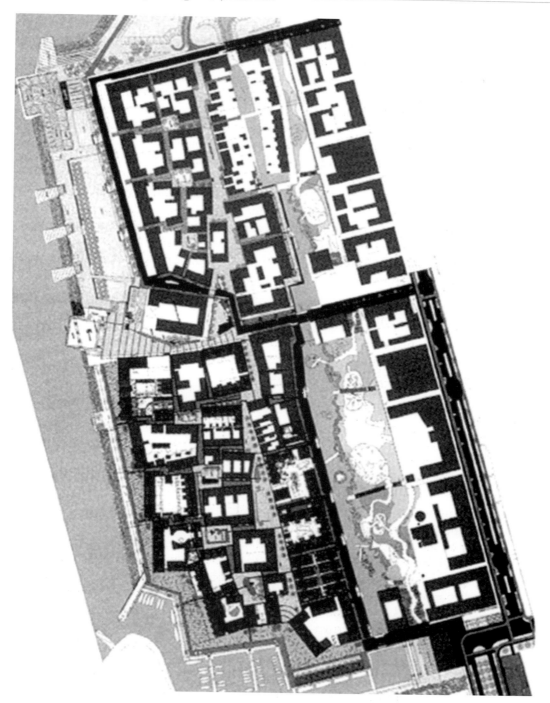

Figure 7.14 Bo01 site plan (Jan-Erik Anderson/Eva Dalman)

Bo01 has created a new residential area of 500 dwellings, together with commercial and social facilities, which are adjacent to the existing trade exhibition halls, office units and community buildings. There were two main areas of development, the first being the permanent new housing of which the Bo01 buildings were the first stage, and the second being a more transient exhibition area. The urban design framework of the development was set by the site location, which had to respect the westerly exposure to the sea and wind, though this also offers dramatic views over the water towards Copenhagen. As a result, the most westerly blocks were designed to be taller to provide more shelter for the other areas of the scheme; plate 29 shows the impressive western side of the development. Buildings ranged in height from one and a half to six storeys and, within the new blocks, 50 furnished showhomes were presented to demonstrate the benefits of the more than 20 individual schemes. Plates 30 and 31 and figure 7.15 illustrate examples of the architecture.

The landmark building for the site is the Calatrava-designed *Turning Torso* largely completed during 2003. This building is a 45-floor tower reaching about 190 m in height, each floor level having an area of about 400 m^2. The tower is subdivided into segments of five floors, forming nine

Figure 7.15 Multi-storey timber housing at Bo01

cubical units that gradually turn through 90 degrees as the tower rises from the centre of the Bo01 site. The tower contains approximately 135 high-quality apartments; their design is to be flexible in order to match occupant requirements. Intelligent control systems abound in order to match the aspirations of the exhibition for high-class design.

Malmö has recently opened a new university and, also designed for the exhibition, was a novel concept for student living. Five-metre cube room compartments were proposed; five sides were made of concrete and one of glass and each contained all the necessary basic items for student life—a lower level living/study area and an open mezzanine level for sleeping. The idea behind the proposal was to prefabricate these modules off-site and then assemble them into a block of more than 100 apartment modules together with associated communal facilities.

Landscape is an important issue for the site, both to provide shelter for buildings in this exposed location and to provide pleasant and stimulating outdoor space for the inhabitants living at high density. The development contains two green park areas, a waterfront promenade, a marina and various sheltered areas within the site. There are also several residential courtyard areas or private spaces, which include ponds, water features, wild plants and green roofs (see plate 32). A water course/canal runs through the site from north to south, and a wooded area called the Willow Forest was created on the north-east portion of the site in which ten secret or hidden gardens were located, together with other landscape features including outdoor sculptures. Private garden areas are relatively small or are communal for each block or group of dwellings, but this is a consequence of the need for higher densities in urban development and evolving styles of city living.

Energy design

The standards of building are sufficiently high that the need for heating is already well controlled. However, in Bo01 the aim has been to be completely self-sufficient in energy. An underground aquifer has been used as a source of energy for heating and cooling. Ten 90 m deep boreholes were drilled in two groups of five within the site; five act as cool sources, five as warm sources. A heat pump enables the underground water at 15°C to be raised in temperature to a more useful 67°C and this is then used to provide the heat for the district heating system. Over 85 per cent of the heating requirements are supplied by the district heating and the remainder is sourced from solar energy. Conventional flat-plate solar panels are located on nine buildings and have a combined area of 1400 m^2; a further 200 m^2 of high-efficiency evacuated tube collectors are also used and together these supply the remaining 10–15 per cent of heating demand.

Electrical energy for the site is provided by wind and solar sources. Photovoltaic solar cells are installed on some of the buildings around the site and make a small contribution to the needs (about one per cent); the remaining 99 per cent is provided by a wind power station approximately 3 km from the site. Sophisticated environmental control of the dwellings is installed (see figure 7.16).

Water and waste systems

Water supply and sewage systems are connected to Malmö's mains network. However, attempts have been made not only to use the most efficient appliances to reduce water usage but in particular to focus on waste water treatment. The waste water normally contains significant

Figure 7.16 Building and environmental control systems were installed at Bo01

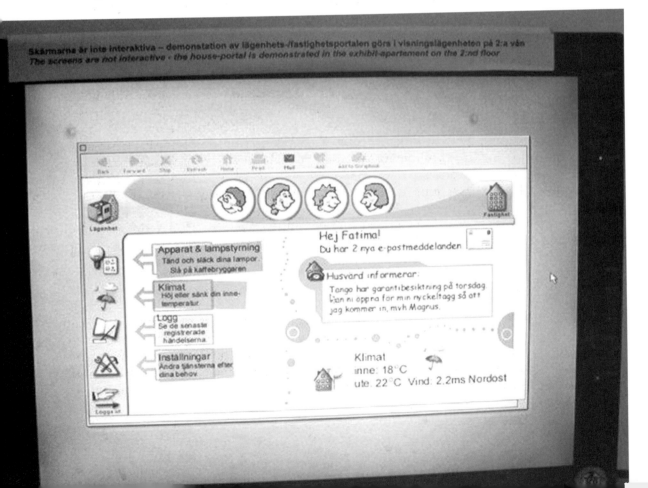

levels of phosphorus, which is an important part of the eco-cycle; therefore, at Bo01, systems to extract the phosphorus content were put in place. Since the phosphorus is associated with food waste, this had to be considered and two forms of food disposal are used. In one the food waste is sorted by the house occupant and placed in paper bags, which can then be thrown into one of the hatches of a novel subsurface mobile vacuum collection system (shown in figure 3.15). This material is then diverted to holding tanks and subsequently collected by waste disposal trucks for processing. In a smaller number of properties (about 70) waste disposal units in the kitchen sink are used to grind food waste before flushing it into the normal water sewage system; this leaves the treatment processing to the conventional network. The efficacy of the different systems will be analysed as part of ongoing research associated with the Bo01 development.

The site also has variations on the disposal system for other materials. Sorting rooms are provided at, or adjacent to, each property block, which enables maximum recycling to take place. A second vacuum disposal system also operates for residual waste, that is waste that cannot be recycled, and the material collected is normally disposed of by incineration, providing additional heat for the district heating system.

The European Village

As part of the exhibition site but separate from the main housing district development, a small village area was created to showcase individual examples of good ecological design from around Europe. Twenty schemes were selected for building during the period in which the main Bo01 Expo was being held, with the aim of completion by the time the exhibition closed. Not all of the houses could be built, however, because of timescale pressures from the developers with whom the architects were working. Nevertheless, nine countries took up the challenge: Norway, Poland, Denmark, Hungary, Latvia, Slovenia, Lithuania, the Czech Republic and Sweden. Between them they built 12 different houses. One of the purposes of the European Village was also to stimulate discussion on construction and housing issues at European Community level.

Discussion

Bo01 set out with very wide-ranging and admirable aims and should be seen as part of the attempt by the City of Malmö to regenerate and reinvent itself. The backdrop to the exhibition has been the development of strategic planning and associated thinking pursued by the local and national governments. The Bo01 project tried to address the intellectual, social and emotional needs of creating a sustainable society as well as the environmental and technical needs. The resulting development is certainly of high quality and is very attractive to certain groups of potential owners; the fact that it is a more sustainable option is a little underplayed.

The scheme exemplifies the dilemma of redevelopment: whether to focus on social and affordable housing which can sometimes be uninspiring, or to showcase the best in design as a stimulus to further progress. There is also the further question of whether high-technology solutions, whilst they are clearly effective in creating style and comfort, can be the ultimate solution to providing a sustainable city. There are certainly many good things about Bo01 and many things to admire and strive for; ultimately, only time will tell if this type of proposal to help define the City of Tomorrow will be replicated.

The sustainability of high density, Hong Kong, China

Dr Edward Ng, Professor, Department of Architecture,
Chinese University of Hong Kong

Background

Hong Kong is one of the major metropolises in the Pacific Rim, ranking alongside cities such as Tokyo, Shanghai, Los Angeles and Sydney. Geographically, it is made up of a peninsula that is part of continental China and over 200 surrounding islands. Until the British founded it in the mid-19th century, the area had only a few villages and around 1000 inhabitants. The early trade settlements from the West appeared in Victoria Habour; now numerous tall buildings surround the same piece of water. At present, an area of some 200 km contains most of the urban built-up zones and supports the life of some 7.5 million people. Hong Kong is now ranked as one of the major financial centres in the world. It has a GDP of some US$25 000 (on a par with the UK and USA). Hong Kong has the world's busiest container port and houses some of the world's most profitable enterprises. An airport the size of Gatwick and Heathrow combined, built on land completely reclaimed from the sea, has recently been constructed, and over 15 million visitors pass through annually. Hong Kong is a high-rise jungle of a city and the tallest building in the world, some 600 metres high, is currently being built.

Yet amidst all the hustle and bustle of the economy and international travel, Hong Kong also boasts a collection of country parks, covering almost 50 per cent of its land area, and it houses one of Asia's most important wetland areas. It is home to 100 or so unique and endangered pink dolphins, and also within its tight boundaries it is still possible to find fishing villages and settlements almost untouched by the onslaught of modern civilization and economic activity. Hong Kong is a land of paradoxes. It seems to defy gravity and common sense. Given the circumstances and the dilemma, how should one proceed to define sustainability in Hong Kong? If there is such a thing as sustainable architecture in an ultra-dense, ultra-compact metropolis, what is it? And how should it be critically understood? To what shade of sustainability could it be conveniently referenced? Plate 33 shows a view of apartment building in Hong Kong amidst green hills.

Geographically, the city is located at the south-eastern corner of continental China. Its climate is sub-tropical, and from October to March it is temperate with pleasant breezes, plenty of sunshine and comfortable average daytime temperatures of around 20°C. Occasional cool fronts from the north can lower the temperature to below 10°C in urban areas, nonetheless, these are the best months of the year. The other half of the year it is hot; humidities climb to over 80 per cent and daytime temperatures, which can reach 36° C, averaging 28°C. Tropical cyclones from the Philippines visit Hong Kong from time to time during the summer months, bringing with them heavy rain and high winds of 150 km/h or more.

Dealing with the climatic environmental characteristics of Hong Kong in general building design is not difficult, but attempts to classify Hong Kong under any known social, cultural, urban, and environmental and sustainability theory have been less successful; as the locals say, 'there is only one Hong Kong'. Hong Kong's uniqueness makes the resolution of sustainable design considerations distinct.

Sustainability and energy use

Since the Hong Kong Chief Executive's policy address in 1998, environmental sustainability has been a catch-phrase in the city. The Hong Kong Institute of Architects (HKIA) has set up an Environment and Sustainable Development Committee to try to coordinate matters in the built environment. It undertook a series of events and seminars under the *Greening 2000* and *Greening 2001* banners, and a new, joint professional, Green Building Council is to be established. If one goes through the web pages of government agencies and the city's main enterprises, the message that 'we are green' is apparent and advances in sustainability seem to be taking shape.

A number of prominent local designers reckoned that Hong Kong is already doing a lot of what needs to be done correctly and can provide lessons from which other large cities may wish to learn. Hard figures support that claim too (table 7.2). The per capita energy consumption is very low compared to cities of equivalent size and economic standing, such as Singapore. What is more important is that the energy is being used very efficiently to generate wealth and a material quality of life.

There are reasons why the per capita energy usage in Hong Kong is so low when compared with other advanced cities. Hong Kong has always been a *sustainable* city, long before the term was used by environmentalists. Since 1949, when the Communists came to power in China, Hong Kong has been a destination for economic and political emigrants. These people, millions of them over a period of some 30 years, came to Hong Kong and brought with them nothing but a hope to ensure and sustain a better quality of life for them and their next generations. This desire to make a successful different life has remained the spirit of Hong Kong. The city has no natural resources of its own; apart from the air one breathes, everything, including water, has to be imported. This historical perspective may help many to understand the mental attitude of its inhabitants towards their surroundings.

In the 1960s, when the territory was confronted with a large body of likely immigrants living just over the border, the government embarked on a long-term urban planning exercise that would allow the city's total land area of $1000\,km^2$ (much of which cannot be built on) to sustain the lives of up to 10 million inhabitants. A few key strategies, discussed below, led the way and seem to have been successful.

Table 7.2 Energy consumption and CO_2 emissions: Hong Kong and other key industrialized cities

	Emission		Consumption	
Location	CO_2 per capita (metric tonnes)	CO_2 (kg per person per $ of GDP)	Kg of oil equivalent per capita	$ GDP per kg of oil equivalent
Hong Kong	3.7	0.2	1931	12.0
China	2.8	1.0	902	0.7
Singapore	21.6	0.9	7835	3.8
Japan	9.3	0.4	4058	10.5
USA	20.0	0.7	8051	3.4
UK	9.5	0.5	3992	4.8

Transport

Energy used for transport represents 35 per cent of all energy used and is the highest single sector usage in Hong Kong. This is comparable to other industrialized countries as a percentage, but is less in absolute terms. For instance, in Hong Kong, 18 per cent of transport energy is used by private vehicles, whereas in the UK it is 62 per cent; the difference is in the use of public transport options.

Due to the hilly topography of Hong Kong, some 60 per cent of the land is uneconomical for buildings. This led the early urban planners to adopt a high-density land development policy that was based on using only a few main transport arteries. The arteries are well planned and the average vehicle speed during peak hours is still around 25 km/h.

Each day 10 million passenger journeys are made on public transport systems which include two high-capacity railways, trams, buses, minibuses, taxis and ferries. There are 280 licensed public transport vehicles for every kilometre of road, over 500 bus routes are in operation, and the Mass Transit Railway provides 2.2 million journeys each day. Although three tunnels are in service, the ferries still take 150 000 passengers across the harbour each day, and also serve many of the inhabited islands in Hong Kong. In contrast, there are only 300 000 private cars in Hong Kong.

Two factors contribute most to the success story of public transport. Firstly, the fares are low, and this is made possible by the volume of passenger traffic. In addition, the major infrastructure providers are given land rights over their stations for property development. Most of the cost of constructing new lines comes from the profit made on these developments; the fare is merely for operational costs, and because of this, the relationship between a station and its surrounding buildings and occupants is very close. It is possible to walk from one's home, use public transport and arrive at the office without crossing a single road.

Three-dimensional pedestrian movement systems

In addition to the public transport system, the city areas of Hong Kong have another design feature that makes movement through it on foot a pleasure. Firstly, in the central business district and other satellite town centres, buildings are connected together with elevated pedestrian walkways. These walkways not only serve as circulation routes, they are also integrated with retail outlets. Secondly, some of these walkways are connected to outdoor elevator walkways that take people all the way from the seashore to the hills. When they were first designed they were for movement only; however, a few years later the walkways have completely revitalized and regenerated some of the neighbourhoods through which they

Figure 7.17 Public transport is one of the key features of Hong Kong's operation (Edward Ng)

Figure 7.18 Connected walkway and escalator systems enable easy pedestrian movement
(Edward Ng)

pass. Nowadays, it is seen as a miracle in urban design that old districts have been socially sustained through simple and unintentional intervention. Plate 34 shows some of these walkways.

Perhaps the first lesson from Hong Kong is that it is important to see the city as a movement system. In this respect a successful, efficient and sustainable city is not about roads for cars and tracks for rails; the transport infrastructure is, and must be designed as, part of the built environment. For high-density cities, the pedestrian element of the system is as important as the vehicular system. The more one encourages pedestrians to move around on foot or by other convenient systems, the less the reliance on private vehicles.

Compact multi-use buildings

Apart from the movement systems, the second main reason for the high efficacy of the city has to be the use of its buildings, and a number of key policies prevail. Firstly, there are few distinct zones to demarcate the city; all classes of use, residential buildings, public housing, commercial buildings, offices, schools and other amenities, co-exist in close proximity, and sometimes within one another. In Hong Kong, this is known as *mix and multi-use*. Since movement using transport costs energy, the close proximity of amenities and functions in Hong Kong is important for an energy-efficient city to operate. It is possible for an average household (and 90 per cent of households can be considered 'average' in urban design terms) to carry on their daily lives, for example, shopping, going to school, buying goods, visiting a health centre and so on, completely on foot.

The policy of mixed-use architecture also promotes a more harmonious social relationship; millionaires rub shoulders with pensioners in the shop; high-cost private apartments are located next to public rental housing. This generates a more tolerant culture that is essential for a congested living environment. Moreover, the gregarious and tolerant mentality of an average inhabitant of Hong Kong can best be seen in the houses (though *pigeonholes* might be a more apt term) in which they live. Fifty per cent of the housing stock, or some one million units, are public housing. On average, a small residential unit for a family of three to four has an area of only about $40\,\text{m}^2$; a larger unit is just under $50\,\text{m}^2$. For such a small unit to function, the spaces have to be multi-use, as well as the buildings. It is common for some families to use the living space as a bedroom at night. The size of the units also has the effect of reducing the air-conditioning load during the summer, this being 19 per cent of energy use in an average household.

Density

For Hong Kong to work, the keyword is density. In the middle of the city, one travels through a three-dimensional urban and traffic matrix that is the densest in the world. In each square kilometre of land some 50 000 inhabitants live and are provided with all the utilities, amenities and transport required to sustain their life, work, schooling and recreation.

The newly constructed residential sites in satellite towns around the city are designed with a net residential density of 2000 to 2500 inhabitants per hectare. Apartment blocks some 100 m high are packed so closely together that the distance between them is often as little as 30 m. To ensure that no valuable land is wasted, the blocks are built on top of multi-storey podiums, which house most of the amenities that are required to support the community. The buildings are thus compact, efficient, mostly mixed-use, and are provided with well-planned amenities within walking distance. The towns are such that they can be served by a highly efficient and cost-effective public transport system. Any space left over is given to charitable organizations for school buildings and community centres. The remaining areas, unusable for anything else, become parks and leisure ground. In short, nothing is wasted. In fact, the urban jungle has a lot of concrete and few trees, but it occupies so little space that trees could continue to grow around it.

If there is a need to characterize Hong Kong, one might argue that whilst the rest of the world is pressed to achieve a *light green* version of sustainability, Hong Kong, given its unique circumstances, is being forced into a *dark green* version of the same. It has proved itself to be a viable alternative. Perhaps in 20 years time, when use of land resources in other parts of the world approaches the same severity experienced in Hong Kong, the dark green version will begin to make sense to a wider audience.

In summary, the low energy consumption of Hong Kong can be attributed to the following:

- High development density.
- Establishment of specific key transport arteries and urban development areas.
- Efficient and affordable public transport systems.
- Efficient and three-dimensional pedestrian movement systems.
- Mixed land and building use.
- Close proximity of amenities and functions.
- Compact and multi-use living spaces.

Figure 7.19 The high density of Hong Kong (Edward Ng)

Environmental issues

To look at buildings in isolation and to evaluate th
energy used, the material spent and the waste th
point. In a dense built environment, it is the combi
themselves and the collective supporting mechanisr
minimum effort and maximum efficiency that rea
meaningless to attempt to solve the issue at the buil
solution must surely rest at the macro and governm

Environmental cost can be defined as the adverse effects of human activities. In high-density cities, where things are so close together, environ-mental effects are amplified. For example, traffic fumes on an open road can easily be dispersed by winds, but in built-up areas they are difficult to disperse and, more seriously, the same amount of pollution will affect more people. Another example is concerned with waste, both human waste and general waste. In high-density cities, the amount of waste produced per unit land area is high, and it is much more difficult to find land for its disposal. Taking another example, the waste heat generated by numerous small air conditioners will have an effect on the microclimate: temperatures in urban areas increase, causing increased air-conditioning load, and the vicious circle continues. In Hong Kong, during hot summers, a whole row of air conditioners can shut down automatically due to the very high outdoor ambient temperature caused mainly by their close proximity.

Wastes

In 1998, the government, noting the imminent waste problem, established a number of strategic schemes to tackle the problem. These were a strategic sewage treatment and facility enhancement programme, and a waste reduction framework plan.

Hong Kong produces some 2.2 million cubic metres of sewage every day. About 95 per cent of the population is now served by the public sewerage system, with over 98 per cent of the sewage produced being collected and treated. Whilst new towns have been provided with modern secondary sewage treatment works, the sewage infrastructure for the older urban areas is outdated. The sewage infrastructure is now being upgraded under the Harbour Area Treatment Scheme (HATS) and a territory-wide sewerage rehabilitation and improvement programme.

In 1994, the government conducted a waste reduction study that resulted in the Waste Reduction Framework Plan, which aims to reduce waste by 40 per cent. A key focus of the plan is to drastically reduce construction and demolition waste produced by the building industry by 80 per cent through sorting, reuse and recycling, avoidance technologies and incentive schemes. As part of the initiative to reduce construction waste, the Housing Department of Hong Kong, responsible for some 50 per cent of residential units, is taking the lead. In 2000, the housing authority implemented the Environmentally Responsible Procurement Policy, aiming to bring environmental impact assessment into the equation of general procurement. A scheme that allows life-cycle analysis and costing to be factored in tender procedures is currently under study. The authority also commissioned studies and is putting plans together to reduce construction waste through prefabrication of components and major building elements as well as using reusable metal formworks in lieu of wood formwork. Recycled aggregates are being used for concrete, and wastes are now sorted on site for recycling; also, most established contractors now have an environmental and waste policy. In 2000, government works contracts included a requirement for waste management plans. Another strategy is to provide tenants with a shell and core unit that they could fit-out themselves. This reduces wastes generated by interior redecoration. The private sector is following the public lead.

Air pollution

Air pollution is always a major problem in big cities and has an adverse effect on human health; it can also have a visual and psychological impact and consequent effects on tourism. Hong Kong has two main air pollution issues. One is street-level pollution and the other is smog. In busy streets, air pollution is mainly caused by motor vehicles, particularly diesel vehicles such as trucks, buses and light buses. The pollutants are then often trapped between the very tall buildings lining the streets. To tackle this problem, the government introduced a programme in 2000 with targets to reduce emission from motor vehicles by 80 per cent (particulates) and 30 per cent (oxides of nitrogen) by the end of 2005. The key strategies are: to adopt tighter fuel and vehicle emission standards; to adopt cleaner alternatives to diesel where practicable; to control emissions from remaining diesels with devices that trap pollutants; to strengthen vehicle emission inspections and enforcement against smoky vehicles; and to promote better vehicle maintenance and eco-driving habits. The government earmarked HK$1.4 billion for this programme and the investment was designated to help the owners of diesel taxis and light buses to cover the cost of switching to cleaner fuel alternatives, and to help owners of older vehicles to install devices that trap pollutants. The government also provided a one-off grant for replacement of a diesel taxi with one that operates on liquefied petroleum gas (LPG). The purpose is to encourage a quick switch of the 18 000 diesel taxis to environmentally cleaner vehicles. By early 2002, more than 75 per cent of taxis had switched to LPG.

The government is also working with its counterparts in China to tackle the problem of air pollution regionally (whilst Hong Kong has a population of 7 million, the region is home for 40 million and covers an area of 42 000 km^2). Two culprits have been identified: power plants and emissions from light industries, but at present progress remains slow. Ideas such as pollution tax have been proposed, but the key problem is political and will remain so for a number of years.

Noise problems

Despite the gregarious mentality of the inhabitants of Hong Kong, noise is a common subject of complaint. There are three sources of noise: traffic, construction and aircraft. Of these, traffic and construction noise are the most problematic in dense living quarters. Approximately one million people live with loud road noise.

The Third Comprehensive Transport Study, completed in October 1999, provided the focus for noise problems. The study aimed to determine how to achieve and maintain an acceptable level of mobility for passengers and freight by all transport modes up to 2016. A strategic environmental assessment (SEA) was conducted which assessed noise along some 200 major roads in 1997, and some 429 000 residents were already found to be exposed to excessive traffic noise. If there were no restraint in the growth of traffic, 50 per cent of the population would be exposed to excessive noise by 2016, and so a number of noise improvement measures were recommended to complement the proposed transport strategy.

The Hong Kong Planning Standards and Guidelines have addressed noise since 1985 and standards have been progressively tightened. Two sources of traffic noise are particularly addressed: one is from new roads, the other from existing roads. In the design and improvement of a number of major urban areas, various techniques have been used, depending on site conditions, and the government has introduced new policies. These fall into the following categories:

- Use of noise barriers, noise canopies and noise tunnels.
- Use of low-noise road surfaces.
- Use of amenity blocks to shield residential units.
- Use of platforms or podiums over the road to contain noise.
- Redesign of residential building blocks to face away from noise sources.
- Use of noise-blocking fins under windows to shield against noise.
- Use of sound insulation.
- Traffic management systems to reduce load.
- Diverting traffic away from dense living quarters.

- Better planning of new towns.
- Tightening of motor vehicle noise standards in line with those in Europe and Japan.
- Designating Noise Control Areas.

Construction noise has also been a major problem, with pile-drivers sometimes operating 12 hours a day in urban areas, affecting one in 12 people. The Noise Control Ordinance came into effect in 1989 and included controls on construction noise that have been progressively tightened. Piling is limited to three to five hours a day in built-up areas, quieter piling equipment must be used, and other forms of noisy activities are controlled.

Urban heat island effect

The effect of constructing buildings close together results in the microclimate phenomenon of the *heat island*. During the summer months, outdoor air temperatures are of the order of 28°C, which goes up by 2–3°C depending on wind conditions and the canyon effects of tall buildings. A bigger problem not encountered elsewhere is the concentration of air-conditioning units ejecting heat to the external air.

Two government-level initiatives tackle this problem. Firstly, legislation requiring air-conditioned office buildings to reduce cooling needs by improving façade design was implemented in 1995. Secondly, the government recently announced a number of Practice Notes to promote green features, for example the use of balconies, cross-ventilation windows, sky gardens and so on.

By far the most ambitious scheme of the government is the experimentation with the Central District Cooling System. The scheme, if funded, will first serve the South East Kowloon Development (the empty site of the old airport, some 180 ha). The idea is to remove the waste heat portion of the equation by locating chillers far away from the buildings. Seawater cooling will be used. Based on a recent study, the initial and operational costs of a 200 MW plant are estimated to be around 25 per cent less than current systems. Energy and running costs aside, the scheme will significantly reduce waste heat and improve the microclimate thermally.

Natural light and ventilation

When buildings are located too close together, they shield and shade each other. This has the effect of reduced natural light and ventilation. In dense urban Hong Kong, the key question to be asked is: where is the limit and how close should one get?

216

Current building regulations of Hong Kong in this field are over 40 years old, and circumstances have changed so much that adherence to the laws now no longer guarantees adequate performance. The government is aware of this anomaly and commissioned a study in 2000 to examine modifications for implementation in the near future.

Verbena Heights

In 1992, one architect in Hong Kong, Anthony Ng, began to promote sustainability, and his award-winning design is still forward-looking in this respect. The building is a housing estate development called Verbena Heights. It was built for the Housing Society, a provider of cheap and affordable units for low-income groups; therefore the costs are very important. Yet the architect, for the first time in the history of Hong Kong, ventured into a series of studies trying to incorporate sound environmental strategies into the design. Wind and natural light, solar energy, water conservation, green materials and waste management were each part of the design agenda.

The result is seen in its unique form: instead of typical cruciform blocks, Verbena Heights is slab-like; its stepping roofs help with wind movement. At the pedestrian level, carefully designed voids ensure cross-ventilation; so much so that wind canopies had to be installed to reduce the wind velocities at key points. The development is shown in plate 35.

Recent studies by university researchers indicate that the final result lives up to the claim: it can achieve far better light and natural ventilation performance than its counterparts, even given the high site development density of some 3500 inhabitants per hectare. Also important is that the inhabitants are happy and are generally aware of the welcoming breeze in the summer.

It is unfortunate that the success story has not been repeated since. There are poor imitations, especially from those wishing to benefit financially from the green agenda. Features have been installed to give the building the appearance of sustainability, but sometimes these additional devices actually reduce performance instead of enhancing it.

Other environmental measures

There are other measures that are being attempted in Hong Kong, including the following:

- Protection of existing landscape, using nature and marine protection zones.

- Land reclamation policies.
- Reconnection of pedestrian routes along the waterfront, and more pedestrianised zones.
- Introduction of 'green lungs' into existing urban areas through urban renewal projects.
- Increasing number of cycle lanes, especially in new town planning.
- Implementation of environmental indexing and assessment tools for buildings.
- Implementation of schemes for life-cycle analysis and life-cycle costing.
- Renewable energy studies, especially wind.
- Public education.

However, given the current economic situation, most of these initiatives will not be fully implemented.

Discussion

The success of land use and energy efficacy achieved through compactness, high density and administrative measures helps Hong Kong to be the most efficient city of high economic standing in the world. Many lessons can be learnt and some have been described here.

Hong Kong is a temporal place. Most immigrants are from mainland China and they still regard China as their real home; for them, Hong Kong is a place to *make it* and this attitude is the most precious resource of the city.

The city has ridden through many crises: the Cultural Revolution in China in the mid-1960s, the oil crisis in the 1970s, mass emigration of talent in the 1980s and, most recently, economic restructuring. The next potential crisis is likely to be environmental. Hong Kong has no natural resources of its own; everything has to be imported. What if energy becomes so expensive that the city can no longer afford it? What if resources are no longer available? Should people do something about these questions now? The answer to this is obvious. These are not only Hong Kong's problems, these are the problems of the world. Large and economically powerful established nations will suffer most, thus they have more to worry about. Hong Kong will suffer but has the capacity to change, perhaps better than most.

The future of Hong Kong will not be the same, but it will be an extension of the present. Hong Kong must come to a point of realizing that furthering only its economic wellbeing is not the only avenue. Instead, working towards a balance of economics and a fine quality of life in social and environmental terms is a more sustainable model. Many high-ranking thinkers in the government and business realize this. The protection of the remaining natural landscape and heritage, the seeking of ways to improve the quality of the living environment, reduced reliance on non-renewable energy sources and education of future generations to respect the planet are the tasks of this generation.

On a satellite map of south-east China showing Hong Kong and its neighbouring areas of Shezhen and Guangzhou (population 40 million people), one distinct feature of the map shows up: the area that is most green is Hong Kong. This is hardly surprising as 70 per cent of its 1000 square kilometres is still parkland or rural areas. The important task is to ensure that the current features of Hong Kong are enhanced to enable it to stay that way.

Chapter 8

The way forward

Lessons from experience

The task of this final chapter is to draw together some of the major themes from the preceding sections and to suggest means to advance the cause of environmentally sustainable design in a profitable way.

Firstly, there are a number of issues raised by the investigation of the case study developments; these show that there is no one model of planning, design and development that should be pursued above others. Varieties of approaches have been, and continue to be, used with varying degrees of success. The example of Bo01 in Malmö contrasts vividly with that of Hong Kong. In the first a well planned and specifically sustainability-oriented community has been produced; in the second there has been very little sustainable planning as such, the benefits have arisen as a result of necessity rather than advanced design. Even so, the limits for conventional development in Hong Kong are being recognized and some attempts to anticipate the future are being put in place. Fortunately, it already has many good facets of urban development to build upon, even if this kind of living would not match everyone's aspirations. Ideally, one would wish to combine the best features of both in order to have a vibrant, organized and resource-efficient future.

The more general message of the case studies is that a greater degree of urban environmental sustainability is possible if it is planned in advance; if it has local understanding and involvement; and if it is coordinated by knowledgeable and enthusiastic professionals and managers. The key is to have good information presentation and dissemination to the local community so that they are more empowered to support the decision-making process that so affects the potential for long-term sustainability, and to modify their investment and purchasing behaviour so as to influence the financial considerations.

There are other messages too: firstly, that there is already much expertise and willingness in both local government and communities to pursue the environmental agenda; and secondly, that there are already in existence many support systems, such as those arising from LA21 activity.

On a more general level there is also much to commend a sustainability-focused approach from not just an environmental perspective but also a social and, perhaps more critically, an economic point of view. It is important to realize that attention to all-round good quality environmental design of the built environment brings benefits in many areas. Improving the efficiency of building construction and operation together with better resource-efficient design is good business practice. There are also many opportunities for business development to yield future profits, such as in the use of new technologies, new materials, new energy sources and optimizing the infrastructure—collectively known as *smart growth*. There are also improvements offered by use of high-quality prefabrication techniques with inbuilt design for future disassembly and reuse. The number of financial institutions and businesses making decisions based in some part on environmental grounds is expanding by the day, and the impetus this brings cannot easily be avoided.

There are some concerns however. At the present time substantial funding is being used to aid in the regeneration of existing communities in developed countries; this comes from investment by governments and from the private sector. Whilst this investment offers great opportunities to produce sustainable design, there is a risk in the lack of differentiation between *sustainable development* and *regeneration*. The two phrases are often used to mean the same thing, as indeed they can in certain circumstances. The pitfall that must be avoided is this: in attempting to rebuild economies, industries and new urban environments, it must not be possible to replace the old with just a simple, brighter, newer, but ultimately almost as inefficient, wasteful and polluting form of the old. The new built environments created in processes of regeneration have to be sustainable in the long term; the environmental costs of additional refurbishment and upgrade of such new development for *real* sustainability in the future would be extremely expensive and resource intensive. In fact, there already should be more focus on reuse, recycling and refurbishment of the existing building stock as an alternative to new build. This can still prove profitable since many existing buildings have intrinsic value and some of the oldest are more climate-responsive in design than more recent examples. The conversion of some industrial and commercial buildings in city centres has already been carried out successfully and with profit; the task is to ensure that the conversion takes not the cheapest, but the most sustainable route.

Support to achieve profitable sustainability

There is already much support for the mechanisms that can achieve environmental sustainability coupled with profitability. Chapter 6 showed the economic case that might be made, and this is reflected in a number of initiatives and the attitudes of a range of professionals. Examples would include the popularity of conferences such as those organized in the US by the Green Building Council, and those in the UK, including the 'Green Buildings Pay' events organized by the Royal Institute of British Architects (RIBA); the Construction Industry Council 'Profiting from Sustainability' conference; the 'Smart Development' conference; and the 'Sustainability accounting in the construction industry' event, all held in recent years. Each of these events helps to broadcast and support the message of the benefits of sustainable development.

More than this, there are enormous resources already in the public domain to support ecologically focused design and development; the bibliography lists many examples, and in particular there is great value in the websites, which are frequently updated with the latest practical information. A list of key sites would include those for ICLEI (International Council for Local Environmental Initiatives), Smart Growth and Sustainable Development/Smart Communities Network, Austin's Greenbuilder webpages, EcoCity Cleveland, the Rocky Mountains Institute, the Sustainable Development Commission, Forum for the Future and the Commission for Architecture and the Built Environment, amongst many others. Sustainable design and development is already good business as a number of organizations have shown, such as SustainAbility, ECOS, and other consultancies that deal with environmentally sensitive design.

Another area in which there has been much development is that of producing assessment tools and schemes to help evaluate the environmental impact of development. These are now reaching a sufficient level of sophistication and robustness that they can be more easily employed to make judgements about scheme proposals, their environmental effects, and how to mitigate them.

Moving forward

This final section makes a series of recommendations for future development that can support sustainability with profit and that, hopefully, minimize adverse impacts on the environment, for everyone's benefit.

- At the national level, priorities must be set for environmental sustainability that ensure a consistent framework and one which promotes and values good environmental design.
- The scale at which sustainable development can realistically be undertaken, and undertaken with a view to optimizing long-term and sustainable *profit*, is that of local council or neighbourhood for the public sector (this should link to broad policy development in the private sector), and this must be strategically planned and managed.
- To support sustainable development in a form that is robust and profitable there should thus be a new revised and revitalized role for strategic planning. This should act as a means for carrying out sustainable environmental management in a way that addresses urban and neighbourhood development from more than just a land-use planning perspective.
- The role of the strategic planning/urban management professional must engage with wide-ranging issues including: infrastructure; planning, layout and use; quality of development and design; transport systems; energy supply systems; water supply; and waste disposal. Global and national issues must also be related to the local scale and local understanding.
- Neighbourhood planning and development should take a broader *bioregional* view over the long term and produce a sustainable urban design and development framework for guidance. Neighbourhood design and development guides and action plans should then evolve that have the support of the local community.
- There is a need to create a team with wide-ranging skills to offer single-point responses to technical, social, cultural and economic

issues. This team must be able to coordinate the production of relevant information about good sustainability practices and to publicize exemplars of best practice.

■ To enable effective strategic urban sustainability, mandatory and coordinated environmental assessment of urban and building development is needed. The resulting findings must be disseminated in an effective way to the local community so that members of the general public can be made aware of the implications for quality of life issues and wellbeing.

■ There should be cash-neutral schemes for imposition of suitable environmental taxes, and the associated distribution of grants, rebates, permissions etc. to encourage development in line with local policies; and local councils/authorities should themselves use best practice in their own operation.

In conclusion, sustainable development with profit is possible, and that it is already occurring in some places cannot be disputed. The development of strategic planning at the local scale into a process of urban environmental management and quality building design can aid this advancement, but only if local communities and the general public begin to understand the implications of unsustainable practices. The key is to bring environmental, social, cultural and economic influences together at the local scale where their impact can be observed and evaluated in order to enable the creation of a more cohesive urban and built environment that not only offers high design quality, but long-term sustainability too.

Bibliography and websites

Bibliography

The following list of relevant publications represents a cross-section of the existing knowledge and expertise, and sets the background against which the present text was produced. Some texts offer quite a variety of views, and the inclusion of a text here should not imply any endorsement of the ideas and principles contained therein but rather the invitation to explore and absorb the information that each provides.

Abley, I. and Heartfield, J., *Sustaining Architecture in the Anti-Machine Age*, John Wiley and Sons, 2001

Anink, D., Boonstra, C. and Mak, J., *Handbook of Sustainable Building*, James and James, 1996

Baker, N. and Steemers, K., *Energy and Environment in Architecture—A technical design guide*, E & F N Spon, 2000

Baldwin, R., Yates, A., Howard, N. and Rao, S., *BREEAM 98 for Offices*, Building Research Establishment, 1998

Ball, A., *Sustainability Accounting in UK Local Government—An agenda for research*, Certified Accountants Educational Trust, London, 2002

Barton, H. (editor), *Sustainable Communities—The potential for eco-Neighbourhoods*, Earthscan, 2000

Barton, H., Davis, G. and Guise, R., *Sustainable Settlements: A guide for planners, designers and developers*, Local Government Management Board, UK, 1995

Barton, H., Grant. M. and Guise, R., *Shaping Neighbourhoods—A guide for health, sustainability and vitality*, Spon Press, 2003

Benson, J.F., and Roe, M.H., *Landscape and Sustainability*, Spon Press/Taylor and Francis, 2000

Bentley, I., Alcock, A., Murrain, P., McGlynn, S. and Smith, G., *Responsive Environments: A manual for designers*, Architectural Press, 1985

Boyle, G. (editor), *Renewable Energy*, Oxford University Press, 1996

Brandon, P.S., Lombardi, P.L. and Bentivegna, V. (editors), *Evaluation of the Built Environment for Sustainability*, E & F N Spon, 1997

Brownhill, D. and Rao, S., *A Sustainability Checklist for Developments*, Building Research Establishment, 2002

Building Research Establishment, *Climate and Site Development (Part 1, General Climate of the UK; Part 2, Influence of Microclimate; Part 3, Improving Microclimate through Design), BRE Digest 350*, Building Research Establishment, 1990

Burke, G., *Towns in the Making*, Edward Arnold, 1971

Button, K.J., and Pearce, D.W., Improving the urban environment: how to adjust national and local government policy for sustainable urban growth, *Progress in Planning*, Vol. 32, pp. 135–184, Pergamon Press, 1989

Carley, M. and Kirk, K., *Sustainable by 2020—A strategic approach to urban regeneration for Britain's cities*, The Policy Press, 1998

CIC, *Profiting from Sustainability*, Conference Proceedings, Construction Industry Council, London: http://www.cic.org.uk/conference/ (accessed June 2003)

CIRIA, *Sustainability Accounting in the Construction Industry*, CIRIA Publishing Services, London, 2002

Cofaigh, E.O., Olley, J.A. and Lewis, J.O., *The Climatic Dwelling*, James and James, 1996

Corporation of London/DEFRA, *Financing the Future—The London Principles*, Corporation of London, 2002

Department of the Environment, *The UK Environment*, HMSO, 1992

Department of the Environment Transport and the Regions (DETR), *Planning for Sustainable Development: Towards better practice*, HMSO, 1998

Department of the Environment Transport and the Regions (DETR), Energy Efficiency Best Practice Programme, *Building a Sustainable Future—Homes for an autonomous community (General Information Report 53)*, DETR/BRECSU, 1998

Department of the Environment Transport and the Regions (DETR), Report of the Urban Task Force, *Towards an Urban Renaissance*, HMSO/E & F N Spon, 1999

Department of the Environment Transport and the Regions (DETR), *Planning Policy Guidance Notes PPG3—Housing*, HMSO, 2000

Department of the Environment Transport and the Regions (DETR), Commission for Architecture and the Built Environment (CABE), *By Design—Urban design in the planning system: Towards better practice*, HMSO, 2000

Department of the Environment Transport and the Regions (DETR), Energy Efficiency Best Practice Programme, *The Design Team's Guide to Environmentally Smart Buildings (Good Practice Guide 287)*, DETR/BRECSU, 2000

Department of the Environment Transport and the Regions (DETR), Energy Efficiency Best Practice Programme, *The Hockerton Housing Project—Design lessons for developers and clients (New Practice Profile 119)*, DETR/BRECSU, 2000

Department of the Environment Transport and the Regions (DETR), Commission for Architecture and the Built Environment (CABE), *By Design: Better places to live—A companion guide to PPG3*, HMSO, 2001

Department of the Environment Transport and the Regions (DETR), Urban Green Spaces Task Force, *Green Spaces—Better places*, HMSO, 2002

Droege, P., *Postglobalization: Cities in the age of climate change and fossil fuel depletion*, http://www.solarcity.org/solarcity/postglobalisation.htm (accessed June 2003)

Edwards, B., *Green Buildings Pay*, Spon Press, 2003

Edwards, B. and Turrent, D., *Sustainable Housing—Principles and practice*, E & F N Spon, 2000

English Partnerships/The Housing Corporation, *Urban Design Compendium*, Llewelyn-Davies, London, 2000

European Commission, *City and Environment*, Office for Official Publications of the European Communities, Luxembourg, 1994

Forum for the Future, *Changing Business*, Forum for the Future, London, 2002

Frey, H., *Designing the City—Towards a more sustainable urban form*, E & F N Spon, 1999

Goulding, J.R., Lewis, J.O. and Steemers, T.C., *Energy Conscious Design—A primer for architects*, Batsford, for the Commission of the European Communities, 1992

Goulding, J.R., Lewis, J.O. and Steemers, T.C., *Energy in Architecture—The European passive solar handbook*, Batsford, for the Commission of the European Communities, 1992

Haughton, G. and Hunter, C., *Sustainable Cities*, Jessica Kingsley Publishers, 1994

Hawkes, D., *The Environmental Tradition*, E & F N Spon, 1996

Hillier, B., *Space is the Machine*, Cambridge University Press, 1996

Jenks, M. and Burgess, R., *Compact Cities*, Spon Press, 2000

Jenks, M., Williams, K. and Burton, E., *The Compact City*, Spon Press, 1996

Johnson, B. and Hill, K., *Ecology and Design—Frameworks for learning*, Island Press, 2001

Joseph Rowntree Foundation, *Made to last: Creating sustainable neighbourhoods and estate regeneration*, Joseph Rowntree Foundation, York, 1995

King, S., Rudder, D., Prasad, D. and Ballinger, J., *Site Planning in Australia—Strategies for energy efficient residential planning*, Department of Primary Industries and Energy, Commonwealth of Australia, 1996

Layard, A., Davoudi, S. and Batty, S., *Planning for a Sustainable Future*, Spon Press, 2001

Littlefair, P.J., Santamouris, M., Alvarez, S., Dupagne, A., Hall, D., Teller, J., Coronel, J.F. and Papanikolaou, N., *Environmental Site Layout Planning*, Building Research Establishment, 2000

Lyle, J.T., *Regenerative Design for Sustainable Construction*, John Wiley and Sons, 1996

Macy, C. and Bonnemaison, S., *Architecture and Nature*, Spon Press, 2003

McCarthy, C. and Battle, G., *Sustainable Ecosystems and the Built Environment—Multi-source synthesis*, Wiley-Academy, 2001

Meadows, D.H., Meadows, D.L., Randers, J. and Behrens III, W.W., *The Limits to Growth*, Pan, 1974

Mendler, S.F. and Odell, W., *The HOK Guidebook to Sustainable Design*, John Wiley and Sons, 2000

Mitchell, G., May, A. and McDonald, A., PICABUE: A methodological framework for the development of indicators of sustainable development, *International Journal of Sustainable Development and World Ecology*, Vol. 2, pp. 104–123, 1995

Moughtin, C., *Urban Design—Green dimension*, Butterworth Architecture, 1996

Olgyay, V. and Olgyay, A., *Design with Climate*, Princeton University Press, 1963

Oseland, N., *To what extent does workplace design and management affect productivity?*, published on website of the Office Productivity Network (http://www.officeproductivity.co.uk/) (accessed June 2003)

Papanek, V., *The Green Imperative*, Thames and Hudson, 1995

Pardoe, G.K.C., McVeigh, J.C. and Mordue, J.G., *Energy Demand and Planning*, Watt Committee on Energy Series, Spon Press, 1999

Pearce, B., Roche, P. and Chater, N., *Sustainability Pays*, Co-operative Insurance Society, London, 2002

Rao, S. and Brownhill, D., *Green File*, European Green Building Forum 2 (European Commission DG Transport and Energy), April 2001

Rao, S, Yates, A., Brownhill, D. and Howard, N., *EcoHomes—The environmental rating for homes*, Building Research Establishment, 2002

Rapoport, A., *House Form and Culture*, Prentice Hall, 1969

Ravetz, A., *Remaking Cities*, Croom Helm, 1980

Roaf, S., Fuentes, M. and Thomas, S., *Ecohouse—A design guide*, Architectural Press, 2001

Rudlin, D. and Falk, N., *Building the 21st Century Home—The sustainable urban neighbourhood*, Architectural Press, 1999

Rydin, Y., *Urban and Environmental Planning in the UK*, Macmillan Press, 1998

Smith, M., Whitelegg, J. and Williams, N., *Greening the Built Environment*, Earthscan Publications, 1998

Smith, P.F., *Architecture in a Climate of Change—A guide to sustainable design*, Architectural Press, 2001

Smith, P.F., *Sustainability at the Cutting Edge—Emerging technologies for low energy buildings*, Architectural Press, 2003

Smith, P.F. and Pitts, A.C., *Concepts in Practice: Energy*, B.T. Batsford, 1997

Thomas, D., *Architecture and the Urban Environment—A vision for the new age*, Architectural Press, 2002

Thomas, R. (editor), *Sustainable Urban Design*, Spon Press, 2002

Thompson, J.W. and Sorvig, K., *Sustainable Landscape Construction*, Island Press, 2000

Uno, K., *Environmental Options: Accounting for sustainability*, Kluwer, 1995

Vale, R. and Vale, B., *Green Architecture*, Thames and Hudson, 1991

Vale, R. and Vale, B., *The New Autonomous House*, Thames and Hudson, 2000

Watson, R.T. and the IPCC Core Writing Team (editors), *Climate Change 2001: Synthesis Report of the Intergovernmental Panel on Climate Change*, Cambridge University Press, 2001

Weber, M., *The City*, The Free Press, 1958

Wooley, T. and Kimmins, S., *Green Building Handbook, Volume 2*, E & F N Spon, 2000

Wooley, T., Kimmins, S., Harrison, P. and Harrison, R., *Green Building Handbook*, E & F N Spon, 1997

Yeang, K., *The Skyscraper Bioclimatically Considered*, John Wiley and Sons, 1996

Websites

All websites were checked for validity in mid 2003. The host domain address generally gives access to opening pages from which more detailed information can be viewed; in some cases the opening page links to an enormous range of subdirectories but it was felt inappropriate to list all these as such directories change much more frequently than the host domain. Websites for the case studies have not been annotated and contain different levels of information, often with a wide variety of subsections. As in the case of the preceding bibliography, the inclusion of a website or webpage here should not imply any endorsement of the ideas and principles contained therein, and, given the nature of the internet, the invitation is simply to explore in more detail any areas of interest.

General sites

Advanced Buildings—*site that provides a wide range of useful information on technologies and products to improve energy and resource efficiency:* http://www.advancedbuildings.org/

AECB—*website for the Association of Environmentally Conscious Builders:* http://www.aecb.net/

AGORES—*the European Commission Web Site for Renewable Energy Sources*—*acts as a gateway to wide-ranging information supporting the European Union's strategy for renewable energy:* http://www.agores.org/

American Institute of Architects—*Committee on the Environment*—*website provides information exchange and project data source including green awards:* http://www.aia.org/cote/

Amsterdam Environmental and Building Department—*information on regulations, information, advice and projects in Amsterdam:* http://www.dmb.amsterdam.nl/index-eng.html

Arcosanti—*website provides information on the ongoing architecture/ecology project by architect Paolo Soleri in Arizona:* http://www.arcosanti.org/

Australian Building Greenhouse Rating Scheme—*information on the application of this procedure:* http://www.abgr.com.au/

BEES—*Building for Environmental and Economic Sustainability version 3.0 assessment method*—*website contains information on the model and its use:* http://www.bfrl.nist.gov/oae/software/bees.html

BEQUEST—*environmental assessment/indicators website at the University of Salford*—*details information from European project (note*—*site under review*—*address may modify):* http://www.surveying.salford.ac.uk/bqextra/main.htm

BRE—*Building Research Establishment*—*general site with access to a wide range of information on UK building research:* http://www.bre.co.uk/

BREEAM—*Building Research Establishment Environmental Assessment Method website*—*links to details of the methods and their use in offices, homes and other building types, with some useful downloads:* http://products.bre.co.uk/breeam/

BSR—*website for Business for Social Responsibility*—*a global organization supporting member companies*—*some information freely available on activities and reports:* http://www.bsr.org/

BURA—*website giving information about activities of the British Urban Regeneration Association including overview of publications:* http://www.bura.org.uk/

C.A.B.E.—*the Commission for Architecture and the Built Environment*—*aims to foster quality in the built environment and provides much useful guidance and downloadable information:* http://www.cabe.org.uk/

CAT—*Centre for Alternative Technology*—*website describes this eco-centre's activities, projects and publications with some useful information available:* http://www.cat.org.uk/

Center for Resourceful Building Technology—website for project providing information on research, education and demonstration for environmentally responsible practices in construction: http://www.crbt.org/

CERES—Coalition for Environmentally Responsible Economies—a US-based network that acts to support organizations working for a sustainable future: http://www.ceres.org/

Citistates—network organization for journalists, speakers and civic leaders concerned with sustainable metropolitan regions—contains some reports and articles plus links and information: http://www.citistates.com/

Cleveland EcoCity Project—site provides much useful information about the potential for ecological design, smart growth and transportation in the Cleveland area of Ohio: http://www.ecocitycleveland.org/

Community Based Environmental Protection—website for US Environmental Protection Agency's community-based approaches to dealing with environmental management—contains some useful information and links: http://www.epa.gov/ecocommunity/

Community Building—website for community builders in the US—provides links to information sources and resources: http://www.vision-nest.com/cbw/

CRISP—website for recently completed European project for a network dealing with construction and city-related sustainability indicators: http://crisp.cstb.fr/

Design For Homes—a UK site that gives information to aid home design—registration gives access to more facilities, includes some CPD type material: http://www.designforhomes.org/

The Earth Pledge Foundation—aims to promote and disseminate information on innovative techniques and technologies—site contains basic information and links: http://www.earthpledge.org/about.html

Eco-Portal—website for environmental sustainability information gateway—provides numerous links and site search options: http://www.eco-portal.com/

ECOS Corporation—website provides information on its business-oriented activities to support sustainability in a commercial context: http://www.ecoscorporation.com/

EDA—the Ecological Design Association aims to increase awareness of environmental issues in the building professions—website has information on its activities: http://www.edaweb.org/

Energy Efficiency and Renewable Energy—website of US Department of Energy—resources and links to wide range of information including many documents: http://www.eere.energy.gov/

Energy Rated Homes of America—website for an organization that coordinates Home Energy Rating Schemes (HERS) operating in different states across the USA: http://www.erha.com/

English Partnerships (National Regeneration Agency)—a detailed website providing details about sustainable regeneration and best practice to support high quality sustainable growth in England: http://www.englishpartnerships.co.uk/

ENVEST—Building Research Establishment website with details concerning the software tool for assessing environmental impact and whole life costs: http://www.bre.co.uk/services/ENVEST.html

Envirolink—website of online environmental community with categorized listings of information and further links: http://www.envirolink.org/

Environmental Building News—website for online magazine containing information on environmentally responsible building design and construction—range of useful information, some on subscription: http://www.buildingGreen.com/

Environmental Design and Construction—online version of magazine with news and information on products, techniques, resources and suppliers: http://www.edcmag.com/

Environmental Home Center—Seattle-based online store and source for green building materials: http://www.environmentalhomecenter.com/

Environmental Profiles—Building Research Establishment website providing information about this system which allows measurement and certification of building materials: http://www.bre.co.uk/services/Environmental_Profiles.html

Envirosense—consortium of building product and equipment manufacturers with information and links to products and projects: http://www.envirosense.org/

European Commission websites—each acts as a portal to information and numerous links:
Transport and Energy: http://www.europa.eu.int/comm/dgs/energy_transport/;
Energy: http://www.europa.eu.int/comm/energy/;
Environment: http://www.europa.eu.int/comm/environment/;
Transport: http://www.europa.eu.int/comm/transport/

European Energy Cities Project—website for an association of local authorities which provides information on sustainable local energy policies—contains project and good practice information in searchable database: http://www.energie-cites.org/

FirstRate—website with information on energy rating system for Australian buildings: http://www.seav.vic.gov.au/buildings/firstrate/

Florida Sustainable Communities Center—an archive site (no longer active) but with some useful links and information for the Florida area: http://sustainable.state.fl.us/fdi/fscc/

Forum for the Future—website of UK based group supporting sustainability through solution-oriented approaches—wide range of information and reports available: http://www.forumforthefuture.org.uk/

FSC—Forestry Stewardship Council—website of organization promoting responsible forest management: http://www.fsc-uk.info/

Global Ecovillage Network—website for networking organization supporting sustainable settlements: http://gen.ecovillage.org/

Green Architect—part of Architectural Record website dedicated to green architecture—information includes reports, awards and links to products and techniques—free registration gives more access: http://archrecord.construction.com/features/green/

Greenbuilder—site for sustainable building sources and resources including the *Sustainable Building Sourcebook* in downloadable format: http://www.greenbuilder.com/

Green Building Advisor—website for information about Green Building Advisor software package available on CD ROM for architects and designers: http://www.greenbuildingadvisor.com/

Green Building Challenge—website for project that ran 1998–2002 involved in promoting green building design and assessment tools for a range of building types—free registration gives access to downloads: http://greenbuilding.ca.iisbe/gbc2k2/gbc2k2-start.htm

Green Building Council—website for the US organization representing building industry leaders—has information on assessment, case studies and reports, also has a members-only section: http://www.usgbc.org/

Green Building Council of Australia—website has information on resources and implementation of environmental rating scheme being developed: http://www.gbcaus.org/

GREENPRO—online internet library of eco-building information and products for the UK—requires subscription (also for 'Building for a Future' magazine): http://www.newbuilder.co.uk/

GRI—Global Reporting Initiative—website for institution that is involved in developing and providing information about sustainability reporting guidelines: http://www.globalreporting.org/

Groundwork—a federation of trusts in the UK that aim to build sustainable communities in poor areas through environmental action—website has details of activities and projects: http://www.groundwork.org.uk/

HUD—website for US Department of Housing and Urban Development—information on Department's activities related to homes and communities: http://www.hud.gov/

ICLEI—International Council for Local Environmental Initiatives—a wide-ranging website with best practice case studies from around the world; some information and case studies available free: http://www.iclei.org/

Intelcity Project—examines new opportunities for sustainable development of cities through the intelligent use of information and communication technologies: http://www.scri.salford.ac.uk/intelcity/

International Initiative for Sustainable Built Environment—associated with the former Green Building Information Council—provides database of information to subscribing members: http://www.iiSBE.org/

International Institute for Sustainable Development—aims to advance sustainable development by developing policy recommendations—website gives access to a range of the institute's documents and reports: http://www.iisd.org/

IPCC—Inter-governmental Panel on Climate Change—full texts of reports on climate change and other information published since 1998 available online: http://www.ipcc.ch/

LEED—Leadership in Energy and Environmental Design—information on this assessment procedure and downloadable versions of the scheme: http://www.usgbc.org/LEED/leed_main.asp

Los Angeles Eco-Village—*provides information on the Eco-village since its inception in 1993:* http://www.ic.org/laev/

NABERS—National Australian Building Environmental Rating System—website with information on the development of this new scheme: http://www.ea.gov.au/industry/construction/nabers/

NatHERS—website with information on housing energy rating system and software: http://www.nathers.com/

National Council for Science and the Environment—*US based site has as its aim the improvement of the scientific basis in environmental decision making—website contains some resources, reports and conference presentations:* http://www.ncseonline.org/

Natural Logic—*website for a company that provides consultancy, software, training and other services to support business advantages of good environmental performance:* http://www.natlogic.com/

The Natural Step—*website for an organization that provides expertise to companies to help integrate sustainability into business:* http://www.naturalstep.org/

New Buildings Institute—*website of a not-for-profits organization aiding design of better built environment—some downloadable reports:* http://www.newbuildings.org/

NREL—National Renewable Energy Laboratory—website contains wide range of information on activities and projects: http://www.nrel.gov/

ODPM—Office of the Deputy Prime Minister: contains lots of useful information generated by the UK government in the form of reports, guidance and policy documents, most freely downloadable: http://www.odpm.gov.uk/
(site related to planning issues: http://www.planning.odpm.gov.uk/*)*

One World Network—*gives access to worldwide regionally focused civil society networks with information and links on a wide range of environmental and other topics:* http://www.oneworld.net/

Planning and Development Network—*operates as an information exchange/links site for the urban planning and development community:* http://www.planetizen.com/

RegenNet—website for information network for regeneration partnerships: http://www.regen.net/

Residential Energy Services Network—*website for an organization that is helping to develop the market for energy rating of residential properties in the USA through Home Energy Rating Systems (HERS) and Energy Efficient Mortgage (EEM) programmes:* http://www.natresnet.com/

Residential Environmental Design and Sustainable Architecture—*acts as an information exchange and links site for green architecture, contains some useful articles and reviews:* http://www.reddawn.com/

234

Resource Renewal Institute—site supports the institute's activities in working towards a sustainable future including material to enable 'green plans' to be produced, with useful documents downloadable: http://www.rri.org/

Rocky Mountains Institute—wide range of information, links, and reports (some free) covering more efficient use of natural and human capital: http://www.rmi.org/

Santa Monica Sustainable City Program—website for this project including policy, community goals and city plans: http://www.ci.santa-monica.ca.us/environment/policy/

Schumacher Society—website of the society that focuses on social and environmental sustainability with details of its educational information including downloadable lecture pamphlets: http://www.schumachersociety.org/ or http://www.schumachersociety.org.uk/

Smart Architecture in the Netherlands—a site covering smart, green architecture in Holland, site contains an interesting 'grid' presentation of information on architects, projects, concepts and techniques from around the world: http://www.smartarch.nl/

Smart Communities Network—a major site from the US Department of Energy promoting smart growth and sustainable development with energy efficiency, contains a vast amount of information on many green topics—principles, programmes, projects, systems, etc: http://www.sustainable.doe.gov/

Smart Growth Online—broad information on smart growth principles and issues with categorized links to sources of information: http://www.smartgrowth.org/

Solar City—website for a task force of the World Council for Renewable Energy—website contains several downloadable key reports plus links and reports on activities: http://www.solarcity.org/

Stockholm Partnerships for Sustainable Cities—gives information about an awards programme combined with networking exercise that gathered information about sustainable urban based projects: http://www.partnerships.stockholm.se/

SustainAbility—website describes activities and services of this sustainable development consultancy: http://www.sustainability.com/

Sustainability Now—the website of the Association of Engineers and Geoscientists of British Columbia—Committee on Sustainability, website has downloadable modules and guidance on sustainability for members of the association: http://www.sustainability.ca/

Sustainable Buildings Industry Council—organization that advances good, affordable, sustainable building design—website provides details of workshops and other activities plus publications and software (to be ordered at cost): http://www.sbicouncil.org/

Sustainable Building Sourcebook—website for access to this resource: http://www.greenbuilder.com/

Sustainable Business.com—organization providing products and services to support sustainable business: http://www.sustainablebusiness.com/

Sustainable Cities—website for the European Sustainable Cities Project and Campaign—provides information about projects and events: **http://www.sustainable-cities.org/**

Sustainable Communities Network – website of organization linking citizens and communities to sustainability resources: **http://www.sustainable.org/**

Sustainable Development—a comprehensive 'virtual library' listing of several hundred websites dealing with sustainable development categorized under a wide variety of headings: **http://www.ulb.ac.be/ceese/meta/sustvl.html**

Sustainable Development—website describing the UK government's approach with numerous links to documents and further information: **http://www.sustainable-development.gov.uk/**

Sustainable Development Commission—website with much useful information for UK: **http://www.sd-commission.gov.uk**

Sustainable Development News Service—provides news and information on events and resources: **civitas.barcelona2004.org/**

Sustainable Energy Development Authority—website for organization based in NSW, Australia, with information on sustainable energy production and use: **http://www.seda.nsw.gov.au/**

Towards Sustainability—acts as a portal to useful information on sustainable development with information on design, events and links: **http://www.towards-sustainability.co.uk/**

United Nations—HABITAT Best Practice Database with information on over 1600 projects—several of the subject categories relate to sustainability— subscription required to access detailed information: **http://www.bestpractices.org/**

URBED—Urban and Economic Development Group—an independent research and consultancy group working in urban regeneration and sustainability— website provides information on activities and projects: **http://www.urbed.co.uk/**

Whole Earth—represents network of information sources: **http://www.wholeearth.com/**

World Conservation Union—partnership organization supporting nature, ecology, conservation and sustainability—website provides information about publications and activities: **http://www.iucn.org/**

Case studies websites

Leicester

http://www.leicester.gov.uk/
http://www.environmentcity.org.uk/
http://www.environ.org.uk/
http://www.iesd.dmu.ac.uk/
http://www.energysense.demon.co.uk/

Newark and Sherwood

http://www.newark-sherwooddc.gov.uk/
http://www.sherwoodenergyvillage.co.uk/
http://www.hockerton.demon.co.uk/
http://www.nsenergyagency.co.uk/

BedZed

http://www.bedzed.org.uk/
http://www.zedfactory.com/
http://www.peabody.org.uk/
http://www.bioregional.com/
http://www.sutton.gov.uk/

Austin

http://www.ci.austin.tx.us/
http://www.austinenergy.com/
http://www.centex-indicators.org/
http://www.cmpbs.org/
http://www.earthly-ideas.com/
http://www.greenbuilder.com/

Chattanooga

http://www.chattanooga.gov/
http://www.chattanooga.com/
http://www.csc2.org/
http://www.avsbus.com/
http://www.etvi.org/

Portland

http://www.ci.portland.or.us/
http://www.planning.ci.portland.or.us/
http://www.sustainableportland.org/
http://www.p-m-benchmarks.org/
http://www.green-rated.org/
http://www.portlandgreenmap.org/
http://www.sustainablenorthwest.org/
http://www.climatesolutions.org/
http://www.energy.state.or.us/

Melbourne

http://www.melbourne.vic.gov.au/
http://www.seav.vic.gov.au/
http://www.vic.gov.au/

Sydney–Olympics 2000

http://www.oca.nsw.gov.au/ (information archive)
http://www.sydneyolympicpark.nsw.gov.au/
http://www.olympic.org/

Bo01

An extensive site (http://www.bo01.com) was built for the duration of the exhibition; unfortunately this is no longer live—some information, however, is available through the City of Malmo's site.
http://www.malmo.se/
http://www.map21ltd.com/scan-green/bo01.htm

Hong Kong

http://www.arch.hku.hk/research/BEER/
http://www.susdev.hk/
http://www.edwardng.com/

Index